Roads & Kingdoms presents

GRAPE, OLIVE, PIG

Also presented by Roads & Kingdoms
RICE, NOODLE, FISH

GRAPE, OLIVE, PIG

Deep Travels Through Spain's Food Culture

—

BY MATT GOULDING
EDITED BY NATHAN THORNBURGH
DESIGNED BY DOULGAS HUGHMANICK

AN
ANTHONY
BOURDAIN
BOOK
HARPER
WAVE

GRAPE, OLIVE, PIG

HarperCollins books may be purchased for educational, business, or sales promotional use. For information, please e-mail the Special Markets Department at SPsales@harpercollins.com.

FIRST EDITION

Designed by Douglas Hughmanick

Cover images: © Stocksy and © Shutterstock

Library of Congress Cataloging-in-Publication Data

Names: Goulding, Matt, author. | Thornburgh, Nathan, editor.

Title: Grape, olive, pig : deep travels through Spain's food culture Matt Goulding ; edited by Nathan Thornburgh.

Description: First edition. | New York, NY : HarperCollins Publishers, 2016. "An Anthony Bourdain/Harper Wave Book."

Identifiers: LCCN 2016018185 (print) | LCCN 2016018774 (ebook) ISBN 9780062394132 (hardcover) | ISBN 9780062394149 (eBook)

Subjects: LCSH: Food habits—Spain. | Food—Spain—History. | Spain—Description and travel.

Classification: LCC GT2853.S7 G68 2016 (print) | LCC GT2853.S7 (ebook) DDC 394.1/20946—dc23

LC record available at https://lccn.loc.gov/2016018185

16 17 18 19 20   OV/RRD   10 9 8 7 6 5 4 3 2 1

For Laura, the part of Spain I'll always love most.

Table of
CONTENTS

IN CORRESPONDENCE WITH BOURDAIN:
How this book was born

Dear Tony,

I went out last night for a quick drink down the road—cold, dark vermouth from a dim bodega in the shadow of an ancient church. A friend showed up with the promise of the best *croquetas* in town (he was right: the crunch of a *chicharrón*, the molten savory flow of jamón lava). The night marched on—from oil-slick anchovies to pimenton-dusted octopus, small tubes of cerveza to big bellies of Beefeater—as my plans to return to work vanished in a slipstream of crushed grapes and pork fat. I woke up to a half-eaten shawarma on the bed stand and a note scribbled on a napkin: "Great Ball of Pig? Grape. Olive. Pig."

The most common reaction to *Rice, Noodle, Fish*, our love letter to Japanese cuisine, has been three words long: "I am going." That's what we set out to do—inspire and contextualize travel while leaving readers room to make their own discoveries. But now that we have a look, a style, a voice, it would be a damn shame not to take it to another delicious corner of the world. And I think I have just the place.

"We changed the history of the world," a chorizo-cheeked chef once told me in Madrid. Maybe it was the gin talking, but he had a point. The Spaniards brought tomatoes and chocolate and chilies to the Old World, sugar and wheat and smallpox to the New World. They forged one of the world's first fusion cuisines—not fusion as a six-letter word, but a cuisine of confluence, where the slow tide of Phoenicians and Romans, Jews and Moors and Catholics washing over the Iberian Peninsula gently but resolutely shaped its character. Like the sting of a Padrón pepper, it creeps up on you gently: in the hint of cinnamon in grandma's meatballs or the stain of saffron in a proper paella. More a whisper than a full-throated pronouncement.

Not that the Spaniards don't know how to shout. After all, this is the country that invented foams and spheres and the forty-course tasting menu. But Spain's greatest virtue lies in that time-tested Mediterranean formula: beautiful local ingredients, impeccable technique, and a ravenous appetite for all manners of flora and fauna. The Spaniards suck the brains from shrimp heads, crunch sardine spines like potato chips, throw elaborate wine-soaked parties to celebrate spring onions. There are stories to tell here.

From what I've heard in our conversations, you know exactly what I'm talking about. Food that will make your toes curl. People you want to name your children after. The fact that we first met over roasted snails and cava in the Catalan countryside brings this thing full circle.

We'd go with the same squad from Roads & Kingdoms: Doug Hughmanick painting with pixels, Nathan Thornburgh flexing from the edit desk. And assuming those nice folks down on Broadway dig on canned seafood and blood sausage, Harper Wave putting the ink to paper. What do you think?

Saludos,
Matt

Dear Matt,
So, it's the end of an epic meal in Andalusia, as so many in Spain seem to be, and I'm sitting at the table, enjoying a few moments of woozy happiness when the chefs emerge from the kitchen and join me. They are friendly, but strangely . . . wary.

FOREWORD

—

"You know, señor Anthony, that we in Spain like you very much. We like your book. We like your shows . . ." There was an uncomfortable silence as I waited for the "but" that seemed sure to follow. ". . . but people say things. Here in Andalusia, in Madrid, they say you are close . . . TOO close to the Basques."

Which is, of course, kind of true. My first and closest connections to Spain came through the great Basque chefs Juan Mari Arzak and his daughter, Elena. It was culinary educator Luis Irizar and his daughters who first led me, stumbling through the nighttime streets of San Sebastián, eating wonderful things unlike anything I'd experienced before. Juan Mari has since become as close to a father to me as anyone since my dad passed. The phone still rings late at night and it's him, the two of us struggling in our broken French and Spanish to communicate but somehow always managing.

And of course, the equally obstinate Catalans grabbed hold of my heart early and often. Ferran and Albert Adrià making it their personal mission to show me how good, how insanely good, ham could be. How stuff that came in a can could be divine. Showed me—as they showed the world—the glorious extremes of human creativity. It's not that I loved the South of Spain any less. It's just that I came late to the party.

Spain, for me, is a country of grown-ups. When I'm asked where I'd like to die—specifically at what table—I always picture myself in Spain, sagging to the ground with a blissful expression on my face at Etxebarri, an austere yet revelational restaurant in the mountains near San Sebastián where most dishes have only three ingredients: the principal protein (a single perfect prawn, a spoonful of fish eggs, a slab of exceptional beef), olive oil, and salt.

It's fitting that you choose Spain to follow *Rice, Noodle, Fish*. There are, I've long believed, similarities between the two countries and their approaches to food: the embrace of single ingredients done as well as possible, the love of tradition, the mania for great seafood. The "poteo," that uniquely awesome bar crawl, bouncing from place to place, scooping delicious, delicious things into your mouth between glasses of wine: wild mushrooms, little plates of slow-braised cheek, slices of acorn-scented, fat-rippled ham, ridiculously tiny sea cucumbers, squid and octopus seared on the *plancha* . . . grilled turbot . . . slow-cooked tripe with hunks of chorizo. . . . Going out to eat dinner at midnight. Think about Spain and the mind reels.

You could hardly pick a better place to eat, to write about, to die.

Cheers,
Tony

Dear Tony,

Like you, my love for Spain was born in the north. It struck first in Barcelona—eighteen years old and goose-bumped by everything that passed before my eyes. Later, I fell in with the Basques, learned the art of *pilpil* and *pintxos* crawls at the hands of Luis and Visi Irizar. Finally, I found a more permanent solution to my courtship with this country: I fell hard for a Catalan girl and somehow convinced her to marry me.

I've called Barcelona home since 2010, and I've used the years since to roam the peninsula like an Iberian pig in search of fallen acorns. I've eaten baby goat with the horsemen of Andalusia, crushed sea urchin in the cider houses of Asturias, scraped *socarrat* from paella pans with the *abuelas* of Alicante. My appetite for this country knows no one taste or territory.

Make no mistake, this ain't Japan. I can't hide behind my gaijin status here. I married into this country and claim to understand its cuisine. At the very least, I've consumed enough calories over the years that I'd be a knucklehead not to have learned something along the way.

The book I'm thinking about is a more personal, intimate book than Japan. To write it any other way would be to ignore the role my family and friends have played in shaping my understanding of this country and its people. Here, I am part insider, part outsider—a position not without its possible perils, but maybe it gives me something to say.

These are well-traveled grounds I traverse. The titans of the Wandering Scribes' Club—Dumas, Orwell, Papa—have been peddling their opinions on Spain for centuries. More than the foreign contingent, though, the Spaniards claim a long tradition of heavyweight epicures who wield their pens as voraciously as their forks. Néstor Luján, Simone Ortega, José Carlos Capel—men and women with big thoughts about food and huge footprints in the kitchens across Spain. All of this is to say that I would be wise not to fuck this up.

Luckily I've had a lot of really smart people along the way to guide me to the good stuff. Rice masters. Fish whisperers. The brothers Adrià. My in-laws. Your buddy José Andrés has been my most trusted consigliere on all matters of the stomach. He cracked open in me a wide and wonderful curiosity for Spain many years ago, which I've been probing ever since.

More than specific restaurants or dishes, it's the people and the stories behind the food that I want to build this book around. A pack of sisters who brave the elements to scrape gooseneck barnacles from the cracks and crevices of the Galician coast. A band of fishermen off the coast of Cádiz who maintain the world's oldest fish hunt. And in the sunbaked mountains near Granada, in the cave community of Fuente Nueva, my wife's eighty-seven-year-old great uncle, Chacho Federo, the last of a dying breed of Andalusian shepherds.

I've been pocketing these stories for years, saving them in the dank bodega of my mind like a bottle of '74 Vega Sicilia, waiting for the right moment to decant and drink. Now's the time.

Un abrazo,
Matt

Matt,

Might I respond to your last with a resounding "Fuck You!"

You got me beat. By a mile. No matter how much I love Spain, no matter how many friends I think I have, however well connected I thought I was, how sincere my love for the food, the lifestyle . . . you've got me beat. By a mile.

You fucking LIVE in Barcelona. Who doesn't want to live in Barcelona? You had the good sense to marry a Spaniard—which means, in my limited experience, that you often come home to find an *ibérico* ham casually deposited on the kitchen counter next to a knife. You are on close terms with Juan at that incredible counter in the Boqueria. You go out to dinner at midnight, start drinking again at noon, nap around three, nibble on olives and little bites of awesomeness when you rise, and pretty much live the dream.

So, yeah, fuck you, Matt. I hope the next Roads & Kingdoms book is on Orlando.

Suerte,
Tony

Chapter One

BARCELONA

On Saturday, April 17, 1999, at 11:58 p.m. in Café Ramirez on the bottom floor of the Maremagnum Plaza in the port of Barcelona, I fell in love with Spain for the first time. I was eighteen years old, traveling around with twenty-eight other students from the Cary High School Spanish program. Our fearless leader, Señora B.A., had studied abroad in Barcelona, and she hoped to show her students a piece of the culture that transformed her life so many years earlier. Her heart was in the right place, but she was simply outmatched by a group of hormonal teenagers four thousand miles removed from classrooms, homework, parental authority.

We arrived at Maremagnum thirty minutes earlier, a thick pack of teenagers looking to soak up the legendary club scene of Spain. Except that, when we got off the elevator, the dance floor was empty—not a soul besides the bouncer and the bartenders. I grabbed my two closest friends and retreated down into the commercial complex below in search of alcohol. This wasn't just my first time drinking in Spain; it was my first time sitting at a bar, first time speaking Spanish outside of the classroom. I dug deep: *Un* whiskey *cola, por favor.* The bartender gave a little grin, put two cubes of ice and four fingers of J&B in a tube-shaped glass and topped it off with Coke. Success! Spanish in action.

For the next two hours, we put three

years of Spanish class into extraordinary practice. The bar technically closed at midnight, but the owner and the group of thirty-something Catalans were so amused by this rogue crew of Spanglish-speaking Americans that they locked the door with us inside and kept the drinks flowing. With every sip, the Spanish slipped past my lips with greater ease. I started to dig out words I didn't know I knew, combined in ways that kept the conversation marching forward: Not just where are you from, but what do you do, what do you think, what do you believe. When we finally climbed down off our stools, a few sips past the stroke of two, my entire body was on fire. We made a pact right then, before riding the elevator back up to a by-then-packed disco: We would spend the next ten days putting it all on the line—drinking absinthe off La Rambla, eating tapas in the backstreets of Toledo, dancing until sunrise in Madrid—but we would do it all in Spanish.

🍇 🫒 🐖

On Tuesday, March 27, 2002, at 11:47 a.m. at stall #570, the María Pujol Frutería two-thirds of the way back in the Mercat de la Boqueria in the Ciutat Vella of Barcelona, I fell in love with Spain for the second time. I arrived in the city six weeks earlier and settled in for my semester abroad in the Catalan capital.

My only request was that whomever I lived with allow me to cook my own meals. College awakened in me an intense desire to experiment in the kitchen, and more than studying, I looked forward to raiding the Spanish markets for new ingredients to discover. Since most host families rely on cooking for their student guests for extra income, the study abroad program paired me with Teresa, a single Catalan woman in her late forties, who not only didn't cook anything, she didn't eat either. Instead, she drank two bottles of Bach Brut Nature cava a day on her little patio in the Gràcia neighborhood of the city. At first Teresa proved a fun hostess; in the window between when the first bottle woke her up and the second bottle put her down, she'd engage me in intense conversations about the post-9/11 world America was shaping (like most Spaniards, she longed for the Clinton years). But as her drinking and depression grew in tandem during my first six weeks in Spain, I decided to seek out my own accommodations. Just so happened David Klinker, a friend from UCLA, had a room opening up in an apartment he was renting with a Catalan, an Italian, and a pair of Germans.

At that hour on a Tuesday, I should have been in my Catalan history class, learning about the heroics of Jaume I and Lluís Companys, but we had a big dinner party planned that evening and I needed a head start on the shopping. I had only recently discovered the Boqueria, the thirteenth-century market at the heart of the Barcelona food chain, and it quickly became my new classroom, a Technicolor collision of produce, protein, and human activity that provided the perfect backdrop to the two things that mattered most to me in 2002: cooking and speaking Spanish.

"Back for more, eh?" *Wait, is he talking to me?* I scanned the crowd, saw myself surrounded by a sea of Catalan grandmas with their little produce carts. Just a few words, but words of immeasurable value; words that meant some part of me belonged to this distant landscape.

After these elaborate dinner parties, we would invariably pile onto the metro and make our way to the Raval, to L'Ovella Negra, a loud, dark, cavernous drinking hole known for its density of international revelers. I spent most of my time at the foosball tables watching El Viejo, the old man rumored to be the greatest *futbolín* player in all of Spain. He wore a jacket with medals pinned on his right breast like a decorated general, and sat there sober, stone-faced, chewing on the butt of a cigar, waiting for his prey to come to him. El Viejo was doling out one of his typical thrashings to a team of stunned Germans one night when David spotted a beautiful Catalan girl across the room. We grabbed a pitcher of sangria, made our way over, challenged her and her friend to doubles. After a few rounds, we all went out dancing. Two years later, David married Marta on Coronado Island in Southern California.

I lived in Santa Cruz at the time and drove down the coast to the wedding in a one-hundred-dollar used Peugeot I bought with money from my first writing gig. By that point, Barcelona was almost an abstraction—a surreal six months transformed into a warm, sunny island in the recesses of my memory. The place destined to live on as an ellipsis in my life.

On Friday, September 23, 2010, at 6:07 p.m. on the terrace of La Paciencia at the base of La Rambla del Raval, I fell in love with Spain for the third time. I was late, but I needed to buy a cheap cell phone, just in case. Laura was there at one of the metal tables, sipping a *caña* of Estrella Damm.

I arrived in Barcelona four days earlier roughed up from the life I left behind. I had spent the previous five years living between Manhattan and Allentown, Pennsylvania, working as the food editor at *Men's Health*, writing with my former boss a series of nutrition books called *Eat This, Not That!* It wasn't supposed to be a series, but after the first book sold a million copies in its first year, the project took on a momentum of its own. Eighteen books in five years, combined with a day job and the intensity of life in Manhattan had pushed me to the breaking point. I grew up treating the word *no* as an allergy, believing that few good things come from those two letters, and the buffet of life that is New York in your twenties preyed upon my weakness. My body showed signs of cracking, my head not far behind. I needed a change. I broke up with my girlfriend of four years, said good-bye to my friends, packed a single bag, and left my apartment in the East Village. My plan was as simple as it was unoriginal: Move to Italy, write a novel, fall in love with an Italian, and spend a life eating pappardelle and drinking afternoon *amari*.

Barcelona was a pit stop on my way to paradise, a chance to see some old friends and revisit some of my favorite haunts before pushing on to bigger things in Italy. Before leaving, I e-mailed David and Marta, happily ensconced in their Southern Californian existence, and asked if they had any friends in the city who might want to grab a beer or a cup of coffee while I was in town.

"My sister-in-law, Laura, lives there," David wrote. "Be careful with this one. She's a bit shy. No guarantee she'll respond." I sent her an e-mail, but David was right: no response.

Counting down my days to Italy, I traveled up to Girona for a dinner at El Celler de Can Roca, destined to be crowned the best restaurant in the world in the years to follow. The dinner showcased everything I had been reading about in the years since I left Spain—a mixture of technical innovation, whimsy, and concentrations of outrageous flavor and texture that moved me deeply over twenty-two courses and four hours. A single giant shrimp broken down into seven different aquatic expressions; an earth-shattering beef tartare covered in crunchy *pommes* soufflé and tiny pellets of mustard ice cream; a dessert served in a halved soccer ball presented as *"un gol de* Messi." As dinner wound down, I sat with the Roca brothers—Joan the chef, Josep the sommelier, Jordi the pastry chef—and listened to them say very smart things about food and life in Spain.

Afterward, I sat alone on the steps of the church perched above old Girona and looked out across Catalunya. Did I just have the best meal of my life by myself? Were those tears of joy or fear or desperation I fought off during dinner? What the fuck am I doing here?

Back at the hotel, I opened up my in-box and found an e-mail from Laura in Spanish. "I'm sorry for not responding earlier. I just found your e-mail in my spam folder. I'd love to have a beer before you leave for Italy. How about tomorrow at 6:00 p.m.? You choose the place."

Little did she know that I had already mapped out a plan as soon as I sent that first e-mail, a little bar crawl that would allow me to feign a backstreet Barcelona knowledge in a casual, seemingly spontaneous romp through the Raval. I didn't want to be another American passing through, even if that was exactly what I was.

After beers at La Paciencia we pushed deeper into the neighborhood, to El Celler

BARCELONA WAS
A MISTRESS WE
SHARED.
EVERYTHING
WE DID, WE DID
TOGETHER.

d'en Frank Petersen. Owned by Armando, a Guinean immigrant with a high-wattage smile and wry sense of humor, the bar is one of the last of a dying breed of old-school bodegas, places where Spaniards go for a quick drink and a snack while buying wine for the week from giant wooden barrels. Bring in anything—a leather wineskin, old water bottles, a Dutch Oven—and Armando will fill it for you for two euros a liter.

We ate sheep's milk cheese and drank cheap barrel wine. We talked about her sister, about Laura's job at Catalunya's biggest bank, about my marathon meal at Can Roca. I asked her one of my favorite questions to spring on new friends: What would her last meal on earth be? She didn't hesitate: "A plate of *jamón*, toasted bread rubbed with tomato and olive oil, and a slice of my dad's *tortilla*." I felt my heart skip a few beats.

We moved on to the bar at Dos Palillos, a polished Japanese-Catalan restaurant with a hip clientele and a long menu of Eastern-inflected tapas. We ate *ibérico* pork dumplings and giant red shrimp washed down with cava, which I discovered was Laura's lifeblood. I asked her what it was like having her sister so far away; she asked me why I left New York. At 10:00 p.m., we parted ways. Laura had a late dinner with a group of friends; I had plans to drink with a chef I had met a few days earlier. We shared a taxi uptown, and when I dropped her off at the restaurant, I gave her the number to my new red plastic ten-euro mobile. Just in case.

I spent the next few hours at an awesome piano bar, the kind you daydream about from across the Atlantic, drinking cocktails and bantering with the chef and his wife. But I wasn't there; I was still back in the streets of the Raval, reliving the last few hours in my head, wondering if she found that taxi ride as excruciating as I did.

At 2:00 a.m. my little red cell buzzed in my pocket for the first time.

¿Qué haces? *What are you up to?*

I put my trip to Italy on hold and spent the next two nights wandering the Ciutat Vella until daybreak. We treated the narrow passages and hard angles of the

Old City like a Rubik's Cube to solve to-gether. On the third night, I invited Laura over to my rented apartment and made her the dinner I had been cooking in my head since the moment we met at La Paciencia: gnocchi with duck ragù topped with a bit of shaved orange and bitter chocolate. We rolled the gnocchi together, drank cava, ate vanilla gelato with coarse sea salt and emerald olive oil—one of those nights that lives on a loop in your head.

Ana Laura Pérez Gonzalez was born on June 19, 1987, in Igualada, a town of fifty thousand in the interior of Catalunya. Her parents came to the region as teens, both part of the Andalusian exodus to the north—her mother from Jaén, the olive oil capital of the world; her father from the cave communities outside of Granada. Ángel ran a branch of CatalunyaCaixa, one of the region's largest banks, and Laura was, in some way, set to follow in his footsteps: She studied accounting at the University of Barcelona and worked at a local branch of the Caixa. She had traveled outside the country just twice—to France with her family and to California for her sister's wedding—but said she was anxious to see more of the world.

There were many things to love about Laura: her generous sense of humor; her mixture of school-girl innocence and old-soul wisdom; her ability to derive deep reservoirs of pleasure from life's little moments, like cracking the burnt-sugar crust of a *crema catalana*. And, to be completely honest, what struck me most that first night as we hopped around the Raval were her long brown hair, chestnut skin, wide, bright eyes that convey nothing but warmth and humility. I felt the earth opening up inside me.

But it wasn't an entirely monogamous love. Barcelona was a mistress we shared, and everything we did we did together. We ate *jamón* and roasted pepper sandwiches at Can Paixano near the port, elbow-to-elbow with the mass of old Catalans and young travelers that storm the old bar for its salted pork and cheap house champagne. Drank elaborate gin tonics in big-bellied cabernet glasses with horn-rimmed hipsters at Pesca

Salada in the Raval. Took walks down to the beach for the smoked paella and bay scallops at Kaiku—at the edge of Barceloneta, a few steps from the Mediterranean.

With every day came memories of a place I wanted to make my own years earlier: the early-morning light against the palm trees and arches of the Plaça Reial; the skateboarders—the world's best—attacking the smooth ledges and stone gaps of the modern art museum; the old men in Speedos playing *petanca* at the beach, their skin like overcooked hot dogs; the way Catalans wish the entire bar a good day as they come and go.

Whatever tide of doubt and confusion that came pouring out of me days earlier on the steps of Girona suddenly seemed very far away. Why start from scratch—language, friends, local knowledge—when I had roots in Barcelona? Why chase an Italian when you can give yourself to a Catalan?

I traded my temporary apartment in for a long-term rental and unpacked my bag.

Every great ancient city needs a powerful origin story; Barcelona's starts with Hercules. Four hundred years before the founding of Rome, on the hunt for the Golden Fleece with Jason and the Argonauts, our hero loses one of his nine ships to the rough seas and begins a desperate search to recover it. He finds it washed up on the shores of Catalunya, and Hercules and his crew are so taken by the area's beauty that they build a city and name it after the ninth ship: *Barca Nona.*

In truth, the Romans built Barcelona, at least the first lasting iteration of it. They called it Barcino, a seat of governance for the Iberian outpost of the empire—not big enough to merit a coliseum or an amphitheater like Tarragona to the south, but important enough to construct a two-mile defense wall to protect the five thousand or so inhabitants living in Barcino by the second century.

In the thousand years after the fall of the Roman empire, Barcelona became a revolving door for the forces that stirred across Western Europe: Jewish settlers seeking a place beyond persecution, Visigoths in search of a seat for their volatile empire, Muslim forces looking to extend their growing presence in Iberia. The golden age of Barcelona came in the early part of the fourteenth century, when deep coffers and naval dominance gave the Catalans control over most of the Mediterranean: first they took Sicily, later Constantinople, Athens, Corsica, Sardinia, and Naples. While trade, banking, and art flourished, the master builders of the fourteenth century constructed the stone core of Barcelona that still stands today, and the sense of a national Catalan identity began to take shape. As Colm Tóibín, the Irish author who has lived on and off in the city for years, observes in *Homage to Barcelona*: "This feeling that as intellectuals, humanists, inventors, writers, and entrepreneurs they had risen above Spain would never leave Catalan consciousness."

By the time Cristóbal Colón returned to Catalunya in 1493 to announce to Ferdinand and Isabella his discovery of a New World passage, Barcelona had already lost much of its wealth and prominence around the Mediterranean. The statue commemorating the Italian explorer at the base of La Rambla today is marked by two historical curiosities: the first being that he stands pointing southeast across the sea, away from America; the second that the statue celebrates the very voyage that was a deathblow to the Mediterranean trade routes that gave Barcelona its importance.

For the next two centuries, Catalunya struggled to retain its autonomy amid the rising power in central Spain. On September 11, 1714, after withstanding fifteen months of a punishing siege by the forces of Philip V, the Catalans lost the War of the Spanish Succession and officially became a part of Spain. This wasn't just a political annexation, but a systematic dismantling of Catalan culture: books were burned, classrooms shuttered, and churches remade as all signs of Catalan language and heritage were banned from the region. September 11 remains Catalunya's national day, when flags and firecrackers and the words of "Els Segadors," the national anthem, fill the

First light on the backstreets of the Gothic Quarter.

streets: "Triumphant Catalunya will once again become rich and full."

By the beginning of the twentieth century, those words came to life in the streets of the Gothic Quarter as a new wave of Catalan nationalism took hold in the city. After two decades of political turbulence among the anarchists, communists, and conservatives vying for power, two radical figures, Francesc Macià and Lluís Companys, swept the 1932 elections on a platform of national pride and promptly made Catalan the official language of the new government. A resurgence of Catalan art and literature took hold across the region, but the high times were short-lived. Fascism was afoot across Europe, and General Francisco Franco was on the march from his exile in the Canary Islands.

At the dawn of the Spanish Civil War, Barcelona was a hotbed of political angst and escalating violence. Anarchists struck first, burning buildings and executing city officials and members of the city's clergy by the hundreds, followed by the Soviet-backed communists looking to exploit the splintering city. By the time Franco arrived, Catalunya was in disarray, most of its leaders having escaped to France as political refugees. That didn't stop Franco and his fascist allies, Germany and Italy, from carpet-bombing Barcelona and systematically erasing all traces of Republican sympathy. Mass executions, political imprisonments, torture: the scars from this dark, cruel period cut so deep that many in Spain still refuse to discuss what happened here in the 1930s.

It wasn't just leftist sympathizers Franco snuffed out; he intended to blast Catalan culture out of existence. If your parents named you Jordi at birth, you were now Jorge; if you wanted to speak Catalan, you did it behind closed doors. Camp Nou, FC Barcelona's massive soccer stadium, famously became one of the few places wear Catalan pride persisted publicly, establishing the team's political roots and giving FC Barça its now legendary slogan: *Més que un club*. More than a club.

With the death of Franco in 1975 came the uncorking of Catalan culture as the region embraced its language, history, and cuisine with the intensity of a nation rediscovering itself. All of these good vibes and big ambitions won Barcelona the 1992 Summer Olympics, an opportunity that the architects of the Catalan resurgence harnessed to erase decades of dormancy and catapult Barcelona to international stardom.

Today the battle for Catalan independence rages fiercer than ever. The secession movement took on new momentum in the wake of the Spanish Crisis, a crippling economic downturn that left national unemployment at record levels. Catalans, tired of answering to a central government they view as corrupt and unjust, have turned out en masse in protest and in referendums to show their support for independence. Depending on whom you talk to in Spain, it's either the latest iteration of Catalunya's superiority complex, or the inexorable march toward the independence Catalunya has always deserved.

Regardless of how this all plays out, it's clear that the rift between Catalunya and the rest of Spain has gone well beyond name-calling and petty stereotypes and into more nefarious territory. Like a couple's quarrel gone off the rails, both sides are saying and doing things that they simply can't take back. Whether by decree or by default, Catalunya will be an island in the sea of Spain for many years to come.

I may have already written the ending to my Spanish telenovela, but not everyone read the script. A few days after moving into my new place, my little red phone buzzed again: "We need to talk." The four most dreaded words budding love has ever known.

We met at a shitty café down the street from my apartment. I didn't want to ruin a good bar with a painful conversation. And it was: "This isn't the right time for me. I like you a lot, but I'm not ready for this." I rolled the words in Spanish around in my head, stared at them from every angle, hoping to wring from them some alternative truth. I tried my own words—something feeble about the risks in life worth taking—but they fell to the ground, lifeless.

We parted ways with a vague promise

to continue to hang out around town. I sat stunned in my apartment for days, replaying the magical week, trying to understand where I had gone wrong. I probed David for information, hoping Marta might have some insight into the sudden about-face, but they didn't want to get in the middle of it.

I tried to push on with life in the city. I wrote in the mornings, took long bike rides up the coast in the afternoons, got beers with friends in the evenings. Above all, I did what I loved to do most in Barcelona: I ate.

I ate in a way I never could when I was dumping my last Euros into beers and baguettes during my student days. I ate razor clams and Galician beef in polished places praised by the global food cognoscenti. I ate *conservas*, Spain's exemplary canned seafood, washed down with dark vermouth from bodegas in Poble-sec. I ate shawarma in the Raval, where spinning towers of meat fill the neighborhood at all hours with the smell of garlic and mystery spices. I ate suckling pig roasted in the oven of my rented apartment with everyone I knew in the city gathered around one small table. I ate my way around neighborhoods I had never known before—Poblenou, an industrial barrio in transition; Sarrià, with its wine bars packed with upper-crust Catalans—and Barcelona was brilliant throughout.

But I wanted to share all of these moments with Laura, and I struggled to get past the sting of disappointment that I couldn't. I didn't like the dark alleys my mind was leading me down, so when two friends proposed a trip to northern Italy for truffle season, I packed my bag and said good-bye to Barcelona.

In Piedmont we ate nothing but fragrant tubers for three days, aided in our excess by a retired policeman who took us truffle hunting in the hills above Barolo and sent us off with our pockets stuffed with diamonds. A few days later, a train pulled into Bologna Centrale and spit me out into the city that I had originally planned to live in. I found a room in an apartment with a graduate student and a guitar player and enrolled in an Italian school a few blocks from Piazza Maggiore.

In Bologna, I found a blueprint for the life I had fantasized about during all those sleepless nights working on the books. I spent my mornings soaking up Italian lessons with a small class of international students; I spent the afternoons trying it out in the little vegetable stands and meat-and-cheese shops and fresh-pasta emporiums that line Via Pescherie Vecchie. A lifelong love of ragù blossomed into a full-blown obsession that sent me by bike and train to all corners of Emilia-Romagna, chasing down the esoteric little differences found between one village's recipe and the next. I found the café of my and every American writer's dreams, filled with animated Italians and oil-thick espresso and a liquor shelf heavy with bitter spirits. I spent many three- and four-spritz afternoons there, trying to write my way out of whatever mess I made in Spain.

But there wasn't enough Aperol and agnolotti in all of Italy to lessen the gravitational pull from across the Mediterranean.

Things that had absolutely nothing to do with Laura—a statue of Poseidon, a bad pop song, a bubbling tower of *lasagne verdi*—stirred in me deep pangs of longing. I tried everything to fight off the magnetic pull: I called friends in New York and told them to talk sense into me, I went out drinking with lovely young women from my class, read about ragùs of mythic origins waiting to be devoured. But none of it worked.

When I read online that LCD Soundsystem, one of Laura's favorite groups, was to play at the Razzmatazz club in Barcelona on the night of November 7, I bought two tickets, canceled the rest of my Italian course, and said good-bye to Bologna.

On my train ride to Rome, I wrote an e-mail to a close friend in the States.

As much as I may love its beaches and bars and avant-garde structures, as happy as I am playing Ping-Pong with Salva and watching Barça games with the Jefe and wandering the jumbled streets of the Raval with a thick international posse, I am really going back for one reason: her.

Barcelona has long had a magnetic pull on its visitors. Hemingway found its bars to be some of the finest watering holes in Europe. Orwell felt so strongly about the city and the region that he took up arms and spent months in the cold, muddy battlefields in northern Catalunya, fighting the fascists. Federico García Lorca, the great Andalusian poet, came to Barcelona in 1925 as a guest of Salvador Dalí and promptly fell in love with Catalunya—its bars and cafés, its community of artists and intellectuals, its free spirit. At the end of a performance of his controversial play *Yerma* in 1935, in the months before war broke out, he took to the stage and offered: "My heart is with you. Long live Catalunya!" A year later, Franco would have Lorca executed in Granada.

Their ghosts can be found everywhere: in the seedy Gothic plaza named for Orwell or at the Hotel Majestic on Passeig de Gràcia where Lorca spent four of his last months on earth or on the dust that covers the absinthe bottles at Bar Marsella, seemingly untouched since the days when Papa tussled with the green fairy here.

It's hard to think of a city that wears its charms more conspicuously than Barcelona. They're all there for you to absorb, one by one, mountain and sea, wide, majestic avenues and tiny, lonely backstreets, oil-slicked shoebox bars and opulent eateries of innovation. Spend a perfect day in Barcelona—one that starts early wandering the streets of the Gothic Quarter (magical at dawn before the city fully stirs), moves on to breakfast at the Boqueria (perhaps a plate of garbanzos spiked with blood sausage and raisins from Pinotxo, washed down with a few glasses of jet-cold cava), followed by some time lost in the grip of Gaudí (the psycho-naturalism of Parc Güell, maybe, or the dueling apartment buildings of Passeig de Gràcia) before retiring to the beach for a crock of soupy lobster rice and a siesta on the sands of the Barceloneta, a recharge for the nighttime tapas crawl through Gràcia or Born that will carry you from bar to bar into the early morning—spend a perfect day in Barcelona like this and you'll find yourself saying: "What if . . ."

El Quim, at the heart of
the Boqueria, all fired up.

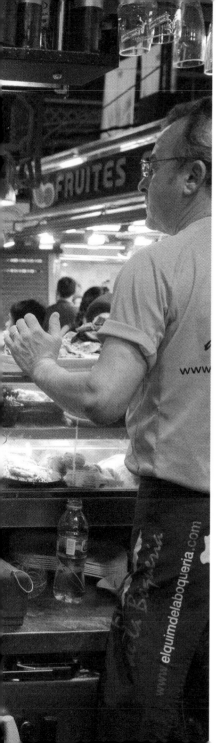

One time, over a late breakfast at El Quim de la Boqueria, a high-traffic bar in the center of the market serving an expansive menu of seasonal Catalan cooking, I met a short, bald man from Hong Kong and his chopstick-thin girlfriend. The two of them sat at the bar for the better part of two hours, silently dismantling every last inch of the menu: grilled asparagus and fried artichokes, braised oxtail, giant plates of seared crustaceans, eggs fried in olive oil and blanketed with baby squid.

Finally, after sucking the last shrimp head and swilling the last drops of cava, the man patted his lips with a napkin and turned to me. "I am a businessman from Hong Kong and I have traveled all around eating at the best restaurants in the world, but I've never eaten as well as I do at this bar. I want to marry her, but first I needed to bring her here, to see that she loved it as much as I do. Tonight, I will propose to her."

Barcelona will do that to a man. Inspire travel from the corners of the globe for a small taste. Make perfectly brilliant destinations elsewhere feel dim by comparison.

But all of this love for the Catalan capital comes at a cost. Barcelona is now the third most-visited city in all of Europe, after only Paris and London. Its port houses two of the world's largest cruise ships, the 6,328-passenger *Allure of the Seas* and its sister *Harmony of the Seas*, twin menaces of the Mediterranean that, along with a fleet of countless others, have ushered in a homogeneous cruise-ship economy. You need only follow the souvenir shops and the paella signs to understand the trampled trail of the eight-hour tourist: up La Rambla, around Plaça de Catalunya, climbing Passeig de Gràcia past Gaudí's two famous apartment buildings, and ending beneath the towering spires of the Sagrada Familia. The architects of post-Olympic Barcelona never imagined the city in the grip of such a mongrel mass of British stag parties, Russian yacht barons, and Chinese tour buses.

To make matters worse, 2014 marked the end of a grandfathered lease agreement that capped rent for old, family-run businesses deemed a vital part of the city's social fabric. The rent on toy stores and candy makers and small workshops occupying the most coveted real estate in the high-traffic corners of the old city rose by thousands of euros overnight. The rise of shoe stores, souvenir shops, and bike rentals continues to consume the city's historic heart.

Citizens have revolted. Catalans, adhering to a long tradition of airing their grievances as publicly as possible, organize in front of city hall in Plaça Sant Jaume to remind the politicians of the body they were elected to govern. Red spray paint on ancient walls issue stiff warnings to foreigners: GUIRIS GO HOME! Banners and flags across the Ciutat Vella that hang from balconies across the old city paint a troubling picture: SHHH! LET US SLEEP! WE WANT A DIGNIFIED BARRIO!

In 2015, Ada Colau and her band of progressive socialists swept into office on a campaign to fight the forces of Barcelona tourism. Proposals on the table include a moratorium on all new hotels, adding tourist taxes, capping cruise-ship parking, and actively combating luxury tourism. "I don't want a city that only snobs come to," she told the press. Some say this is biting the hand that feeds the city, spiting an evergreen industry that has buoyed Barcelona as the rest of the country suffers through a financial crisis. But most citizens applaud her crusade, desperate for some signal from the government that this city is still theirs.

I arrived to Barcelona-El Prat airport at 3:00 p.m. on November 7 with two tickets to LCD Soundsystem, a liter of Campari, a quarter wheel of Parmagiano-Reggiano, a bottle of fifty-year-old balsamic vinegar, a quarter kilo each of thinly sliced mortadella, *culatello*, and *finocchiona*, plus two freshly dug white truffles roughly the size of a small boy's fist. An excessive haul, I admit, but once you go on a pantry run, the procuring takes on a momentum of its own.

The only thing I didn't have was a firm plan. I had rented an apartment on Carrer dels Escudellers in the Gothic Quarter for three nights. Two days earlier, I sent a text to Laura:

Will you be in Barcelona on Saturday night? I have a friend who has a package for you.

I am a man of the grand gesture, the meticulous construction of the big moment, and the text bought me just enough time to figure it out. I dropped the supplies off at the apartment and walked furiously around the neighborhood, looking for inspiration. I passed by Maoz, a falafel shop on Carrer de Ferran I used to frequent in 2002, and as I stuffed my pita with pickled peppers, a lightbulb began to flicker. I tore out a page from my notebook, scribbled a few words in Spanish, folded the note, and passed it to the dreadlocked blond working the fryer. "A young brunette Catalan about this tall is going to come here at 7:00 p.m. When you see her, please pass her this note."

I ran down the street to a small corner market, wrote down another few words on a notebook page that I folded and handed to the Middle Eastern man behind the register. "A young brunette Catalan about this tall is going to come in here around 7:15 p.m. and is going to buy two oranges and a head of garlic. When she does, please hand her this note."

At 6:00 p.m., I sent Laura a message.

Me: Be in front of Maoz Falafel shop on Ferran at 7 p.m.

Her: I don't understand. Are you here?

Me: Don't worry. All will become apparent soon enough. Just be there at 7.

Her: Alright.

The text led her to the first note, the first note led her to the second, and the second led her to me, sitting on the steps of Plaça Tripi with the third and final note. She didn't say anything, just opened it.

Te echo de menos. I miss you.

What followed felt like a courtship sequence from a Wes Anderson film. Rounds of tapas and cava at two of my favorite little bars, followed by a two-hour, head-rattling, soul-shaking performance from LCD Soundsystem in front of 1,500 rabid Spaniards. We stood in the front row and danced like a pack of teenagers on MDMA. After-

ward, we went to Dos Cielos, a Michelin-starred restaurant on the twenty-sixth floor of the Hotel Me, where we drank gin tonics and ate snacks with the chef while all of Barcelona shimmered below us.

At 5:00 a.m., we ended up in the kitchen at my rented apartment, and I put the Italian treasure to work: a plate of Parmesan chunks and thin slices of cured pork, a Campari spritz made with the oranges Laura had purchased earlier in the market, and to close, a plate of eggs fried in olive oil. Laura held her plate as I showered it with thin slices of white truffle, an overwhelming fragrance of funk and pheromones filling the room. If I got down on a knee right then to propose, I was certain she would be mine.

But I was alone in that thought. Laura ate her eggs, drank the last of her spritz, and stood up to leave. "It's been a beautiful night, but I really should go." We walked in silence down to the metro stop on La Rambla. We stood there at the top of the stairs for a minute, the sunrise like a fire in the sky over our heads. "I'm still not ready."

The next few days I spent a long time

lying on the couch, playing psychiatrist with myself, wondering if I was in love with this woman or the idea of this woman—the beautiful Spaniard playing the world's most exasperating game of hard to get. It wasn't just a person or a feeling I was chasing, though; it was an entire life whose dimensions I already played out in my head: the meandering road trips down south to see her family, the elaborate dinner parties where four or five languages stitched the night together. Laura became an avatar for all that my life was missing in America. As someone who hadn't stopped moving since high school—who had ended his previous three relationships by packing a bag—I finally found a reason to slow down. Or so I thought.

I regrouped. I rented another apartment, the eighth in three months, this one on Carrer de les Carretes, a chippy corner of the Raval where a mixture of hash dealing and street soccer turned my front door into a hazard zone. I worked on a book proposal. I read Henry Miller and Montalbán. I tried to fold myself into the rhythms of the neighborhood.

Technically part of the Ciutat Vella, the Old City of Barcelona, the Raval has long been a cultural foil to the more refined living of the Gothic Quarter on the other side of La Rambla. Historically, it was known as the Barri Xinès, the Chinese Quarter, a red-light district with a spicy braise of artists, prostitutes, and immigrants looking to lay down a foundation in Spain. Old-timers talk about their parents warning them of alchemists and bloodsucking vampires that roamed these streets looking for children. Despite its position near the port and La Rambla, the Raval has largely avoided the T-shirt shops and one-euro tapas bars that clog Old Barcelona. Instead, you'll find Muslim butchers and tiny cocktail bars, secondhand clothing stores and Middle Eastern spice merchants. It's a neighborhood where lives are lead publically—on the street corners and in the cafés, down streets so narrow you can smell what the other side of the street is having for dinner. Look up and you will see the worlds of its citizens hanging from the balconies: undergarments and empty butane tanks, gasping plants and jackets on their last winter season. Flags for independence, flags for Spain, flags for a dozen different countries.

I saw Laura once a week, usually on Wednesday or Thursday after she got out of class, and together we continued to discover new corners of the city. After the truffle sunrise, I stopped pushing for romance, stopped interpreting every smile and sideways glance as a door slowly opening. But these nights were potent reminders of how much more I loved this city with her by my side.

At the end of November, I received an invitation to dine at El Bulli. At the time, it was the most famous restaurant in the world, the cradle of Spain's culinary renaissance. Its chef, Ferran Adrià, had recently announced that he would be closing the restaurant in six months, and the world's eaters promptly lost their shit. I lost my shit, too, and spent days debating who to take: One of my gastronaut American friends, who would fly over in a second just to eat this one meal? Maybe a Catalan or Italian friend in Barcelona, someone who would forever cherish the memory? As much as I tried to fight it, though, I had to accept that there was only one person I wanted to go with.

Laura took some time to consider and sent an e-mail. "I would really love to go. As long as you're okay with us going as friends." For some reason, seeing our status so naked on the screen was a tipping point. This—all of this—was a mistake. The yo-yoing emotions, the self-delusion and self-pity, the insistence on making Barcelona work without her: these were all signs of a man slowly coming undone. I decided that I would have dinner at El Bulli with my lovely friend Laura, and when I went back to the States for Christmas, I would stay.

If I was going to leave Spain, I would go out in style. I bought a leg of *ibérico* ham and a wild turkey from the Boqueria, plus a basket of foraged mushrooms, a branch of Brussels, and a mountain of root vegetables and invited everyone I knew in Barcelona over for Thanksgiving. A lifetime of watching proud fathers carve bronzed birds in American movies had the Euro crew deeply intrigued. We smoked spliffs and roasted vegetables. We danced and mashed potatoes. My Italian friend Alice slid her salted hand beneath the bird's skin to season it more thoroughly. We lit candles and laid blankets and spread a dozen dishes out across the floor and at 1:00 a.m., thirteen Europeans sat down to their first ever Thanksgiving dinner. I gave a speech.

At 3:00 a.m., the group shuffled off for a final drink at a bar down the street. I stayed behind to do the dishes. As I stood in my kitchen, surveying the remains of the meal, I heard a gentle knock on my door. I opened it to find Laura standing in the dim light of Carrer de les Carretes. "I thought you might need some help."

🐦 🐖 🐷

When people thought about eating in Europe in the 1980s and 1990s, they dreamed of Provence, Tuscany, Paris, Rome; they didn't think Spain and they didn't think Barcelona. Not that Spain's place on the bottom of the totem pole was justified. The regional cooking of this country has always been based on an infallible formula—exemplary raw ingredients, a world-class pantry, and an abiding simplicity that informs as much of the world's notion of the Mediterranean diet as Italian and French cuisine.

Catalunya is home to Spain's most sophisticated regional cuisine. Its connection to France (Catalunya once extended well north of the Pyrenees) created a deeper reservoir of techniques and influences, while regional wealth—from textiles and trade—meant people had the means to pay for the good stuff, and enough free time to spend preparing and eating it. In a country where most canonic dishes contain no more than a handful of ingredients, Catalans embrace nuanced combinations like *pollastre amb escamarlans*: chicken braised with crayfish in a mole-like mix of nuts, aromatics, and dark chocolate, underlining a region-wide penchant to play sweet against savory, *mar* against *muntanya*.

It's the breadth that makes Catalan cuisine so impressive: In the interior, in places like Lleida and Girona, you find a rich tradition of game and snails and slow-cooked stews. Along the coast, some of Europe's best seafood (deep-water shrimp from Palamós, exemplary anchovies from L'Escala) finds its way into preparations both simple (*plancha*-cooked crustaceans with nothing more than olive oil and coarse salt) and complex (the rich, savory fish stew known as *suquet*). Everywhere you find vegetables, artichokes, asparagus, and teardrop peas from Maresme in the spring; *escalibada*, a salad of ember-roasted onions, peppers, and eggplant; and *samfaina*, a ratatouille-like vegetable stew, at the peak of summer; and in the last gasps of winter, the legendary *calçotadas*: spirited fiestas of charred spring onions dipped in *romesco* and washed down with great quantities of vino *tinto*. But these treasures, like the region itself, remained largely a secret to the rest of the world—further obscured by forty years of dictatorship that strictly forbade anything that looked, sounded, or tasted Catalan.

In 1984, a twenty-two-year-old Catalan named Ferran Adrià took over the stoves at a beachside restaurant in an isolated section of the Costa Brava and slowly began to change that. El Bulli had opened twenty-three years earlier as a roadside grill and miniature golf course for vacationing families who came to Cala Montjoi in the summer months. By the time Ferran signed on, the restaurant had earned a reputation as a place for fine dining, but no one, not even the young chef himself, was prepared for what would happen next.

Working with his partner Juli Soler and a small brigade of young, ambitious cooks, including his younger brother Albert, he began slowly deconstructing the foundation of classic haute cuisine and rebuilding dishes with tastes and textures the world had never seen. Now mythic creation stories from those early days abound: of Ferran dropping strange ingredients into the fryer, or of the brothers Adrià making discoveries in hardware stores and pharmacies in sleep-deprived moments of lucidity.

In the same way Gaudí approached the construction of Sagrada Familia as a sequence of problems to be solved—how to support the massive spires, how to make the facade drip like candle wax—Ferran asked difficult, at times absurd questions, then set about answering them: Can we deliver the essence of a sauce without its cloaking heaviness? (Yes, with CO_2 canisters.) How can we make this olive taste more like an olive? (By dipping concentrated olive juice into calcium alginate to form a sphere.) We can turn solids into liquids, but what about liquids into powders? (*Sí*, with a sprinkle of maltodextrin.)

To keep up with the innovation, the team closed the restaurant six months a year and retired to a workshop on Carrer de la Portaferrissa in Barcelona to develop new dishes for the coming season, unveiling the results in dramatic thirty-five-course bursts of post-haute creativity. Some called it heretical, others called it genius, but everyone waited breathlessly to see what would come out of the kitchen next.

In Ferran, Spain found its new Picasso, its Dalí, its Gaudí. The twentieth century began with a boom of radical innovation in painting, sculpture, and architecture, and now the twenty-first opened with a revolution in the kitchen—one fueled by the belief that food should do more than simply be delicious; it should provoke, entertain, and challenge the diner.

More than an island of radical innovation, El Bulli was an incubator for a new class of ambitious young chefs who together created a common language that helped recast the image of Spanish food globally. Over the years, the chefs destined to change Spain's culinary trajectory all put in their time behind the stoves at El Bulli: José Andrés, Joan Roca, Carles Abellan, Quique Dacosta, Andoni Luis Aduriz. And the foreign talent that came to the Costa Brava—René Redzepi, Grant Achatz, and Massimo Bottura among them—would go on to alter the dining landscape in their respective countries. (Four of the top six restaurants on the 2015 list of the World's 50 Best Restaurants are captained by Bulli alums.)

At the height of its reign as the world's most influential restaurant, El Bulli attracted up to two million reservation requests for just eight thousand seats a year.

The bite-size brilliance of Tickets,
one of Spain's most magical restaurants.

For those 1,992,000 souls who didn't get in each year, Catalunya and Spain were now on the food map. And those first few waves of chefs trained in the Bulli brand of radical rule-breaking were only too happy to welcome them into their restaurants across the region. As the French grit their teeth, publications around the world cheerfully reported that Spain was now beating France at its own game.

That legacy still stands today. As of early 2016, Catalunya is home to the world's number one restaurant (El Celler de Can Roca), the most Michelin-starred female chef on the planet (Carmen Ruscalleda), and, most important, a culture of innovation and free-wheeling experimentation that continues to expand the definition of Spanish dining—and dining itself.

After closing the restaurant in 2011, the El Bulli team decamped to Barcelona.

Albert struck first, and quickly went about showing the world that he's much more than the younger brother of the world's most famous chef. In a stretch of three blocks along Avinguda del Parallel, he has created a restaurant row for the ages: Hoja Santa (modern Mexican), Pakta (Peruvian-Japanese), Bodega 1900 (classic Spanish), and Tickets, the mothership, a modernist tapas wonderland serving some of the most delicious, thought-provoking food on the planet. In less accomplished hands, all of this would feel like culinary parlor tricks, but nobody on the planet can condense more flavor and texture into a single bite than the man behind so much of El Bulli's success over the years. Albert's latest creation, Enigma, will use thirty-five chefs to feed thirty-two diners a night in a progressive dinner that will no doubt break rules and defy expectations. According to both Adriàs, Enigma will be the closest thing to a reboot of El Bulli in Barcelona.

Ferran, for his part, now heads up the Bulli Foundation, a massive team of researchers and chefs whose aim is to further expand the boundaries and definitions of creativity in the kitchen. He will soon move the project from a warehouse at the foot of Plaça d'Espanya back to Cala Montjoi, where the revolution began.

We didn't go to El Bulli as friends. We drove up the coast a day early, stayed in Cadaqués with a balcony overlooking the Mediterranean, ate seafood and drank cava, and walked the tiny streets of this white-washed village hand in hand. In the days after the Thanksgiving surprise, I didn't ask her why she came back, afraid that even mentioning it might rupture whatever fragile alliance we were then forming. But that night in Cadaqués as we lay in bed, the moonlight bouncing off the Mediterranean and flooding our little seaside room, I asked what brought her back that Thanksgiving night. "Maybe I finally trusted that you weren't going to leave. Or maybe I was just in a better place with myself. But by the end of the night, I knew I wasn't ready to leave."

Our first date, at least in any formal capacity, was a five-hour, forty-five-course dinner at the world's most famous restaurant. We started with the flurry of tiny snacks and cocktails that marked the beginning of every meal at El Bulli. Most looked like escaped patients from the Wonka Institution: a transparent chip of crystallized olive oil, raw sugar, and coarse salt; an edible sandwich of mojito made with a dissolving meringue baguette and a neon gel of apple and mint; a frozen balloon of Gorgonzola cracked open at the table and seasoned with grated nutmeg. After a dozen handheld courses, a plate arrived divided into a ying-yang configuration: on one side, hazelnut puree topped with osetra caviar; on the other, a dark osetra puree topped with shiny orbs of hazelnut caviar—to this day one of the most brilliant and delicious dishes I've eaten. We had entered uncharted waters.

The hallmarks of the Adriàs' cuisine, the new language that their legions of apprentices and admirers would appropriate for decades to come, manifested themselves dish by dish as the night inched on:

A textbook tiramisu fashioned from whipped tofu, dark miso, concentrated soy and sake, as intensely savory as the classic version is sweet. *Whimsy.*

A warm cappuccino of bitter chocolate and concentrated hare stock. *Inverted expectation.*

Two of Spain's most famous soups combined in a single ivory bowl: gazpacho and *ajoblanco,* the former as a light clarified granita, the latter an intense emulsification of almonds, garlic, and olive oil. *Deconstruction.*

Baby endive, half of them braised, the others nearly raw, wrapped in parchment paper and torched, then bathed in walnut butter and tiny orbs of olive oil caviar. *Pure. Fucking. Technique.*

A shallow crystal bowl covered with a thin layer of ice and scattered with matcha tea powder and raw sugar, meant to be cracked like a frozen pond in the winter. *Art imitating life.*

The real beauty of the meal, though, was watching Laura lose herself in its sprawling dimensions. She grew up a meat-and-potatoes girl, subsisted largely on tomato salads and *bocadillos de jamón* in her college years, and counted cod a la microwave as her most accomplished recipe. This was her first fine-dining experience, and she embraced it with gusto: not just devouring dozens of ingredients she'd never seen or heard of before—sea cucumber, barnacles, hare blood—but attacking my plate in the moments I spent furiously scribbling notes between bites.

Not everything was delicious; a few dishes were downright puzzling. Adrià has long said that he's not in the business of giving pleasure; he cooks in order to produce emotion. And there was no shortage in the range of feelings he pulled out of us that night. Like a hallucinogenic experience, we cycled through stages of nervous energy and quiet contemplation, inexplicable nostalgia and intense, childlike joy. If I really look back at my romantic life, it can be boiled down to one simple objective: to find the best dining partner possible. And here she was.

When the magic box of mini desserts arrived, both our brains and our bellies were too stuffed to go on, so Laura emptied its payload of miso peanuts and green tea truffles into her purse.

Afterward, as we sat on the terrace overlooking Cala Montjoi, sipping strange potions from tiny glasses, I made a confession: "Two weeks ago, when you sent me that e-mail about being friends, I decided I was leaving Spain."

"And now?"

"I think I'll stick around a little longer."

In January 2012, we moved into an apartment in the heart of the city. Five months later, along the rocky coast of Cadaqués, a town we had grown to love together, I proposed. A year later, in a Spanglish ceremony officiated by both our fathers, we were married at the same spot.

For three years, I lived illegally in Spain, slipping in and out hoping no one would notice. They didn't, and now I am officially a resident of Europe—my sponsor a lovely Catalan-Andalusian with eyes like oceans, a heart of melted butter, and a special set of prescription lenses that magically enhance my virtues and mitigate my faults.

After the wedding, we talked seriously about finding a new place to live. Laura had left her job at the bank to work for Roads & Kingdoms a year before, which meant we could conceivably live anywhere in the world. We tried to go about the process as methodically as possible, sketching out an algorithm based on a list of the qualities we valued most in a home: culture, food, weather, location, health, price, friends, and family. We created a roster of possible candidates and ran each one through the algorithm: San Francisco, Raleigh, Saigon, New York, Bologna, San Diego, Kyoto, Charleston. No matter how many candidates we threw at it, no matter how we tweaked the algorithm, Barcelona trounced the competition.

It's not just the excellent city beaches, the looming mountains, the Mediterranean climate, the gentle cost of living, the universal health care system, the world-class restaurants and nightlife: It's also my new family, a brother, sister, and two parents who count me as one of their own; a group of friends that mirrors a UN assembly; and the Catalans themselves—not as instantly accessible as Spaniards to the south, but once they let you into their lives, you won't want to leave. It's the balance: the fact that people don't treat their smartphones as crutches in social situations (and that five years later, my "smartphone" is the same plastic ten-euro phone I bought the day I met Laura), that I can write in peace for five hours before the East Coast has its first coffee, that I'm never a Gothic stroll or coastline bike ride or random train ride away from a release valve. It's all the stuff that doesn't fit into an algorithm.

Before you ditch your apartment in New York, let me warn you: There are things about Barcelona that will fuck with your head. The crushing crowds, which between April and October turn the Old City into a theme park. (A friend of mine likes to joke that residents should be paid for being actors in the city's tragicomedy.) The torpor: Little problems can take weeks to fix, servers and store employees can make you feel very small, and nothing is open on Sundays. The crime—not dangerous crime, not don't-walk-down-this-street-at-night crime, but opportunistic crime: vultures picking the bones for protein. In five years in Barcelona, I've had two bikes, a phone, a computer, a camera, and a passport stolen from me.

You learn tricks along the way, the little pressure points that crack the city open, minimizing its flaws, maximizing its awesomeness. We live on Via Laietana, a thoroughfare created in 1908 to shuttle traffic from the port uptown, effectively dividing the Ciutat Vella in half: the Gothic Quarter to the south of Laietana, and Born and its towering church and boutique-filled backstreets to the north. Twenty years ago, you came here for heroin; now you come for three-hundred-euro jeans and cold-pressed juices.

Like the old couples who shuffle arm and arm through the Gothic Quarter and who refuse to cede their turf to tourism, we learned the beauty of Barcelona is best taken in as the sun comes up. At 8:00 a.m., the light splinters through the narrow streets and lights the facades of old buildings on fire.

Few cities wear their layers of history as visibly as Barcelona. Our morning walks start at the base of Plaça dels Traginers, where the last pieces of a Roman defense wall mark the borders of Barcino, the an-cient city center. We walk up Carrer dels Lledó, my favorite street in the city, past the bellhops at the posh Mercer Hotel, past the Scottish woman arranging her artisanal cheeses at La Seu, past the workforce waking up with the day's first *café con leche*, until we hit the Plaça del Rei, one of the city's most magnificent squares. Beneath the wall of surrounding stone, on the same steps where Isabella and Ferdinand received Columbus upon his first return from the New World, we sit and soak up the last moments of silence.

Learn the backstreets of Ciutat Vella and even in the fiercest torrents of foreign invasion you're never more than two turns away from a private moment. Pinched between two narrow backstreets and opening up to a small fountain and five sides of stone, Plaça de Sant Felip Neri is an urban oasis, a place we go to hide from the chaos of the surrounding city. It wasn't always so: On the morning of January 30, 1938, Franco's army dropped a bomb in the plaza that killed forty-two people, most of them children from the preschool next door. The facade of the church, the same one where Gaudí attended evening mass while building the Sagrada Familia, is still cratered from the bomb blast.

As the city begins to stir, so does the appetite—you'll need the little tricks now more than ever. Barcelona is not a great breakfast city—breakfast in Spain being so perfunctory that many skip it entirely in favor of a midmorning *bocadillo*. You can go strong, like the handful of old-timers who still believe in starting their days at full speed, and eat fried blood and onions in the Mercat de la Barceloneta or braised tripe at Pinotxo in the Boqueria. Better to ease into the day with 150 grams of churros from Xurreria dels Banys Nous—where the oil is cleaner and the churros hotter than places charging three times what this father-son operation does.

The *Menú del día* rules the lunch scene in Barcelona, where working Catalans expect three courses, plus wine, water, coffee, and bread for under fifteen euros. It's a good way to eat from day to day, and a fine way to familiarize yourself with the classics of the Catalan kitchen, but your life won't be changed by a *Menú del día*. For that, you'll need to be more exacting in your efforts: Suculent in the Raval for classic Spanish comfort food with measured moments of flare: mackerel escabeche, braised pancetta and white beans with a poached egg, baby octopus goosed with nuggets of foie. Or La Cova Fumada in Barceloneta for small oily fish *a la plancha*, plus a pile of grilled artichokes dipped in *allioli*.

As night falls, there is very serious eating to be done around town. Bar Brutal pairs the city's funkiest list of natural wines with light, sharp, seasonal cuisine. Somodó, captained by a Japanese chef with a long history in Europe, offers a six-course dinner that represents one of the city's best dining deals. A respectable dinner could be had at any of the Michelin-anointed eateries you read about in magazines, none better than Albert Adrià's Parallel kingdom. But nighttime in Spain is best reserved for more fluid affairs—slow, determined tapas crawls that expose you to the places and faces of this city in steady doses. Barcelona isn't a tapas

Saturdays at La Plata, one of the little rituals that make the city ours.

town, at least not in the way that Granada or San Sebastián are—cities where establishments are expressly designed for customers who want to eat one or two specific dishes, then push forward. But with a bit of effort, you can piece together a brilliant tapas crawl through Born or Poble-sec or Gràcia.

Then there are the Places that Shall Remain Nameless. The bodega in Sants with the pitch-perfect *croquetas* and throwback prices. The little wine bar close to Plaça Sant Jaume, a sacred refuge from the camera-clutching masses. The coffee shop with brilliant java where, for the moment, I am the only one clicking away. In a city of Barcelona's immense popularity, having a few places to yourself is sacrosanct.

More than specific establishments, though, you learn to love the little rituals forged between you and the city. Our *ruta de resaca*, the Saturday-morning hangover crawl, always starts at La Plata on Carrer de la Mercè, a southern-style Spanish bar serving just three things: fried anchovies, a tomato-and-onion salad, and grilled pork

37

sausage, all washed down with jugs of barrel wine. The vermouth culture, an old Catalan tradition of drinking sweet vermouth and eating salty snacks before a big family lunch, has come alive in recent years; to best capture its full force, head to Carrer del Parlament at 1:00 p.m. on a Sunday and work your way up the street, one glass and one plate of *boquerones* at a time.

Of all the rituals, though, none is more sacred than foraging for dinner. The system of markets is among the finest in the world, each neighborhood across the city anchored by an enclosed structure—often a work of art in itself—filled with exemplary meat, seafood, and produce stands. The Boqueria is the king of these markets, the king of all markets, the eight-hundred-year-old engine of Barcelona's kitchen. Once a sheep market, then a pig market, then a straw market, it is today one of Europe's largest and loveliest food markets. True, it's been overtaken by tourists in recent years, the most vulnerable vendors trading pyramids of produce and icy rainbows of marine life for prefab smoothies and sushi. But the best stands still survive: Petras, the grumpy mushroom king of this fungus-obsessed dominion; Bacallà Carme Gomà, for all manners of dried and salted fish; and Avinova-Aviram, where all birds of a feather meet their final makers.

On the fringes of the city, massive supermarkets—the one-stop solution—loom ominously, but for now, a prevailing culture of specialization means that dinner could easily entail a dozen transactions between you and the people who know best: Peixos J. Arrom in Mercat de Santa Caterina, where the city's best sushi chefs buy tuna belly and sea urchin; Baluard in Barceloneta and its dozens of heroic fire-baked loaves; Vila Viniteca for the best selection of regional cheese and charcuterie and Spanish wine in the city (my last stop before every trip back to the United States). To cook in Barcelona is a daily miracle of market majesty and human interaction.

It takes time and trial and error to figure this stuff out. At first, as you work to assimilate into a new world, your daily life overflows with holy-shit moments. They hit you unannounced, often with a vicious force: as you stand in line at the fishmonger, riding your bike to the beach, smelling the Mediterranean from your window. It took me a full year just to stop being blown away by the fact that I spoke to my girlfriend in Spanish, and that she spoke to her father in Catalan.

Somewhere along the way, the intense bursts of wonder fade as the holy-shit moments are replaced by the little pleasures of daily life in a deeply visceral world: the small design details that go into everything in this city (the streetlamps, the rooftops, the tables at dive bars), the immigrant vendors selling hot samosas and cold beer for a euro on street corners at all hours of the night, the hush that falls over the city during an FC Barça soccer game, and the cloud of hashish that rises from the narrow streets afterward. This is the secret language of your new home; somewhere along the way, you stop saying *them* and you start saying us.

But every once in a while, out of nowhere, the holy-shit moment still hits me. Usually, it's late at night, when my wife is asleep and I'm alone on the terrace, eight stories up, looking out across Barcelona. I see the low-lit arches of the Plaça del Rei where the Romans made fish sauce, the stone points of the old Stock Exchange where Picasso first learned to paint, the packs of drunk Brits kicking crumpled beer cans like soccer balls under the streetlamps, the shadow of the castle on Montjuïc where Franco unleashed the firing squads on his opposition, the Plaça d'Espanya steps where my computer and passport were stolen, the hundreds of Catalan independence flags that carpet the sides of buildings, the beautiful apartment facade below me, the plumes of steam from my neighbor's kitchen, the arch of the crumbled wall where we start our morning walks. The little signs of a life taking shape. That's when it hits me hardest.

KNOW BEFORE YOU GO

 **Know where you are.**

The Spain you imagine may be a strong, unified country fueled by paella, sangria, and bull's blood, but in reality, language, food, politics, and sense of patriotism vary wildly as you work your way from Catalunya to the Canary Islands. Many Spaniards recognize themselves as Galician or Basque or Valencian first, and Spanish second. You'd be wise to learn as much about the regions you plan to visit as possible — knowing a bit of history, specialty dishes, drinks of choice, even a few words of local dialect can go a long way toward coming across as a savvy traveler.

02 **Embrace the value of *"vale."***

Vale is the salt of the Spanish language, used to season every conversation imaginable. It literally means "worth" and functionally means "okay," but its shape-shifting abilities make it one of the world's most useful words. If a chatty cabbie lets loose a diatribe on dumb tourists or an angry citizen corners you, your smile and your *vale* may be all you have. Depending on tone, inflection, enthusiasm, *vale* can be finessed into dozens of different situations. A slow, drawn out *vale* (*vaaale*) means I get it; a few quick ones — *vale vale* — I'm on it. *¿Vale? Vale.*

(03) Know the tipping point.

Gratuity in Spain is almost unheard of among locals. That's not to say that you shouldn't tip a server at a very nice restaurant (you should—5 or 10 percent will do) or tell a bartender or a cabbie to keep the change if they've served you well, but dropping a big bill at a table will more likely evoke confusion than delight. In recent years, servers at a certain class of restaurant have grown accustomed to foreigners' tipping habits and might even be waiting with open palms for their 15 percent, but if your waiter is expecting a tip, then you're probably eating in the wrong restaurant.

(04) Put your lips into it.

Handshakes and hugs have limited social currency in Spain. When meeting a friend or the friend of a friend, expect the double kiss, starting on the left cheek, then moving to the right. It's not as much a kiss as a light cheek rub with a gentle kissing noise, but as your relationship deepens, so does the physical contact. Same goes for intimate male friends and family members, so get over whatever hang-ups you may have in private and be ready to pucker up.

KNOW BEFORE YOU GO

 **Learn these three words.**

 **Go north.**

Por la crisis: because of the crisis—an all-too-common refrain you'll hear from taxi drivers, bartenders, and anyone you meet during your time here. After spending the better part of the decade in a deep recession, Spain is finally on the road to recovery, but the residue of the crisis still clings to everything in the country. National unemployment floats around 20 percent and austerity has trimmed local budgets down to the bone. People may go out less and spend more carefully, but it would take more than a crushing economic crisis to keep the Spaniards down.

Tourists generally divide their time between Barcelona, Madrid, and Sevilla, but the northern coast combines Spain's most stunning landscape with its greatest cuisine. A plodding road trip from the *pintxo* bars of San Sebastián and Bilbao through the cider houses of Cantabria and Asturias and into the seafood palaces of Galicia will give you a taste of it all. Be sure to build in time for the far-flung mountain villages and coastal hamlets, where honest food and warm-hearted locals make for really good times. (Bonus move: Las islas Cíes, off the Galician coast, have some of Europe's loveliest beaches.)

07 Stock up for Sundays.

Research shows that Spain is one of the
least-practicing Catholic nations in the
world, but Sunday remains a sacred day of
rest for the entire country. The streets may
be filled with locals taking in the afternoon
on their day off, but 90 percent of
restaurants, markets, and bars will be
closed, so stock up on the vitals on
Saturday (*jamón*, cheese, wine, etc.) or be
prepared to eat in a tourist-heavy spot.
Sunday afternoon is the big Spanish meal of
the week, almost universally enjoyed at
home, so you could do worse than to
befriend a local during the week and hope
for an invite come the weekend.

08 Play the market.

From Barcelona's Boqueria to Valencia's
Mercado Central to Madrid's Mercado de
San Antón, Spain's markets are among the
finest in all of Europe, there to be pilfered
and plundered for picnics, snacks, and
makeshift meals. That same plate of
fifteen-euro *jamón* in the restaurant will
cost you five euros at the market. Skip the
smoothies, chorizo cones, and all the other
third-rate prepared food used to lure
tourists and focus instead on the *materia
prima*—the raw ingredients that drive the
best chefs and serious home cooks wild:
cured pork, heroic cheeses, preserved
seafood, and impeccable produce.

EAT LIKE A SPANIARD

Spaniards have long mastered the art of eating well, drinking well, and living long. Here are eight ways you can follow their lead.

BREAK BREAD

A meal without bread in Spain is no meal
at all. Bread is an extension of your
hand—an edible implement used to
convey calories from plate to mouth.
Want to look like a Spaniard? Hold your
fork in one hand, bread in the other,
and make the food below you disappear.

SHOW UP LATE

Spain eats later than anywhere in
Europe—starting around 2:00 p.m. for
lunch and 9:30 p.m. for dinner. Tourist-
friendly restaurants may open earlier,
but just know you'll either be alone or
surrounded by people packing passports.

SNACK LIKE A PRO

Eating lunch and dinner so late requires strategic snacking, an art the Spaniards have mastered. *Almuerzo*, around 10:30 a.m., is time for a *bocadillo* and a beer, while *merienda*, a late-afternoon snack, might mean toast with olive oil and chocolate.

SPEAK YOUR MIND

Argue. About the serving sizes, the price, the direction of the country. Anything, really, but do it with fierce, half-drunken conviction. When in doubt, say that whatever classic dish— paella, gazpacho, garbanzos—you're eating is better en casa.

MAKE IT THE MENU

Lunch is the big meal of the day, and it gets no bigger than the *Menú del día*: three courses—starter, main, dessert— plus bread, wine, and coffee for under fifteen euros. Quantity is as important as quality for most Menu-eating Spaniards, but you'll eat well nonetheless.

STAY ON YOUR TOES

Tapas aren't made to be eaten in a single sitting; they're intended to be part of a long movable feast. A real pro knows who makes the best *croquetas*, the best octopus, the best *patatas bravas*, then goes about building a long, boozy path connecting them all.

KEEP IT SIMPLE

Spanish food is about perfect product
and impeccable technique. Spaniards
don't dig on sauces, condiments,
or intense spice. They dress salads
with salt and a river of olive oil,
seafood with nothing but their own
rumbling anticipation. Enjoy the
beauty of simplicity.

TAKE YOUR TIME

Spaniards can stretch a lunch until
dinner and a dinner until the sky turns
pink again. *Sobremesa* means lingering
long after the meal is done, turning the
table into a way station, a soapbox, a
psychiatrist's couch. Order yourself
another drink and soak it up.

MAKING THE OLD NEW AGAIN

Tomato bread (*pa amb tomàquet* in Catalan) is said to be an invention of southern Spanish immigrants working on the Barcelona rail system in the 1920s. It solved two problems: how to revive stale bread, and what to do with Spain's glut of tomatoes.

SEEING RED EVERYWHERE

As the national dish of Catalunya, you'll find tomato bread on every restaurant menu and every family table across the region. Small, juicy tomatoes grown expressly for this sell at market stands across the region.

TOMATE

BETTER BREAD

In leaner times, *pan con tomate* was made with any old piece of bread in need of revitalizing, but these days, the best is made from deeply toasted *pan de cristal*—airy bread with irregular pockets for soaking up as much tomato as possible.

TO SMASH OR GRATE

Controversies abound, especially over whether the pulp of the tomato should be grated or smashed directly onto the bread (purists say the latter). The only point of agreement is lots of virgin olive oil and coarse salt.

Chapter Two

SALAMANCA

On Friday evening, January 16, 2014, the tiny town of La Alberca in the mountains above Salamanca is busy with preparations for the big day ahead: Mariluz Lorenzo is in the back of her sweets shop, sculpting tempered chocolate and toasted nuts to look like links of blood sausage; Demetrio González fills glass bottles with *licor de cereza*, made with cherries soaked in *aguardiente* for five months until the fruit and the firewater are nearly indistinguishable; the cooks from La Catedral make *patatas meneás*, boiling and mashing hundreds of pounds of yellow potatoes, mixing them with olive oil and smoked paprika until they turn orange, then topping with crunchy curls of fried pork belly and points of pickled peppers; María Martín lays out her best blouse, her handkerchief, the stockings and jewelry—the same outfit she wears every year to the festival, plus a few extra layers to fight the cold winds she's seen in the forecast ("I think this will do just fine," she says to herself in the mirror); the women of Entrevinos, a small wine bar in an alley off the main plaza, polish wine glasses and fry up chunks of *farinato* redolent of garlic and crushed cumin seeds; Ana María González works her way through a long prep list for the various feasts that will take place tomorrow: seventeen kilograms of heart, thirty of ribs, fifteen of pork belly, and thirty kilos of ground pork to be made into chorizo; Hilaria García works the streets, selling up the last of the thick book of raffle tickets she started with a month ago; don Poldo dusts off his magical *castañuelas* and cracks his wrists; Mayor Jesús Pascual Bares runs over the notes for his speech, just a little bit different from the speech he gave last year and the year before that; María Jesús walks the rough stone streets, ringing an iron bell and chanting a prayer to keep away the evil spirits believed to lurk beyond the borders of the village; and in a quiet, damp corner of town, in the same pen he's lived in for the past six months, Antón the pig sleeps soundly, unaware that tomorrow will be his last day on earth.

On that same Friday morning, Santiago Martín is having a tough time getting out of bed. Normally he wakes at 6:00 a.m., eats a breakfast of toasted bread soaked with olive oil and salt, and drinks coffee with steamed milk, then makes it into the Fermín factory outside of town by 7:00

a.m., just in time for the day's sacrifice. He knows that there are 140 pigs to slaughter this morning between sunrise and 10:30 a.m., when the workers break to eat their midmorning *bocadillos*.

But today Santiago is sick, fighting a nagging cold—a by-product, no doubt, of La Alberca's biting winter weather—and he hits the alarm, goes back to sleep, and dreams of something he won't remember when he wakes up two hours later.

Meanwhile, at his plant, the pigs to be slaughtered that day arrive from the acorn patches and begin their inexorable march toward the end. Once in the pen, they sense something is wrong—making little squeals, darting this way and that—but two men slowly and calmly usher them to the edge of the pen and through the small doorway that leads onto the killing floor.

From there, the end comes quickly. A conveyor system moves the pigs onto a narrow, padded escalator, where each animal receives an electric shock, and by the time they land on the belt before the *matarife*, the factory's designated killer, they are unconscious. Andrés Luis is young by *matarife* standards, but he's been on the floor at Fermín for ten years, which means he's killed tens of thousands of pigs in his short life. He works with a remarkable economy of motion, the look on his face frozen in the same state of muted seriousness. To kill, he makes two cuts, the first a shallow slice with a short, stubby knife to the neck to expose as much of the heart as possible, the second with a long, thin blade plunged directly into the heart, which ends the animal's life almost instantly. Combined with the electric shock, this is as swift and painless as death can be.

The pig is attached by its back two feet to a metal hanger, a contraption that hoists the carcass into the air and carries it from station to station until the animal has been divided into its primal parts. The processing is quick and exacting: First, the pig is scalded in hot water, then spun in what looks like an industrial dryer to loosen all the hair from its skin. It passes through flames next to burn off any remaining hairs before arriving to the series of butch-ers who will take the animal apart piece by piece: first the entrails, then the vital organs, then the front and hind legs, ribs, and loin.

In total, a crew of ten can process 140 pigs in just under three hours. The team works calmly, cleanly. There is no way around it: This is a tough business, and the air in the room—warm with the smell of blood and burned hair—will never let them forget where they are. But they take pride in the efficiency and humanity they bring to the messy business of death. In Spain, they don't say they "kill" animals; they "sacrifice" them.

By 10:30 a.m., after all of the day's pigs have been sacrificed, the team transitions from the killing floor into the butchering room, where a conveyor belt moves the primal cuts from one employee to the next, each carving out his or her designated piece with a long, narrow blade before returning it to the belt. Organs and specialty cuts like *secreto* and *pluma* will be sold fresh in Fermín's butcher shop in La Alberca, but most of the pig will be seasoned and cured in

some way: loins are rubbed in smoked paprika and garlic and cured for three months to make *lomo*. Front legs are coarsely ground and turned into chorizo, *salchichón*, and *cabeceros*. And the hind legs move up to the salt room, where they are buried in coarse salt for two weeks before spending the next three years curing ever so slowly into *jamón ibérico de bellota*, the most prized charcuterie in the world, and the heart of Fermín's business.

By the time I finish my tour of the Fermín factory, Santiago has arrived to the office and is busy taking phone calls and meeting with his top lieutenants. His business consists largely of mobilizing a team of farmers, butchers, inspectors, and sales representatives, and he goes about it with the steady, stoic persistence of a marathon runner. He is a large, imposing man with a thick, black beard that carpets the bottom half of his face. His eyes peak out from the thicket of hair and hard features like two lighthouses in a dark sea, conveying information in concentrated flashes. Despite the framed photos of him in crisp

suits shaking the hands of politicians and dignitaries around the world, Santiago looks more like a lumberjack than a businessman, the kind of guy you want on your side when shit goes sideways.

January is the busiest time of the year at Fermín. The acorns begin to fall from the trees in October, marking the beginning of the *montanera*, the period of intense fattening that will ready the pigs for slaughter. Over the past three months, the Fermín pigs have nearly tripled in size, and with the acorn supply dwindling in the dead of winter, their days are numbered. Santiago talks to Victor, the man responsible for raising the company's pigs on a one-hundred-acre farm nearby. The big news today is that a wild boar broke into one of the pigpens and had its way with some of the animals. "We will have to kill those pigs," Santiago says grimly.

His sister Paqui occupies a similar office across the hall, where, as part owner of Fermín, she handles the company's logistics. His brother-in-law, Halem Guerrero, handles the finances. His daughter, Soraya, helps with marketing and public relations. Somewhere in America, his nephew, Raul, is busy introducing *jamón* to a public slow to warm to its joys.

At 1:00 p.m., Santiago emerges from behind the closed door. "Let's eat," he says to nobody in particular.

There is no animal better suited for consumption than the pig. Easy to raise, easy to feed, easy to kill, and easy to butcher, with a pitch-perfect balance of fat and protein: cure it, smoke it, braise it, sear it—the variety of tastes and textures you can tease from pork is unrivaled in the animal kingdom. Perhaps the great twentieth-century philosopher Homer Simpson said it best: "Oh yeah, right, Lisa, a wonderful, magical animal!" Hot dogs and headcheese, trotters and tenderloins, though nearly half of the world's population is religiously precluded from partaking in the earthly delights of cured and cooked pork, pig remains the most essential of edible animals, utilitarian and sensual at equal turns. For every hickory-smoked shoulder, there's an Oscar Mayer wiener, every plump pork chop a crispy piece of bacon—a ying to the yang, fat and succulence, protein and sustenance, a world of food issues expressed through the flesh of its most despised and beloved conspirator. If this year is the year of the pig, may it forever be so.

As some of history's greatest civilizations—the Romans and Gauls, the Celts and the Chinese—knew, pork reaches its fullest potential only when salt enters the equation. The first records of salted meat stretch back three thousand years to China, where industrious eaters worked out a crude version of what would become Jinhua ham. In 160 BC, the Roman counselor and epicure Cato the Elder wrote extensively about the union of pork and salt, leaving behind a detailed manual for how to cure, smoke, and dry ham. Later, the rest of Europe—the French and Germans, Czechs and Poles—followed with their own adaptations of the basic formula of pork, salt, and cool mountain air. Even the early settlers of the New World got in on the act, feeding their hogs peanuts and air-drying them in the style of their ancestors to create country ham.

Cured meat is the story of humans no longer living hand to mouth. By adding salt to anything, you initiate a potentially long, complex process of enzymatic breakdown with a few huge upsides. First and foremost, you dramatically inhibit microbial growth, extending the life of meat by months or years. But more important for our story is the other principle benefit of curing: the alchemic transformation of salt and time, which work in tandem to extract water and convert proteins into amino acids, giving cured pork its savory, umami richness. It's not the history or the ingenuity or the long shelf life that chefs and artisans and distinguished palates the world over crave; it's the intensified flavor.

The Iberians are ancient masters of salt. From Portuguese salt cod to the fish sauce known as *garum* made during Roman times to the culture of salted and cured tuna parts dating back three millennia to the Phoenicians, they have harnessed NaCl as effectively as any civilization. Though bacalao and fish sauce are invaluable contributions to the canon of world cuisine, pork was their masterpiece.

The pig has long been a barometer for the complex religious and cultural changes Spain has undergone over the centuries. After enjoying a sporadic place at the table during Roman and Gothic times, pork was banned during centuries of Moorish rule, eaten only in the northern pockets of resistance. Indeed, pork and pork fat became the official flavor of the Reconquista, galvanizing the Catholics during their brutal seven-century-long expulsion of the Moors. During the ensuing Inquisition—when those lucky enough to survive could either convert or leave the country—conspicuous consumption of pork became a way for Jews and Muslims to demonstrate allegiance to their new religion. What better way to throw off the scent of a skeptical Catholic inspector than to hang salt pork in your pantry or stir a bit of bacon into your beans—a tactic that, according to some food scholars, explains how so many of Spain's iconic dishes ended up with bits of pork in them. In the centuries since, pork has come to dominate Spanish cuisine in a way few animals have elsewhere.

Nearly every region of Spain has developed its own tradition surrounding the killing, butchering, and fabrication of the pig—*la matanza*, they call it, a two-thousand-year-old technique of turning a single animal into a year's worth of eating. The list of regional specialties to emerge from the *matanza* culture is staggering. Mallorcans make *sobrassada*, a soft, spreadable sausage stained red with paprika. In Burgos, *morcilla*, blood sausage, comes laced with grains of cooked rice. The Asturian town of Tineo specializes in *chosco*, a blend of head, tongue, paprika, and garlic smoked over oak and chestnut wood.

Regardless of the region, the most noble part of the pig in Spain has always been the leg, a symphony of skin and sinew, protein and intramuscular marbling, held together by two bones that lend an elegant shape and a sturdy structure for hanging and, later, for ceremonious carving. The front leg, leaner, more vital to a pig's movements and therefore more muscular, is called *paletilla*; the hind leg, more prized for its bulk and fat content, is, of course, called *jamón*.

There are many classes of *jamón* in Spain—everything from *jamón dulce* (basic boiled ham used on sandwiches) to *jamón serrano* (salt-cured for twenty-four months). What makes *jamón ibérico* (what some people call *pata negra* for the black feet of the pig, or *Jabugo* after one of the most famous producing towns) so special is a potent blend of nature and nurture: The breed of pig, a descendant of wild boar, is known for its uncanny ability to filter fat through its muscles. Raised on a diet of grass and cereal grains from birth, the most prized *ibérico* pigs spend the final months of their lives roaming freely in the countryside, fattening up on the fallen acorns that give the meat its intense flavor and sweet deposits of fat. It's hard to imagine a happier time for an animal that lives to eat, and the results are reflected in its ever-increasing bulk; in the final two months of its life, a pig gains between 50 to 75 percent of its total body weight eating acorns. (Lucky for consum-

Roaming the *dehesa* in search of fallen acorns.

ers, all those acorns convert mainly into heart-healthy oleic acid.)

After the slaughter and the salting, the legs are hung in a series of rooms carefully controlled for temperature and humidity. Three to four years later, you have what any reasonable soul would recognize as the most elegant and delicious piece of protein in the world. At two hundred dollars or more per kilo, it is also one of the most expensive.

Most parts of Spain produce ham of some sort, but over the years, three regions have emerged as the heart of the country's *jamón* industry: Andalusia in the south, Extremadura in the far west along the Portuguese border, and Castilla y León to the northwest of Madrid. Each is home to small mountain towns with skilled artisans and the ideal conditions—cool temperatures and constant airflow—for curing ham.

Salamanca, 120 miles west of Madrid, is the heart of Castilla y León. It's a city of stone buildings and student bodies, home to the second-oldest university in Europe and a spectacular collection of old cathedrals, towers, and palaces. Few leisure ac-

tivities in Spain can top a stroll through the old part of Salamanca at night, when the crowds shrink and the subtle lighting against the ancient stonework gives the city a magnificent glow.

Carnivores eat like kings in Castilla y León. Restaurant menus are dominated by oven-roasted milk-fed lamb and crispy suckling pig, inch-thick steaks called *chuletones* cooked bloody, and offal-heavy creations like *chanfaina*, a slow-cooked stew of aromatics and vital organs. With Guijuelo, one of the capitals of Spain's artisan pig industry, close by, cured pork greets you at every turn, in logs of cured sausage and empanadas of chorizo and dangling legs of *jamón*.

Fifty miles to the south, 3,400 feet up in Las Batuecas Natural Park, La Alberca remains one of Spain's best-preserved medieval villages: streets of stone, homes of hardwood, citizens made of the stern stuff acquired in the quieter corners of civilization. People have lived here since before the Romans came to Spain, an ever-adapting receptacle for the Christian, Jewish, and Islamic cultures that dominate Spanish history. Tucked into the oak and chestnut groves of the Sierra de Francia, La Alberca is shire-like in its beauty and charm and self-reliance, the kind of town you dream of stumbling upon after a few dozen wrong turns.

You won't find much in La Alberca in terms of commerce—a smattering of restaurants and bars, shops selling local goods, and, of course, a cluster of butchers selling fresh and cured pork from the Fermín factory down the road. This is a town that survives largely on the bounty of the pig—if you don't work in the factory or in one of the meat shops, your wife or son or brother-in-law surely does.

It's only fitting, then, that its most famous citizen isn't the mayor or a local newscaster or even Santiago Martín, but the pig they call Antón. In the summer, at three months old, he is moved from the countryside to the village, where he spends the rest of the year freely wandering the cobblestone streets, fattening off the generosity of the villagers, who feed him grains and table scraps. The pig is named for San Antón, the patron saint of animals, whose legacy La Alberca celebrates in January in a rousing street party filled with music, dancing, and an abundance of fresh and cured pork.

The tradition dates back to the Middle Ages, when, at the end of the festival, Antón went to the poorest family in town, but these days, the village sells raffle tickets to the hundreds that stream in from around the region to drink cherry firewater and eat blood sausage and maybe, just maybe, win three hundred pounds' worth of the world's most prized pig.

Fermín Martín was always out in front of the pack. As a young entrepreneur he wandered the countryside around La Alberca, going from town to town with a herd of goats, selling them for slaughter. In 1956 he and his wife, Victoriana, moved the burgeoning business to a small house he bought just above the central plaza in La Alberca. The house had two floors—the first floor for killing and butchering the animals, the second floor for family living. Victoriana sold the meat while Fermín handled the business of death. When young Santiago came home from school, he would press his ear to the door to listen for the sounds of sacrifice before entering to avoid any unpleasantness.

Business was slow in the tiny village, so before slaughtering an animal, Fermín would knock on doors and ask the villagers—the town doctor, the mayor, people who could afford to buy meat—if anyone was interested in buying a piece. Back then, every family had their own pig, which they would kill in the streets in December or January, but fresh pork wasn't available the rest of the year, and Fermín saw a chance to change that.

He worked with a partner in those early years, a neighbor and a friend, but soon they both came to accept that the business wasn't big enough to support two families. So they made a pact: the two men would draw straws, and whoever drew the short straw would pack his bags and move to France. To underscore the seriousness of the wager, both men got passports for themselves and their families beforehand.

With his partner out of the way—true to his word, he moved his family to France that same year and became a mechanic—Fermín began to slowly expand production, moving the business to a larger house and gaining a reputation in the county for the quality of his fresh and cured meat.

During this time, his son, Santiago, and daughter, Paqui, left to study in Salamanca. Santiago, not seeing a future in the pork business for himself, went to medical school. After doing his residence, he spent years as a roaming family doctor, often with a trunk full of hams for delivery across the region. In 1983 his father had a heart attack and the family brooded on the fate of the business. With a new factory recently built and debt mounting, Santiago put down the stethoscope and stepped in to run Embutidos Fermín. "It was either put aside medicine or sell the business, and a bit of my macho pride as the only son wouldn't let that happen."

With his full attention turned to Fermín, Santiago began to expand operations, gradually growing the small space just outside of La Alberca into a factory capable of processing enough pig to expand Fermín's footprint beyond the region. "Instead of curing people, I cure hams."

Downstairs, below the factory, is a cavernous brick bunker with a fireplace, a bar, and a long wooden table for group meals. It's dark and dank like the curing rooms upstairs, without flash or pretense; nevertheless, the Martín family has hosted Spanish royalty, famous chefs, the ambassador of China in this subterranean space.

Santiago has invited the whole family to lunch today: his younger sister, Paqui, and her husband, Halem; his older sister, María, and her husband, Pedro, who own and operate the Fermín butcher store in town; and Ana María González, not family by blood, but by bond. Ana came to La Alberca when she was a teenager and was raised by Santiago's parents as a fourth child. She has extensive experience in nearly every corner of the business—from butchering and quality control to sales and administration. She even helped raise the children of the three siblings.

Ana is the family cook, and today's spread, unsurprisingly, centers on a potpourri of pig: wedges of *hornazo*, a local pastry made with lard and stuffed with all manners of cured pork; wood-grilled hunks of prized parts, fresh from the slaughter; and, of course, plates of Fermín *embutidos*: rosy pink slices of cured loin, burgundy coins of chorizo, and two wooden boards paved with *jamón ibérico de bellota*.

Santiago picks up a slice of *jamón* and holds it between us. "This is the only product that Spain can offer to the world that no one else can."

Spain has long suffered from an inferiority complex in the culinary world, the by-product of having France and Italy as its neighbors. *¡España no se vende bien!* It's a refrain you'll hear all over the country: Spain doesn't sell itself well! It's hard to argue the power of Spain's pantry: lusty red wines; bright, bracing whites and sparklings; soulful cheese from goat, sheep, and cow; spices and dry goods worthy of the world's adulation. Spanish olive oils consistently win the big international competitions, beating out the other Mediterranean powerhouses. When it surfaced that Italians were buying up huge quantities of Spanish olive oil, slapping Italian stickers on the bottles, then selling it for three times the price it fetched with a Made in Spain label, a national scandal erupted.

But Santiago is right when he says that *jamón ibérico* is different. It's a category killer, a product so vastly superior to other international interpretations that they don't even merit comparison. Yes, Italy produces fine cured hams, but next to a slice of three-year, acorn-fed, black-footed *jamón*, prosciutto tastes like lunchmeat. If Spain wants to flex its soft power, it has no better ambassador than the *ibérico* pig.

In 1995, Santiago decided it was time to take the taste of Spain to the rest of the world. He targeted wealthy Asian countries like Japan and Singapore, but above all, he wanted to crack into the American market. At the time *jamón ibérico* was still banned by the United States Department of Agriculture (USDA), but the Americans had released a set of regulations and guidelines that served as a road map for importation. With a newly remodeled factory and a firm control of sanitary issues, Santiago saw it as a sure bet for Fermín.

"I was amazed that none of our competitors were trying to break into the biggest market in the world," he says. "I thought we'd be selling *jamón* in the US the next year."

Not so fast, *jefe*. The USDA, with its byzantine laws and joyless enforcers, specializes in keeping culinary treasures out of America. Never mind that the product is two thousand years older than the United States itself, and that *jamón* has little history of health or contamination issues, the USDA put up every roadblock imaginable for importation: grueling plant inspections, endless paperwork, ever-shifting standards and regulations. As the years dragged on, the future of Fermín hung in limbo.

In 2005, after a decade of denials and disappointments, Fermín became the first company to sell *jamón ibérico* in the United States. They've since been joined by competitors like Cinco Jotas and Joselito but maintain a strong foothold in the young market—selling 80 percent of their total production in the States. As someone whose life was improved immeasurably by Fermín's breakthrough, I tell Santiago he and the family are doing God's work, but when he speaks about the troubles of selling Spanish ham in America—the draconian rules of the USDA, the enormous effort it takes to educate a public accustomed to paying a quarter of the price for prosciutto—all the wrong facial muscles go to work. "We thought it would be a gold mine," he says with a deep sigh. "If we don't accelerate, we'll never make our investment back."

Taste a slice of proper *jamón* and you will understand Santiago's frustrations. Acorn-fed ham is so rich with fat that it sweats as soon as it's exposed to air. Rub the fat on your lips like a balm, then place the slice on your tongue like a communion wafer and wait for it to convert you. First you taste the salt, then the pork, then the fermentation, and finally some deep, primal flavor will rise up and scratch at your throat and leave behind a ghost that can haunt your palate for a lifetime.

As Santiago talks, I indulge my habit: not just lacy veils of *jamón*, but planks of *pluma*—taken from the neck—so soft and rippled with fat that it could double as foie and chunks of *secreto*, cut from the skirt of meat below the ribs, with a salty crust from the fire and a marvelous chew. I hold up a slice of *lomo* and let the light illuminate the rivers of fat that run through it. *Lomo* might not have the fame of *jamón*, but Fermín's take on it is stunning, with an earthiness and perfume that recalls toasted hazelnuts and shaved truffle.

The rest of the family doesn't eat much. Maybe they've grown tired of their treasure, or maybe they're worried about tomorrow's pig more than today's. For the past twenty-eight years, Antón has been donated to La Alberca by Fermín. It's a magical tradition, this of the free-roaming village-fed beast, but not one without its unexpected twists. Some unsavory souls in a moving van once kidnapped Antón and made for Salamanca; the police tracked them down on a coun-

"I've never had a problem with a pig in my whole life," says Santiago, with his pet pig Nino.

try road and recovered the pig. A few years ago, a group of hikers found Antón on top of the area's highest peak, miles away from La Alberca; the mayor had to climb up and coerce him back to town. One year, Antón disappeared without a trace. The people of La Alberca accused an old man who had fallen on hard times of killing and eating him. Years later, they found the skeleton of the pig underneath a building where it had been trapped, exonerating the man who had died months before.

At 10:00 a.m. on Saturday, January 17, the fiesta explodes. There is no other verb to describe it. By midmorning, the town has swollen to twice its pre-Antón population and an electric current courses over the rough stones that pock La Alberca's wandering streets. A band sets up in the center of the plaza and a group of middle-aged men and women form adjacent lines and start dancing—partners organized in two lines that spin, dip, and clap in coordinated sequences. Don Poldo, dressed in black from head to toe, leads the charge with his clacking *castañuelas*, echoing the rhythm of the band by flickering his fingers.

Antón barely seems to notice the people pouring into this cobblestoned world of his, petting his back, posing for pictures—now and always, his main objective is food. When he arrived on the streets of La Alberca on June 13, Antón weighed just 120 pounds. Today, he weighs more than three times that, and shows no sign of slowing down.

One by one, the people who spent days or weeks preparing for the event take their places in pockets around the village: Marialusa sits at her regular table next to the fountain, a shawl on her shoulder and a scarf on her head, slicing up chunks of her famous chocolate *morcilla* for a crowd clamoring for a taste. Santiago Hernández Vázquez proudly shows off his collection of killing tools from the *matanzas* of yesteryear, sharpening blades on a wheel of rough stone powered by a creaky wooden pedal. Demetrio and his young son serve up shots of fruit-spiked firewater, using long metal skewers to stab the cherries floating in the bottle and convey them to passersby.

The liquor is sweet and bracing, but the fruit itself delivers all the danger. With the exception of the out-of-towners and their modern-day accoutrements—most come in from Salamanca with smartphones unholstered—this could be a scene from a century of your choosing.

This is my third festival, so the scene has a warm, comfortable glow to it now. Wasn't always so. The first time I came, with José Andrés and a band of American chefs here to take in the pork culture, we all basically lost our minds. We were a roving spectacle for the locals, almost as popular as Antón himself: a group of eight disheveled chefs and an ill-prepared journalist, hangovers stuck to our clothes like wine stains, blinking and drinking our way through cold morning light until José, the year's guest of honor, took to the balcony to deliver a fiery speech invoking the greatness of Spain and its unrivaled culture of pig.

Suddenly, wineskins and herbal liquors materialized and our hangovers were painted over with fresh coats of intoxication. People pulled us this way and that, to one tavern to try this liquor or to another to dance this number, until finally we were all gathered around one long table in the backroom of a bar with people slapping us on the back and men dancing on the bar and José spooning caviar onto slices of *jamón* and placing these absurd little packages directly into our mouths, the pork and the fish eggs caught in a beautiful struggle for the upper hand. I announced then—to a stranger at the bar—that I would be back one day to win Antón.

It is with a small but unshakable sense of pride that I walk the streets this morning, shaking hands with people who remember that day and still call me *el periodista*—the journalist. "You're loving this, aren't you?" my wife ribs me as I introduce her to my drinking buddies. I am not one of them, but she is, and maybe that means something. Or maybe not.

At least we look the part. The Fermín family has dressed the two of us in traditional garb—a charcoal button-down shirt with white pin stripes for me, a billowy flowered skirt, pearls, and a headscarf for

How the sausage gets made on the streets of La Alberca

her. People mistake us for locals and pose for photos. I carry a wineskin slung over my shoulder, which I refill at the bars around the plaza, and all day, strangers come up and they spray tight streams of red wine into the recesses of their mouths.

A news crew from Salamanca interviews me about the market for Spanish ham in the States. "Americans love pork, so there is hope." "But people there know what acorn-fed ham is, right?" "The good ones do."

A multicourse feast unfolds in the four corners of the plaza. An old woman fries dough in olive oil and dusts it with powdered sugar. Cooks from the local restaurants pass out plates of smoky *patatas meneás*. María and a group of older women initiate what can only be described as a live sausage demonstration, folding the seventy pounds of pork Ana lovingly ground yesterday with garlic and pimenton and hand-cranking it through an ancient sausage stuffer into long coils of sheep intestine. Taut and tied, the chorizo goes straight into a cast-iron cauldron of olive oil bubbling over a wood fire. Crowds descend, waiting for a piece of this or one of the other porcine treats emerging from that magic cauldron: crispy brown ribs, fragrant chunks of *morcilla* dark with pig's blood.

The team I saw yesterday working the killing floor at Fermín is all here: the woman with the thick forearms has traded the cleaver for a golden flower of fried dough, the guy who oversees the salting squeezes through the crowd with plates of potatoes for his kids, the *matarife* canoodles his wife in the corner.

In the center of the plaza with his wife, Rosa, at his side, Santiago surveys the scene, a look of stony seriousness—his default expression—on his face. In a sea of pork- and booze-fueled revelry, he is a port of quiet containment, working out the challenges of tomorrow. *Does Raul have the samples he needs for Whole Foods? The factory in Tamames needs reinforcements on Monday. Kill the wild boar. Please don't let the pig go to this shit-eating writer with the cheesy wineskin.*

From time to time, he breaks from his

thousand-yard stare to shake the hand of a villager or an employee who comes to pay his respects.

At noon, with the crowd frisky off the firewater, the mayor takes to a large balcony overlooking the plaza and makes his speech. "We are in the most beautiful town of Spain, if not the entire world!" Then, the year's guest of honor, a novelist who wrote La Alberca into her latest work, steps up to draw a winner from the five thousand raffle tickets ("a new record!") sold this year. I clutch the ten I've bought over the last few days, including three right at the cutoff line, but luck is not on my side: the pig goes to someone from Salamanca.

The feast, though, goes on. By 1:00 p.m., we've been swept up into a bar where wine and swine make the rounds. Santiago's daughter Soraya shares a few stories from festivals past, and the granite facade of her father begins to show signs of cracking. He saves his smiles for when he means them most, which gives moments like these gravity. The whole family is here, including Noelia and Myriam, Santiago's two other daughters who have come in from Salamanca for the party. I ask Noelia why she is one of the few in the extended family not to work for Fermín. "I've watched my dad go to work every day from six a.m. until nine p.m.," she says. "I didn't want to follow in those footsteps."

We cross the plaza to El Balcón, where the band and the dancers have taken over. Don Poldo, the costar of San Antón, dominates the space with his clacking *castañuelas*, capable of shaking from these little circles of wood a world of ecstasy and agony. At eighty-three he is still able to turn his entire body into an instrument. A chorus of *olés* ring out from all over the bar. Wineskins are refilled and passed around the circle, my village people costume by now bloodred around the collar.

One of his daughters lets it escape that Santiago keeps a pet pig at his house: Jacob, with tiny legs and a dark belly that scrapes the ground, his own little Antón, only without the expiration date.

"You can't work in this business unless you care for the animals," says Santiago. "I've never had a single problem with a pig in my life."

Santiago invites us to his house above the village for one last feast of Fermín's finest with his family, and they take off in front of us to get the fire going. We stick around for another drink and a few last rounds of don Poldo's bittersweet vibrations.

When we exit the bar at 3:00 p.m., the plaza is empty. No fried flowers, no hand-cranked chorizo, no camera crews. The morning revelers are on their way back to Salamanca and the locals are sitting down to lunch at private tables across the village. The only noise left in the plaza is the click-clop of Antón's black cloven hooves as he waddles his way around the fountain, alone once again. Maybe his new owner has yet to claim him, or perhaps somebody from Fermín will round him up later, but he continues to roam La Alberca like a free radical, wet nose to the cold stone, sniffing his way from crumb to crumb, doing what he was born to do.

There will be another pig next year, and he will also be called Antón, and he will sweep these streets for six months, fattening himself on the generosity of townspeople who long ago stopped being surprised to see a beast on their doorstep, and on a cold Saturday in January, after the last of the cherry liquor has been drank, the chocolate *morcillas* consumed, the plates of *patatas meneás* scraped clean, the speeches given, the cameras flashed, the music faded, there will be only two things left for Antón: salt and time.

CERDO IBÉRICO

PRESA DE PALETA

AGUJA

PRESO O BOLA

PALETA

CARRILLERA

PALETA

SECRETO DE PAPADA

LOMO

SOLOMILLO

JAMÓN

COSTILLA

• SECRETO O CRUCETA

PANCETTA

FROM SNOUT TO TAIL

You can tell how serious a culture is about an animal by how thoroughly they butcher it. When you raise black-footed *ibérico* pigs on a diet of fallen acorns and open spaces, nothing goes to waste.

The Cured
MEATS

Spain is the land of porcine dreams, where regions are defined by the charcuterie (*embutidos*) they produce. These are six of the provincial stars of the cured pork world.

03

04

05

01 JAMÓN IBÉRICO DE BELLOTA

The king of cured pork

02 CHORIZO RIOJANO

Smoky sausage of La Rioja

03 LOMO EMBUCHADO

Garlic, paprika, loin

04 SOBRASSADA

Mallorca's spreadable pork

05 FUET

Salami a la Catalunya

06 MORCILLA DE BURGOS

Rice, spice, and blood

Life Skills

DRINK LIKE A SPANIARD

Drink Like a
SPANIARD

ORDER LIKE A LOCAL

Spain possesses one of Europe's great regional drinking cultures, where the beverage of choice changes from one town to the next. Want to fit into a crowd of Andalusians watching a bullfight in the bar? Order a *manzanilla* or a *fino* and brace for the blood.

DRINK IT SMALL AND COLD

Artisanal beer is on the march in the north, from producers like Edge and Basqueland Brewing Project, but most Spaniards drink light, regional pilsners—Mahou, Estrella Damm, San Miguel—as cold as possible, in small (8- or 12-ounce) servings.

LET THE VERMOUTH FLOW

Vermouth culture has made a huge comeback in recent years. Sweet, dark house-made *vermú* is popular in the late afternoons, and on weekends as a warm-up before a big lunch.

DON'T SIP THE *SIDRA*

Asturias produces less wine than any other region in Spain, focusing instead on turning its bounty of apples into sparkling hard cider. *Sidrerías* dominate the social and culinary landscape of the region. There are many rules to cider (discussed in Chapter 6), but most important, don't sip it; drink it all back in one animated gulp.

TAKE TO THE STREETS

Most Spaniards wouldn't be caught dead drinking on the street, but the youth have mastered the art of the sprawling outdoor boozefest called *botellón*. Looking to recapture your youth? Grab a bottle and join in.

SKIP THE SANGRIA

Pass on the goblets of purple potion being proffered along Spain's most trampled thoroughfares—La Rambla, Plaza del Sol, anywhere in Sevilla. Sangria is largely a tourist trick—a way for unscrupulous restaurants to charge a premium for cheap wine and sugar.

BASQUE IN THE BUBBLES

Txakoli is the social lubricant that keeps the bars and restaurants buzzing across the Basque region. A dry, lightly sparkling wine poured from on high to aerate it *(a la sidra)*, txakoli pairs beautifully with the seafood and *pintxos* that dominate Basque cuisine.

SAVE THE STRONG STUFF

A warm-up beer or a glass of wine is as much as most Spaniards are willing to drink on an empty stomach. Cocktails (especially "gin tonics") flow freely in the small hours after dinner.

Chapter Three

VALENCIA

If you look closely enough, you will find the entire history of Spain within the perimeter of a paella pan. Olive oil, the golden film that forms the base of every paella, adding depth and a gentle sheen to the bed of grains, is the story of a hungry ancient Rome, expanding its empire across Iberia, one olive tree at a time. Tomato, the heart of the *sofrito* that lends color and a savory-sweet baseline to a proper paella, is the story of Spain's own vision of empire and conquest, and the unexpected treasures it pillaged from the New World. And the heart of paella—the rice, saffron, and vegetables that fill out the pan—speak of seven hundred years of Moorish rule leaving a

footprint on the Iberian Peninsula that informs how Spain eats and drinks and lives to this day.

When the Berbers of Northern Africa made their way up through Andalusia and into the Valencia area during the eighth century, they found a flat coastal land rich with fresh water from the rivers and lagoons that cut through the plains like veins and arteries. They called the area the Albufera, little sea—green and wet and spotted white with ocean birds, a breeding ground for a new culture in Spain and the rest of Europe. Within years of the Moors' arrival, the wetlands were converted into rice paddies used to feed the growing Iberian extension of the Moorish empire. Thirteen hundred years later, massive grain silos stand tall like watchtowers over the Valencia flats, fueling one of the world's most enduring and extraordinary rice cultures.

Paella wasn't the result of a singular creation from an inspired cook, but a slow evolution of necessity and adaptation, a convergence of land and history and circumstance. References to rice *a la valenciana* can be found as early as the seventeenth century, but the paella itself, the wide, shallow pan fundamental to the rice's creation, doesn't surface until the end of the nineteenth century. With it came what we now recognize as the world's most famous rice dish.

The dimensions of the dish are rooted in the ground itself, the Valencian rice and orange fields where farmers and day laborers sought sustenance as they worked the earth. Paella evolved as a reflection of their immediate surroundings: legumes and tomatoes from the gardens, snails clinging to the wild rosemary and thyme bushes wet with rain, duck and rabbit from the marshes

of the Albufera, all cooked over wood cut from the surrounding citrus groves. The cooking vessel, called the paella (Valencian for pan), made perfect tactical sense: ample enough to fit protein and vegetables to energize the hungry workforce, shallow and open to allow for quick cooking and rapid water evaporation, and built to double as both the cooking and serving vessel, a single metal plate where workers could gather around to feast. Slowly, it migrated from the fields and marshes into kitchens and backyards across the region.

But then something dramatic happened: Spain stopped being a bubble and started being a tourist destination. Franco died in 1975, and with him, most of the country rejoiced the end of thirty-six years of hard-fisted dictatorship, a protracted coming out party that culminated with the 1992 Olympics in Barcelona. Somewhere along the way, through a mixture of coordinated effort on the part of the Spanish tourism board and savvy entrepreneurship from restaurant owners the country over, paella was catapulted to international fame—

right there next to sangria, flamenco, and other hallmarks of Spain's global image. Suddenly, paella wasn't a dish made on Sundays in homes around Valencia, but a national icon, something that anyone traveling to Spain expected to find wherever they turned.

You know how the story goes: The dish was diluted, misinterpreted, bastardized, and butchered. Paella got punked. Those pictures you see everywhere in Spain, the Crayola paella—brilliant yellow rice, bright red peppers, emerald green peas—was the by-product of a country trying to fuel the fires of an ascending tourism industry. And even now, forty years later, that industry shows no signs of slowing down.

If you're eating paella in Spain right now, you're probably eating something vastly different from what a family in Valencia eats on a weekend afternoon. Not just hastily prepared with lackluster ingredients and sloppy technique, but often sourced from the likes of industrial food manufacturers Paellador (tagline: available anytime, anywhere) and O.K. Paella

(a name that doesn't inspire much confidence), part of a massive industry of prefab paellas. Tuck into a paella in the Plaza del Mercado in Valencia, on La Rambla of Barcelona, or the Plaza del Sol in Madrid and the chances are it came from a factory.

For years in Spain, I was the guy eating bad paella. My first came on the Passeig de Gràcia in 1999 with my high school Spanish class, a pan of rice as yellow and wet as a banana slug. Subsequent paellas proved every bit as problematic: I remember hacking through one that contained four kinds of meat, three kinds of seafood, and scarcely any rice, and another that arrived to the table scorched on the bottom and raw on top. Even my efforts to eat at the places with awards and reputations were rewarded with mediocre meals. Nothing I came across offered even the slightest suggestion of how paella came to be Spain's culinary calling card to the world.

Confused and disappointed, I swore off paella entirely, convinced that any further investigation could begin to have collateral damage, compromising my faith in the entirety of Spanish cuisine. I imagined that somewhere out there, people were eating versions of this dish that justified its fame, but real paella culture was like a secret society whose password I would never know.

While I walked blindly through the valleys of paella disappointment, a few brave souls were at work on righting the wrongs of the Spanish rice world. In 2013, a group of proud Valencians with a deep love for their region's cuisine founded Wikipaella as a way for a community of rice lovers to preserve a fundamental component of their culinary heritage. Wikipaella was formed around the idea that it's not the tourist who suffers most the slings of unrealized rice potential, but the Valencians themselves, who have watched for years as the world perpetrated unspeakable crimes on their most sacred staple.

The mission was as clear as it was urgent: to protect what's served. A ten-point manifesto on the site lays out the fundamental beliefs that unite this cabal of writers, chefs, and enthusiasts. A few of the highlights:

1. Authentic paella has its origin in the Comunidad Valenciana

5. Authentic paella is the heritage of no one and everyone.

7. We publicly denounce transgressions committed against paella, especially in the Comunidad Valenciana.

10. We carry paella in our hearts and travel with it as far as possible.

José Manuel Garcerá and José Maza form a core part of Team Wikipaella, eager lieutenants on the front line of the rice wars. "We realize the lack of understanding is as much our fault as anyone's," says Garcerá. "We can't even come to an agreement ourselves what constitutes real paella, so how can we expect the rest of the world to?

"In a radius of sixty kilometers, you'll find four very distinct paellas. Someone might say: I'm sorry, that's not a paella. What the hell are you talking about? That's how my grandpa always made it."

With all of this static surrounding a

single dish, they decided to solve the question of what is paella in the most democratic way possible: let the people who make it most define it. They conducted interviews with two hundred restaurants from Valencia, Castellón, and Alicante and created a database that offers a statistical breakdown of ingredients. Go on the site and you'll find that 100 percent of cooks use olive oil, rabbit, chicken, *garrafó*, and *judía ferradura* (large white beans and wide green beans—local legumes that comprise the central vegetable base of a true paella), 82 percent use smoked paprika, and 74 percent use mountain snails. Garlic (52 percent) and rosemary (55 percent) are the most divisive paella ingredients, while artichokes (10 percent) and pork ribs (7 percent) are the biggest outliers.

The map feature allows you to search for restaurants based on the ingredients they use, and—most impressively—to narrow in on the small handful of restaurants out there still cooking rice the traditional way—over wood fires. For those who would rather do the cooking themselves, Wikipa-

ella also offers slick video instruction from the biggest paella players of the region.

Wikipaella caught on quickly, with restaurants and serious home cooks joining the fight against the sinister forces of the rice world; financial support came from La Fallera, the largest producer of rice in Valencia, as well as the Valencian government. "They recognize that paella isn't just a plate of food—it has an economic and cultural value well beyond mere sustenance," says Maza. To stand idly by while millions eat lackluster paellas is to miss an opportunity to spread a true piece of their culture to the rest of the world.

Maza admits that there's an inherent tension between a culture born in the fields and family kitchens and the restaurant industry that has developed around it. "For me, the perfect paella is my mom's. Almost any *valenciano* is going to tell you the same. But there are plenty of restaurants who do it well—and from a technical standpoint, probably better than most of our mothers."

I don't have a Valencian mother. Nor do you, nor do 34 million Spaniards. We need

Paella finishing over the embers of an orange wood fire

to have our breakthroughs wherever we can. It was at one of Wikipaella's favorite restaurants where I finally had mine.

On a long drive back to Barcelona from Andalusia, we made an unintentional detour through Benissanó, a small, unremarkable town about thirty minutes outside of the city of Valencia. I remembered that José Andrés had proclaimed a paella from this town to be his favorite in all of Spain. Soon, I was upstairs in the kitchen of Restaurante Levante, watching a long line of paella pans bubbling away over burning branches of orange wood.

Rafael Vidal, the owner and chef at Restaurante Levante, is paella royalty—his father famously served rice to the king and queen of Spain back in 1977. Since then, Levante has taken its paella game very seriously: growing its own vegetables in a garden next door, trucking in orange wood from nearby groves, cooking paellas the way they've always been cooked.

Upstairs, at Rafael's side, I watched what I would come to learn as the infallible method of paella *valenciana*, scribbling notes furiously in a saffron-stained note-book that I still keep as my road map: *rabbit + chicken deeply browned, then veg . . . tomato cooked until it clings like mud to the veg . . . pinch of saffron, shake of pimenton. Simple but complex, easy but . . . impossible?*

What arrived on the table was like noth-ing I had seen or tasted before, destined to be the benchmark by which I would judge all rice to come.

A perfect paella is comprised of a thin layer of rice, no deeper than a pinky, the color of rusted gold. Meat—chicken, rabbit, snails, the traditional trilogy—should be dark brown and on the bone, chopped in pieces two bites big. Stars of the Valen-cian garden, fat white beans and flat green beans, should hide everywhere in the folds of the rice—like the protein, supporting actors in a larger drama. Rice is the star of this story, its entire place in paella a para-dox: toothsome yet tender, independent but inexorably bound to the larger whole, swol-len with the flavor of everything that came before it in the pan. At the base of the pan, scattered in irregular pockets, you'll find the *socarrat*, the crispy, caramelized grains that drive rice fiends wild with desire.

It's one thing for a naïve American to lose his shit over a few spoons of *socarrat*, but I wasn't the only one at the table having a rice revelation. My wife and her sister, born and bred on *la cocina española*, were having their own transformational moment: "I feel like I've never tasted paella before."

That was it. This lunch was a gateway drug, the first hit in what has become an increasingly desperate addiction to saffron and *socarrat*. Now that I knew how good it could be, I needed more.

🍇 🫒 🐖

A kitchen without rice is like a pretty girl with one eye.

Those are the words of Confucius, born and raised in the world's first and largest rice culture. From its origins in the Pearl Valley of China some eight thousand years ago, rice spread through southern Asia into Africa, landing in Greece a few hun-dred years before Christ. Along the way, it accumulated economical, social, and cul-tural value that would reshape the way the world works. In ancient Japan, wealth was expressed in rice fields. Families in Persia marked their social status by the rice stored in their farmhouses. In Chinese as in Japanese, the word for meal is the same for rice.

Today rice is one of the most important foods in the world—along with wheat and corn, part of the trinity of staple crops that feed most of the planet. More than two billion people count rice as their primary source of sustenance.

What makes rice so damn important, beyond the sheer quantity consumed around the planet, is the number of ways in which we consume it. Ground into a fine powder and mixed with coconut and turmeric, it becomes *bánh xèo*, a crispy crêpe served on the sidewalks of southern Vietnam. Simmered with milk and cinnamon and sugar, it's transformed into *arroz con leche*, a dessert worthy of its prime ingredient's towering stature. Boiled, inoculated with bacteria, and left to ferment, it becomes sake, a tipple of intoxicating depth and variety. Steamed and simmered, fried and wokked, sugared, salted, milked, and fermented, rice is both

the most voluminous and most versatile food we have.

Spain isn't a rice country; it's a bread country, a place where a chunk of baguette isn't just a squishy bit of sustenance, but a plate, a fork, a finger, a microphone. The average Spaniard consumes just under ten kilos of rice a year, slightly more than Americans, but twenty times less than the Chinese. Spaniards don't consume rice as a side dish or an accompaniment to other more substantial plates; rice, when it makes it to the table, is always the star, a conductor for flavor and texture created by the inclusion of vegetables and protein and the careful manipulation of heat. But out of the limited role grew a tradition of extraordinary depth and deliciousness.

That it developed at all is a minor miracle. During the Reconquista, when Christian monarchs reclaimed Spain from its Arabic occupiers, rice became a symbol of a past most of the country wanted to shed. More than a symbolic concern, Spaniards blamed the grain for cases of malaria and yellow fever that decimated the Mediterranean population. But rice would not be uprooted so easily. By the time the Spaniards reclaimed control of the region, Valencia's economy was so intrinsically tied to the production of rice that to abandon the crop would have spelled certain disaster for farmers and traders of the region. More important, it formed a fundamental part of the local cuisine, and the cooks of the region weren't prepared to give up a taste of their identity for anything.

Today Spain still grows some of the world's most valued rice varietals, including Bomba, Calasparra, and Senia. All three are short, plump, round grains capable of absorbing great quantities of liquid (i.e., flavor) while maintaining a toothsome texture, the golden grail of any rice anatomy. The differences between the three are subtle yet hugely important: Bomba, the most widely available and well-known Spanish rice, is the most forgiving, with a generous window of between nineteen and twenty-two minutes of cooking time, giving amateur cooks a wider target to aim for. Calasparra, named for the small town

in Murcia where it grows, has a narrower window but arguably a higher upside. Senia, the most fickle of all, passes from undercooked to overcooked in a span of seconds, but also offers the greatest possible reward: a payload of taste and texture that makes it the go-to grain for Spain's paella masters.

But paella is only one part of the bigger picture. What makes Spain home to one of the world's great and most underrated rice cultures is the remarkable breadth of dishes—an exhaustive list of rice creations involving all manners of flora and fauna. The easiest way to understand the full spectrum of Spanish rice is to think about the moisture level of the final product: paellas form the central part of *arroz seco*, a "dry" rice dish in which the cooking liquid evaporates just as the rice is fully cooked. At the other extreme, you have *arroz caldoso*, soupy rice, a bowl of brothy, starchy sustenance frequently featuring fish and seafood. *Arroz meloso* is the Goldilocks in-between, risotto-like in texture, with just enough residual moisture to make a spoon a more appropriate vessel than a fork. (Though it should be noted that the traditional eating utensil is a wooden spoon, valued because it doesn't heat up as it scrapes the bottom of the pan, saving many a burned lip around the fire pit.)

Within the dry, moist, and soupy rice spectrum, you have a staggering list of possibilities: *arroz con bogavante*, a rich, bracing expression of the ocean, made dark with lobster brains and roe; *arroz a banda*, a more restrained dry rice studded with small pieces of squid, shrimp, and white fish; *arroz con costra*, a knockout punch of various pig parts capped with a crown of egg and baked in the oven. The ingredients you'll find goosing the grains represent an encyclopedic rundown of the Valencian bounty: cauliflower, fava beans, chickpeas, asparagus, squid ink, blood sausage, calf's liver, red shrimp, monkfish.

All of these have their place in the homes and restaurants around Valencia, but paella is the undisputed king of the Iberian rice world. It's more than a staple in the diets of the five million people living in the region, one of Spain's oldest with its

own language and vibrant Mediterranean culture; paella is a way of life, a ubiquitous presence in every major life event in and around Valencia. Baptisms, weddings, family reunions: all are powered by paella. During Las Fallas, the most important festival of the year, where Valencians spend weeks constructing elaborate monuments only to send them burning into the Mediterranean, the streets crackle with the sound of slow-forming *socarrat*.

So fundamental is paella's role in the Valencian life that an entire language has developed around it. To *pagar una paella*, literally "to pay a paella," is to make a bet. When kids are acting up or being indecisive, parents might say: *¿Què farem, paelleta o arròs caldós?* "What should we make, paella or soupy rice?" Most important of all is the word *comboi*, which Valencians use to describe the entire paella experience: the ritual that surrounds the cooking and consumption, a day of gathering with friends and family to eat, drink, and be merry—a fundamental part of the fabric of social life in this part of Spain.

To fully understand the concept of *comboi*, you need to be born into this culture, a luxury life never afforded me, so I did the next best thing: I befriended a Valencian. Salvador Serrano—tall, curly hair, spectacles, bouncy frame like a tennis player—lives his life in a way that defies easy categorization: a schoolteacher with a fundamental distrust of the system, a nonconformist with a soft spot for tradition, someone who likes to eat and drink well but won't be caught dead in a restaurant with linen tablecloths. A man of boundless generosity and wisdom, as our friendship blossomed over Ping-Pong afternoons and FC Barça evenings, he took it upon himself to school me not just in the ingredients and techniques behind a good paella, but in the revelry and camaraderie that surrounds it.

We began to re-create a little slice of his Valencian upbringing on the terrace of his apartment in the old part of Barcelona, channeling the advice of his rice-obsessed childhood friends and using handwritten notes from his mom to practice paella for groups of hungry friends. As we narrowed

the gulf from aspirational *arroz* to passable paella, Salva decided I was ready to further my education in the belly of the rice belt, so we traveled south together to Valencia.

The Comunitat Valenciana stretches some four hundred kilometers down the coast of the Mediterranean, from the Ebro River and Catalunya in the north to the sunbaked border of Murcia in the south. Most of the region's population is pinched between the turquoise sea and the thin, rocky mountain range that rises up from the coastal flats a few miles from the water. These are among the most fertile lands in all of Spain, a rough patchwork of vegetable gardens and rice paddies and the broccoli-top orange groves that have long fueled this region's economy. When you look out across the orchards and gardens and little stone farmhouses that dot the region, you can almost see the plumes of paellas past, the groups of men huddled around the pan, scraping sustenance from its borders.

As you push up against the coastline, the rolling farmland beauty gives way to a certain high-rise tedium. Spain's beaches may be legendary, its tourism driven in large part by the promise of sun and sand everlasting, but the towns that surround the Valencian coast are not always the charming Mediterranean outposts you might expect. With a few exceptions (Catalunya's Costa Brava, Cádiz's charming beach hamlets), the Spanish Mediterranean has been compromised by loose city planning and a thirsty commercialism that lends a monotonous mediocrity to its shores.

When Mercedes Caballer Tarin purchased an apartment in Xeraco back in 1982, the town was little more than tomato farms and a few lonely beach shacks. Today, the main drag is lined with pizzerias and high-rise apartments that remain shuttered ten months of the year. "I used to be able to see the Mediterranean," she says, staring into the concrete wall across from her. "Now, all I see are buildings. It sure would be nice to at least see a slice of the sea from here."

Mercedes, warm and round and bubbling over with energy, represents the best of the Valencian character: huge-hearted, opinionated, possessing an enormous sense of hospitality and a devotion to faith and family. (This year she's playing hostess to the city's roving Virgin Mary statue, which she keeps dressed and polished, watching over her living room.) Like many Spaniards, when the temperatures rise, Mercedes escapes her inland apartment to the beach. She leaves nearby Alzira, a midsize town twenty minutes inland, and spends her summer between the shore, the pool, and the kitchen. When we walk into the apartment shortly after 2:00 p.m., she's just about to scatter rice into a bubbling pan of meat and vegetables.

Mercedes, born and raised in Alzira, cooks a version of paella true to her town: beyond the traditional base of *sofrito*, chicken, and rabbit, she adds pork ribs, strips of blistered red peppers, and, stunningly, meatballs. Peppered with caramelized pine nuts and suffused with the scent of cinnamon, they bring another bite of Spain's Arabic past to a pan already loaded with it.

Mercedes has made paella once a week at home for as long as she can remember.

Same pan, same propane fire, same supermarket ingredients; at this point, her cooking is more an act of muscle memory than conscious decision-making. When I ask for measurements, she looks at me like I've asked for her opinion of America's electoral system. Measurements are for people cooking a recipe; Mercedes is reenacting a tradition that has survived under her roof for decades.

The rice needs to rest ten minutes before it's ready to be served. While we sit on the terrace eating mussels and drinking sweet vermouth, Mercedes changes into a flowery summer dress before returning to parade the pan around the table.

Beyond the exotic Alzira touches, the rice itself is a study of textbook taste and texture: firm but swollen with flavor, generously seasoned, not the rusty color of restaurant rice, but the brighter yellow of Valencian homes, where a few shakes of food coloring is obligatory.

"Who wants the liver?" she asks, pushing the little gray organs in my direction.

"Nobody's going to eat the rabbit head?" She made other rices too—oven-baked rice, rice with eels, three a week for her family of four.

"I didn't like paella as a kid," says Salva. "It was this gross thing my mom would make." I run through a mental inventory of my own weekday meals—casseroles, spaghetti with meat sauce, Stouffer's frozen meatloaf—and fail to summon up much sympathy for Salva. Today, he spends the better part of fifteen minutes scraping the loose grains of caramelized rice stuck to the bottom of the pan.

"I must say, I'm pretty happy with how it came out," Mercedes says, pulling out her smartphone to take pictures of the empty pan. "You're not going to find a paella like this in a restaurant."

The next day, we head inland to Alzira, where Salva was born and raised, in search of more rice. For years, I've listened to tales of Salva's Alzira group of friends and their prowess with the rice pan, studied cell phone shots of their latest creations, adopted their various techniques and philosophies as my own. The group—ten guys in their midthirties who have been best friends since grade school—isn't comprised of crazy foodies or professional cooks, just an average Valencian crew, the type that embodies the *comboi* spirit. For this group and thousands of others like them, the paella pan is the magnet that pulls them together, even now as wives and kids and jobs complicate the picture.

On a gray Saturday afternoon, we gather with the whole squad in a two-story apartment in the hills outside of Alzira. Two of Salva's most dedicated rice buddies have taken up the cooking duties. Upstairs in the kitchen, Rafa Casterá Montalvá, a computer programmer by day, works his touch on an entirely different creation, one of the region's most substantial and significant rice dishes: *arroz al horno*. Born just south of here in the town of Xàtiva, it's an oven-baked construction of geologic complexity, with varying layers of starch, protein, and vegetable—a hulking creation that is best

consumed on a cold winter's evening, or before an extended hunger strike.

Working with his grandma's thirty-five-year-old *cazuela*, Rafa sets about frying each individual constituent in a shimmering layer of olive oil: potatoes, tomatoes, pork belly, pork ribs, blood sausage. A cloud of porcine mist fogs up the windows in the apartment.

Downstairs, Vicent Ordaz Hidalgo, a masseur by trade, is at work on a considerably more restrained creation. Vicent is widely accepted as the rice king of this crew—short, sturdy, quietly confident in the way the best cooks are. (Over the years in Barcelona, Salva has invoked Vicent's culinary maxims so often that I feel his presence every time I dust off my paella pan.) His friends badger him as he cooks, but when he's not around, they speak in hushed tones of reverence about his kitchen skills: "He's a magician. He can do anything with a pan of rice."

Today he's cooking up *arròs amb fesols i nap*, one of the dozens of rice dishes that

PAELLA IS A
WAY OF LIFE, A
PRESENCE IN EVERY
MAJOR LIFE EVENT
IN AND AROUND
VALENCIA.

hasn't traveled far from Valencia, but maintains a deep importance among local eaters. On paper, it sounds like food for a nation at war—rice with turnips and white beans—but over the course of ninety minutes, through the kind of instinctive finesse that comes from a few decades of cooking the same grain over and over, Vicent unlocks flavors of startling depth from six pedestrian ingredients.

"I love it when I add the water and it starts to boil. Nothing reminds me more of my childhood." He brings his whole face down to the pan, allows the turnip steam to wash over him, seems to forget that I'm there watching.

While Vicent makes the final moves, cranking up the heat to tease out the *socarrat*, two friends and their young kids volley a soccer ball perilously close to the fire. Others drink beers and watch the Valencian soccer game on the flat screen. Two women are locked in a deep conversation about the local school system. Despite the abundance of rice-focused restaurants in the region, nobody here can muster even

a modicum of enthusiasm about the prospects of eating rice outside of the house.

"When you eat out, you never know what's happening in the kitchen," says Vicent. "The cooks are stressed, they don't talk to each other, they cut corners. I'm a big believer in the alchemy of community. Something special happens when people gather around the pan, something you can't re-create in a restaurant."

Rafa's *arroz al horno* is a delicious, rib-sticking celebration of excess; Vicent's turnip rice, a subtle, elegant expression of the grain and its ability to transmit texture and amplify flavor. The women and children sit at one end of the table, devouring servings of both from paper plates. At the other end of the table, the men gather around the pan, elbow-to-elbow, armed with nothing but wooden spoons and a jug of wine; no one stands up until the last turnip and last grain of *socarrat* has been scraped out of existence.

Valencia may be shorthand for Spanish rice culture in most people's minds, but Alicante, the province immediately to the south, which forms a major part of the Comunitat Valenciana, is every bit as dedicated to the pursuit of great grains—from the seafood-driven rice dishes of coastal towns like Dénia, to the heartier meat-heavy creations of the interior. It's there, on the edge of Alicante and Murcia, in the tiny town of El Pinós, that you'll find a restaurant serving what everyone from Ferran Adrià to Joël Robuchon says is the greatest rice in all of Spain.

"If there's one rice worth traveling for, it's this one." Strong words from anyone, but when they come from Robuchon, the man named the greatest chef of the twentieth century, who spends a good part of his time these days eating rice in Spain, you make the trip.

When Josefina Navarro and Paco Gandía opened this restaurant in 1985, the idea was to serve a simple menu of grilled meat and sides. That plan lasted about as long as it took for someone to try Josefina's rice. Soon, Paco Gandía was recast as a rice restaurant. Though most of the big

arrocerías serve up a full menu of rices—dry and soupy, based on seafood, meat, or vegetables—Josefina serves just one: *arroz con conejo y caracoles*, a dry, paella-style rice made with rabbit and snails.

She invites me back to the kitchen to show me the whole process—including the snails that just arrived. She pulls off the top to a pot and there they are, stuck to the lid, shells still coated with patches of dirt from last night's drizzle. "We get them from the mountain behind us. When it rains, they fatten up on rosemary." (One of my favorite parts of a good paella recipe is the part giving cooks the option of using either a dozen snails or a sprig of rosemary—both responsible for imparting that green flavor of the garden to the pan.)

Josefina's technique is like none I have ever seen elsewhere in the region. Her day begins at 7:00 a.m., when she fries the rabbit in olive oil with a bit of tomato to form the *sofrito*, then she adds water and the snails and boils the mix for fifteen minutes before leaving it to rest until lunchtime. "Stock is always better when it's rested; that gives it time for the flavor to develop."

This seems like a small and effective innovation, but in certain circles, the idea of premaking stock is heretical. With a seafood paella or other seafood rice dishes, it's necessary, because it's impossible to extract enough flavor from a small amount of fish or shellfish to impregnate an entire pan of rice with the flavor of the sea. Any seafood rice you eat—whether paella *de mariscos* or *arroz a banda*—begins with a stock of simmered fish bones made separately.

Not the case for meat, though—above all paella *valenciana*, which purists say must be made in a single continuous cooking session, is a serious time commitment. The meat must be properly browned, the *sofrito* cooked down, the water sufficiently reduced to intensify the meat-and-vegetable flavor it gives to the rice. It's a ninety-minute endeavor from start to finish, not something most restaurants have the patience or the space to produce. Josefina's premade stock approach is a perfectly logical, if controversial, solution. (Eat rice at a high-end restaurant and you'll taste the next logical expression of this concept: rice cooked with intensely concentrated stock that lends the rice an almost sticky richness.)

Beyond seasoning—salt, saffron, and smoked paprika—Josefina adds nothing else to her rice. Not the legumes of a Valencian paella ("we don't grow *garrafó* here"), not the chicken ("we've always had rabbit nearby"), just eight ingredients and a lifetime of finesse. "I've been doing the exact same thing for thirty years. Same olive oil, same tomatoes, same brand of rice." That last part, of course, is what counts. When it comes to rice, she repeats a common mantra shared by serious rice cooks everywhere in this part of the country: "Bomba is easier to cook, but it doesn't have the same flavor. Senia is very tricky to cook, but the reward is incredible flavor and texture."

When a customer orders, she puts a pan over one of three triangular iron stands (the standard for wood-fired paellas) and builds a fire beneath it. Just as the ingredients vary from region to region, so does the wood. Orange wood is most common (thanks

Josefina's snail and rabbit masterpiece, forged in
the flames of burning vine clippings.

to Valencia's citrus industry), but Pinoso forms part of the Jumilla wine country, so Josefina uses bundles of *sarmiento*, vine clippings from a nearby winery. "Orange wood burns steady, but it doesn't give you the intense flames that I want."

Normally, wood is the quiet accomplice, whispering at the paella but never raising its voice, but Josefina uses her vine cuttings like an ingredient, wrapping the rice in wreaths of flame that impart a more assertive smokiness in the final product. When Josefina has three paellas going at full blast, the kitchen throbs with the warm glow of a dying meteor.

With her stock already made, most of her effort during service goes into regulating the fires—manipulating the bunches of *sarmiento* to raise and lower the temperature at critical junctures. She asks me if I like *socarrat*, and I nod enthusiastically, but when I tell her that one of the two people I'm eating with today doesn't, she adds extra wine clippings under just two-thirds of the pan—a small but extraordinary piece of refinement you won't find repeated anywhere.

You don't need a famous French chef to tell you this rice is a work of art: two grains high, glistening red-gold, not quite stretching to the edge of the pan, where the reduced stock forms a film of concentrated intensity somewhere between a liquid and solid state. The rice is pregnant with every one of Josefina's touches—the braised rabbit, the rested stock, the rosemary-fattened snails, the scent of *sarmiento*. A poem in a pan, the surrounding world outside concentrated down into each single grain.

Later, she takes a seat at the table, which is silent but for the sound of scraping. She seems genuinely shocked that people find their way to Pinoso to eat her rice. "Arzak grabbed a stool and sat in the middle of the kitchen, watching me cook. 'Hey, darling, walk me through what you're doing.' All of the attention was pretty shocking for us. I mean, for the longest time, we didn't even have a sign on the door."

As I make my way toward the end of the pan, a sense of ambivalence takes hold, some strange mix of ecstasy and melancholy, both rooted in the same overwhelming realization: I am having the greatest rice moment of my life.

There may be no word more loaded in the food world than "authentic." It's a descriptor that gets thrown around a lot these days, by chefs and journalists, foodie friends and enthusiastic family members. ("Your dad and I found this lovely little Mexican hole-in-the-wall. Very authentic.") It's not just shorthand for quality, but a marker of deeper cultural significance—one that confers a certain level of exclusivity on the food, its creator, and, more important, its consumer.

Everybody wants the food they're eating to be authentic, even if our judgment of authenticity is more of a sensation than a concrete analysis, an instinct based on the way things—the restaurant, the clients, the people cooking—look. But the second you try to put a definition to it—an authentic Italian pizza, authentic Chinese food, authentic paella—it slips right through your fingers.

Where do we draw the line when it comes to authenticity? Who sets the parameters? Who defines the terms? When does a dish bend and when does it break? Why are cauliflower and fava beans acceptable in a paella but green peas are not? Because grandma never used them? Because their particular brand of natural sweetness detracts from the rice? Or because of some deeper symbolism—the fact that those little green orbs show up on paella propaganda across the country, and that any serious cook must distance him- or herself from the tourism industry's definition of the dish?

(You see this type of selective chauvinism in food circles the world over. Italians will openly curse the presence of pineapple and ham on a pizza, only to turn around and make one with canned corn and sliced hot dogs—the same porky-sweet combo in different clothing.)

As the food world flattens, flavors inevitably get diluted, recipes co-opted, culture decontextualized and misunderstood. Some would suggest that that makes defining authenticity all the more important to protect the dishes we love most. But cuisine is a living, breathing culture, one in which the parameters are always redefined, the signposts always moving. For dishes such as paella, evolving creations developed out of an organic, let's-make-the-most-of-whatever's-available mentality, the desire to codify them seems out of step with the spirit of their origins.

Don't get me wrong. Food controversies are a beautiful thing. Having an entire body of people engaged enough in the importance of what they eat to hurl vicious invectives at anyone sick enough to add onions (*¡qué horror!*) or black pepper (*¡me cago en Dios!*) to a pan of rice is the sign of a healthy culture. These are the kinds of people I want to roll with. From *tortilla* to *cocido* to gazpacho, Spaniards hold very strong opinions about their iconic foods, but no discussion is more rife with social land mines than the paella debate. Talking to a Valencian about rice is like talking to a zealot about religion. Anything other than head nodding or shoulder shrugging is likely to end ugly.

I learned this the hard way years ago, the first time I wrote about paella. It evoked a fit of angry e-mails and diatribes in the comments section of Roads & Kingdoms. Spaniards published articles about my low IQ; some took to social media to say that I should relinquish my role as a writer. What most people, myself included, don't accept is that there is no truth in a food debate, only truthiness.

My time in Valencia eating rice, one after the next, from as diverse a body of sources and circumstances as possible, isn't a quest for the truth, it's a search for an informed opinion. Just as I am arriving at one, I get an invite from the crew at Wikipaella to put it to the ultimate test: as a judge of the 55 Concurso Internacional de Paella Valenciana, the world's oldest and largest paella competition. To be clear, they have me penciled in as an honorary judge, with no official influence in the final results, but full access to the spectrum of rices delivered by today's participants.

Most days, Sueca is an undercaffeinated town of twenty-eight thousand with deep paella roots due to its strategic position in the center of the Albufera. Travel a few steps outside of town and you'll find yourself surrounded by a swaying green sea of rice paddies. But for one day in September every year, this quiet pueblo is transformed into the center of the rice world.

There are thirty-five contestants in this year's event, hailing from all corners of the world. The bulk of the cooks are Spanish, of course, but the competition includes three teams from Japan, one from Germany, one from Peru, and Casa Paella, a catering company from Tasmania known for the quality of its namesake dish. Most of the international contestants qualified for their slots earlier in the year in regional semifinals, and the locals gravitate toward their cooking areas, watching these foreign paella teams the way most people watch a nature documentary. *I didn't know they had paella in Sweden.*

The undisputed crowd favorite is El Chateo, a tapas bar in Sapporo, Hokkaido, helmed by a group of youngish Japanese dudes with wide eyes and excellent hair.

Crowds swarm around their stall. Local TV crews fight for interviews. A forest of selfie sticks sprouts suddenly. An older gentleman with a large belly and bushy mustache breaks through the ruckus with a tray of beers. "You look sweaty," he tells the Japanese cook, who is both sweaty and confused, but he grabs the beer and offers a *kampai* to his new friend.

The prevailing vibe of the day is somewhere between a track meet and a block party. As the contestants build fires and begin browning chunks of chicken and rabbit, a marching band works its way through the crowd, blasting them with brassy tunes. Along the opposite side of the cooking stations, a line of stands run by local restaurants offer up the fruits of the Valencia table: *horchata* (tigernut milk, which was born here before being folded into Mexican cuisine), *all-i-pebre* (a garlicky stew of Albufera eel), and about a dozen different rices, from Technicolor paellas to *arroz al horno* to an *arroz meloso* made with chunks of fresh tuna and caramelized onions.

The dignitaries of the paella world—rice

—

producers, pan makers, saffron dealers—fill out the crowd, moving from stand to stand, holding their bellies, and sipping stock from spoons proffered by contestants in the know. By 2:00 p.m., the crowd is so thick it sticks to your back like a sweaty T-shirt. You can separate the locals from the outsiders by the way they hurl unsolicited advice to every competitor they cross: *Don't take out water! The rice looks too yellow! Stop stirring, stop stirring!* ¡No, hombre, no!

One of those locals is Mercedes, who has come with Salva to take in the spectacle. For a woman like Mercedes, who has spent her entire life cooking three rices a week for her family, the idea of a paella competition is like an ironing competition or dishwashing competition. When she sees the contestants working through the limited pantry provided, she wonders aloud, "But wait, where are the red peppers? No meatballs?" When I assure her that nothing in the crowd will touch her paella, she plants a kiss on my cheek. "I didn't want to say it myself, but I think you're right."

The Wikipaella crew has matched me

The final round of judging at the 55th International
Valencian Paella Competition.

up with an official judge, Rafa Margós, a young, bearded, fast-talking chef. His restaurant Las Bairetas, in the hills of Chiva, is known not just for the quality of the dozen or so rice dishes they cook, but the sheer quantity in which they produce them. His kitchen is set up to cook up to 143 paellas at once over live orange wood fire, a feat of logistics, engineering, and guerrilla culinary skills almost impossible to fathom.

"The old paella dignitaries think that age is a prerequisite for expertise," says José Manuel Garcerá from Wikipaella, who helps organize and support the event. "Rafa is important because he adds some young blood to a community that skews old. This is a guy who was born next to an orange fire."

Rafa and I make the rounds and he takes to schooling me in the art of tasting with your eyes, analyzing the dozens of paellas we pass without breaking stride. "There's way too much meat in that pan. It will never brown properly." "The flame is too low. You need a full, raging fire when you add the rice to make sure the water evaporates correctly." "See that pallid color? That's because they didn't spend enough time building a proper *sofrito*. The final product will be insipid."

Each team is given the same twelve ingredients to build their paella—the closest thing to a region-wide definition of paella *valenciana*—meaning the competition comes down to technique. No tricks, no improvisations, just the raw skill of the cooks. It's a formidable task, but Rafa seems more amused than impressed by the competition. "Nobody running a serious restaurant in Valencia could afford to close on a Sunday." At this very moment, there are more paellas being cooked at his restaurant—helmed by his brothers in his rare absence—than at the whole of this competition.

As the clock winds down, the revelry turns to tension as more than a few teams find themselves behind the gun. One of the organizers makes an announcement over the PA system: "Just ten minutes to submit your paellas for judging!"

Some teams wildly fan the flames, looking for that last blast of *socarrat*-forming heat. Others lay kitchen towels over the rice, hoping to retain just the right amount of residual moisture in the rice. Down at Team Hokkaido's station, the selfies come to a sudden halt as their boyish smiles fade into looks of terror. The Japanese crowd favorites have yet to add their rice to the pan, meaning they'll either be delivering their paella late or raw.

As the contestants ferry their paellas across a bridge over the train tracks and into the massive salon where they'll be evaluated, Rafa and I discuss the prospects. "I've seen some good ones and some very bad ones," he says. "The biggest surprise is the variety. From the same batch of ingredients come a thousand different paellas."

Whatever bonhomie was shared during the cooking has been replaced by a tense silence from the room of judges—many of whom seem more interested in judging each other than the rice. Eight judges, most of them older men from the rice community, most of whom have been involved in the competition for years and view their role on the panel as a sacred status symbol. The lone woman among the group, an older woman from Kyoto, wears a gold kimono a few shades brighter than the rice we're judging.

Each judge carries a small leather briefcase outfitted with evaluation sheets, pens, tasting spoons, and a sheet outlining the parameters. Paellas are to be judged by color, flavor, symmetry, and *socarrat*, all scored on a 0–10 scale, all equally weighted. Before entering the judging hall, a pretty girl in a pantsuit comes by with a tray and asks us to surrender our phones to avoid any outside influence during the official tasting.

The judges are dispatched to different parts of the room for the first round of evaluation. In our table of six pans, you can see the whole spectrum of potential and peril in the world of paella. We unsheathe our official tasting spoons and get down to business.

The first paella, a messy offering crowded with poorly butchered chunks of chicken and rabbit, merits only a small spoonful before Rafa renders his verdict. "It's basically inedible. See the rice on top—it's raw." It's a double-blind tasting, but I wonder if this might be the Hokkaido offering. Twenty-five points.

The next entry looks and tastes unevenly cooked, and elicits an immediate groan of exasperation from Rafa. "This is the problem with Bomba. You end up with raw rice on the top. No good, man." Thirty-one points.

Rafa perks up as he slides his spoon into the third rice. "It's creamy and tastes of a rich meat stock, but there's no *socarrat* to speak of. It's missing that last punch of fire." Thirty-four points.

The fourth rice looks like the kind of paella you'd find on a poster, which isn't a compliment. "Paella is about rice," says Rafa. "I don't want to have to push aside meat to get to the grains." Thirty points.

As we approach the final rice on our table, one of the older judges—suit, tie, hair gel—stops us before we can taste. "This is a trick! Look, you see how little rice they put in the pan? Don't be fooled, this is not a correct paella."

"I don't know," says Rafa, trying to be diplomatic. "It actually looks like a proper paella to me."

"I'm not telling you how to vote. But I've been a part of these events for the past twenty years. I helped pen the official recipe now used by the organization. I've written more than twenty articles published in journals and magazines all over the world about paella. I have them in a folder next door and I'd be happy to share them with you so you can better understand what we're looking for today."

Rafa smiles politely, takes a bite and writes down his score: thirty-eight points, the winner of our group by a healthy margin.

The winning paella from each group is carried off to the finalist table and the jury members are issued fresh spoons and scoring sheets and told to taste the remaining contestants carefully before making their final judgments.

The same distinguished gentleman from earlier has focused his tasting prowess on the most promising paella of the bunch, one that Rafa immediately fingered to be the winner. "Is that . . . is that *ave crème?*" he says loud enough for us all to hear. *Ave crème* is a popular stock cube used in savory dishes in households across Spain, and a common trick among some cooks looking for instant flavor enhancement—the equivalent of doping in the paella world.

Others gather around, taste, debate, mumble everything from doubt to mild disapproval to outright indignation, until it's finally agreed that some unprincipled *paellero* snuck a stock cube into his rice and desecrated the sacred tradition of paella *valenciana*. Instant disqualification.

With the paella imposter out of the way, the winner becomes apparent within minutes. The paella in the pan marked A has a rugged charm, more handsome than beautiful, but with the ruddy, almost rust color characteristic of a rice cooked with a deeply flavorful *sofrito*. More important than the aesthetics, the flavor is deep and well balanced and the texture is exactly what it should be: a warm, subtle sheen blankets the rice while maintaining the singular integrity of each grain.

On our way out, we pass a young news anchor from TV5 doing a stand-up in front of the long line of pans. "It's been a long, intense day of judging. In just a few short minutes, we'll find out who makes the best paella in the world."

I shoot a look at Rafa. He shrugs his shoulders. "Hey, it's television."

An hour later, in a giant ceremony that I'm too stuffed and salted to attend, the organizers will reveal that the winner isn't one of the crowd favorites—not La Picanterra from Cullera or Levante from Benissanó or everyone's new friends from Hokkaido—but from team L'Albufera, a restaurant located on the bottom floor of a hotel in Madrid, where the paellas are cooked on a gas stovetop

Great Grains

THE RICE MATRIX

CONEJO Y CARACOLES

A staple found in the mountainous interior of Alicante, where rabbit and snails are abundant. When done right, it's one of the finest rice creations in Spain—or anywhere.

Where to eat: Paco Gandía, Pinoso; Racoì del Pla, Alicante.

POSEUR PAELLA

Dubious rice creations used to lure in tourists looking for an authentic Spanish experience. Clues that it's fake: wet or neon yellow rice, a mixture of meat and seafood, share's menu space with pizza.

Where to eat: Plaza de la Virgen, Valencia; La Rambla, Barcelona; Plaza Mayor, Madrid.

ARROZ DEL AUTOR

Fancy rice dishes served in small portions at Spain's white-label restaurants. Distinguished by the intensity of the stocks and the esoteric proteins — pigeon, sea cucumber — used to form their foundation.
Where to eat: Quique Dacosta, Dénia; Dos Cielos, Barcelona.

ARROZ A BANDA

A fisherman creation eaten along the Valencia coast. Made by first creating a fragrant stock from small rockfish, then cooking it with the rice and various forms of seafood: sepia, shrimp, small pieces of fish, depending on where you are. Often served with *allioli*, a garlic and olive oil emulsion.
Where to eat: Casa Carmela, Valencia; El Faralloì, Dénia.

05

ARROZ AL HORNO

An oven-baked porcine party of the highest order, combining blood sausage, pork belly, pork ribs, and the leftover stock from *puchero*, a classic Valencian stew.

06

ARROZ CALDOSO

Literally "brothy rice," *arroz caldoso* packs the comfort of a soup with the substance of a dry rice dish. *Arroz con bogavante* is the king of the *caldosos*, but you'll also find it made with crab, shrimp, clams, and even meat.
Where to eat: Casa el Famós Valencia; Compartir, Cadaqués.

07

ARROZ NEGRO

Tinted jet black with squid ink and studded with various and sundry cephalopods and crustaceans. Expect a moist, almost risotto-like texture with an undercurrent of iron and ocean from the coat of ink.
Where to eat: Las Bairetas, Valencia.

One night with the

SPANISH YOUTH

8:00p.m.

—

COPE WITH *COPAS*

The crippled economy hasn't kept a generation of Spaniards from keeping up their country's reputation as a nightlife juggernaut. *Mileuristas*, those making less than one thousand euros a month, party better than *millionarios*. It just takes a bit more planning to have a good time.

9:30p.m.

—

FÚTBOL FRENZY

Saturday night means Spain's *liga de fútbol* is in high gear—the perfect warm-up for a long night out. A beer at the bar buys you a front-row seat to two hours of the Spanish *Liga*. For added entertainment, offer a strong opinion about Messi or Cristiano Ronaldo.

11:30p.m.

—

DIVIDE DINNER

Expect advance notice of the exact price per head for food and wine. Anywhere north of twenty euros would be considered posh. No dinner table heroics. No "I get this one, you get the next." Bills will be calculated down to the last cent and divided accordingly.

12:45a.m.

—

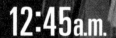

DRINKS AL FRESCO

With the specter of twelve-euro disco cocktails looming, the vital postdinner drinking session moves to the streets. Pair off with friends based on liquor preference (vodka, whiskey, gin), find a patch of cement, and don't move until the bottles are empty.

3:15a.m.

—

TIME TO DANCE

If you're young and drunk in Spain, you're likely to end up at the *discoteca*. Show up before 1:00 a.m. and you'll find the dance floor empty. The night peaks around 4:00 a.m., so pace yourself. Most will nurse a single drink for the remainder, but a round of shots would endear you to your hosts.

6:00a.m.

—

BIKINI SUNRISE

Spaniards don't want to go to bed on an empty stomach. Once the music dies, head to the closest dive bar for a *bikini*, a griddled ham and cheese sandwich, or look for the churros vendors. Few things soak up booze better than fried dough.

TWISTED HISTORY

Churros' history is murky. Some say they came back from China with Portuguese sailors, a play on the salted street food *youtiao*. Others claim shepherds in the south invented them as a way to fill their bellies while on the move with their flock.

SOUTHERN STRONGHOLD

Churro culture is strongest in the south of Spain, where the country's savviest fry cooks reign. They may change shape and name—*porras, tallos, jeringos*—but they all follow the same formula: fried dough, sugar, and optional chocolate for dunking. (Never cinnamon!)

ON CHOCOLATE

IT'S WHAT'S FOR BREAKFAST

Churros aren't eaten for dessert—
they're eaten for breakfast, or
as a snack in the late afternoon,
or as the last thing you put in
your body as the sun rises after
a long night out. Churro stands
are often the first businesses to
open in Spain.

HOT OR BUST

Tourist-heavy spots are fond of
peddling churros that have
been slowly dying under a heat
lamp. Anything other than a hot
churro is worthless, so wait for
a fresh batch, or find a new place
doing brisk churro business.

Chapter Four

BASQUE COUNTRY

The story of modern Basque cuisine doesn't begin with the towering figures of culinary fame that have become household names across Spain: Arzak, Andoni, Berasategui, Subijana. It doesn't begin with long, explosive tapas crawls through the Parte Vieja of San Sebastián or Bilbao's Casco Viejo. It begins in 1946, in the basement kitchen of the Hotel Maria Cristina, where fifteen-year-old Luis Irizar Zamora spent his first days as an apprentice peeling potatoes. It would be three more years before he earned a dime in his role as a young cook, but he was slowly accumulating the skills that would help dramatically transform the shape and trajectory of modern Basque cuisine.

This wasn't just any hotel kitchen that young Luis apprenticed in. This was sacred ground in San Sebastián, the hotel's name taken from the city's most illustrious fan, the young queen regent who in 1893 chose this cool coastal oasis as her respite from royal life in Madrid. Since then, it's been a summer playground for politicians, celebrities, and royalty looking to escape the heat of inner Iberia. Many of the wealthy—including French aristocrats pouring in from the north—traveled with their own brigade of chefs, who began to slowly impart upon the local cooks a body of knowledge and technique that would have a profound impact on Basque cuisine.

Luis had peeled a few potatoes in his early years. His parents ran a family restaurant in Igueldo, a rural outpost not far from San Sebastián, where as a young boy he pitched in where he could. The family had cows and a garden and served the kind of classic Basque food that helped fuel the region's industrializing workforce. But his first professional job, one in a busy hotel kitchen responsible for feeding some of Spain's wealthiest and most powerful people, suggested a great, wide culinary world, and awakened in Luis a desire to explore it all.

The early Franco years was a tough time to be cooking in Spain. Four years of civil war had depleted the national pantry and gutted the agricultural system. Strict rationing made running a high-end restaurant nearly impossible. At his next job, as a kitchen assistant at the polished Monte Igueldo, Luis specialized in culinary contraband, working with French purveyors to sneak caviar, lobsters, foie gras, and other luxury ingredients across the border. "There was no other way to cook seriously during those years."

Despite the lean times, Luis proved a resourceful young worker, doing whatever he had to do to open the next door and continue sharpening his skill set. From black market border runs, he moved south to Madrid to work at the Hotel Ritz and later cooked classic continental fare at Jockey, the type of top-tier places largely insulated from the whims of the outside world. He butchered game, made salads and terrines, worked on the line, accumulating a bank of knowledge that would take him far in the restaurant world.

Luis was the wandering chef before chefs wandered—kept in motion not by money, but by the promise of the next lesson, the new experience that would shape him into a better cook. Today you can trace the grooves in the earth worn by ambitious young cooks traveling between Noma, El Celler de Can Roca, and the other great restaurants of the world, stacking their résumés with short stints in flashy kitchens. In 1950, in Spain, though, you were lucky enough to have a job, let alone an ambitious life plan.

Recognizing the limit to what he could learn in Spain, Luis traveled north to Paris, the center of the gastronomic world, to cook refined French cuisine at the Hotel California. The chef was a tyrant, more feared than loved by his young cooks, whom he tormented for the tiniest transgressions. Smelling possible peril, Luis studied French and worked twice as hard as his French colleagues. The chef took notice, and rewarded Luis by teaching him the secrets to being one of Paris's top sauciers. "The time in France was tough, but I considered it my doctorate."

After France, Luis migrated across the English Channel, following the opportunities as they presented themselves: a stint at a Spanish restaurant with flamenco in London, five years as chef in a high-end Mediterranean restaurant, two years in a classic English pub, where he transposed his scattered biography onto the menu: classic French, Mediterranean, Basque. His next appointment would be his most important to date, as chef at the London Hilton, where he captained a team of cooks responsible for running the hotel's ecosystem of restaurants and banquet rooms, serving an average of 3,500 meals a day. The five-hundred-room Hilton was one of London's most important hotels and business centers, where the English elite sought to outdo each other in escalating shows of luxury and ostentation.

In those early years, Luis had the olive-oil good looks of a rising mob boss, his eyes and his tight-lipped smile transmitting a sly disbelief, as if he never thought his crazy plan would actually work out. Throughout his career, he surrounded himself with a trusted crew of captains and consiglieri, guys loyal to him and willing to do whatever it took to execute his vision. A photo from the Hilton in 1965 shows a team of sixty-six chefs in their whites, Luis sitting in the center, arms crossed, grinning.

During the London years, Luis and his wife, Virginia, had four daughters, and after a decade in England, the chef found himself exhausted and homesick. In 1966, an extraordinary opportunity brought him back to his Basque Country: a businessman named Dionisio Barandiarán had purchased and reformed a hotel in the resort town of Zarautz, and he wanted Luis to run the kitchen and the attached cooking school, the first official culinary school in the region.

Spanish cuisine passed through a dark period in the years Luis spent cooking his way around Europe. When people talk about the cuisines of poverty that developed in rural France and Italy, challenging conditions that birthed such rustic masterpieces as pot-au-feu and *ribollita*, they refer to cultures that transformed scraps of meat and garden vegetables into works of edible art. Spain's wasn't a cuisine of poverty; it was one of desperation. One of the most popular recipes of the postwar years was written by Ignasi Domènech, called *tortilla de patatas sin patatas ni huevos*: potato omelet without potatoes or eggs. Domènech advised his countrymen to use a slurry of flour and water to mimic the egg, and discarded orange peels to approximate the texture of potato.

What began as a profound lack of resources in the famine-riddled postwar years

gave way to an overall absence of direction and leadership in the culinary community as Spain recovered in the 1950s. General Franco, who openly espoused a food philosophy of sacrifice and who showed hostility toward anything hinting at decadence (despite his own well-known sweet tooth), did little to inspire his country's gastronomy. Luis saw in the new position an opportunity to reinvigorate the entire foundation of Basque cuisine. This was a time when required military service and authoritarian rule made it difficult for Spaniards to leave the country. If cooks couldn't travel through Europe, Luis would bring Europe to them. He taught them the mother sauces he mastered in Paris, the pâtés and charcuterie from a stint in Switzerland, the sense of teamwork and organization accumulated during years of running a sprawling hotel team at the Hilton.

On the other end of those lessons was a student body destined to be some of the most famous chefs in the country. Ramón Roteta, José Ramón Elizondo, Pedro Subijana, Karlos Arguiñano: all formed part of

The many faces of Luis Irizar.

that first class of 1966, later dubbed the Triumphant Generation, a family of chefs that would shape Basque cuisine into a potent blend of European haute and Spanish avant-garde.

But before the triumph, a world of challenges awaited Luis and his band of vaunted *vascos*. Toward the end of the Franco years, a new form of civil war broke out, this one waged between the central government and Euskadi Ta Askatasuna (ETA) a vehement group of Basque separatists seeking independence from Spain. Basques have long been known as a proud, independent body. Euskera, the Basque language (an impossible collision of consonants with nothing in common with Spanish), is said to be Europe's oldest, and many scholars believe that the Basques were the first to settle the Iberian Peninsula. ETA sought to carve out an independent nation on the back of this pride, and turned to increasingly desperate measures of violence to make their point—a terror campaign of kidnappings, bombings, and political executions that gripped the country for more than three decades.

The entire region felt the collateral damage. Tourism disappeared, restaurants suffered, hotels emptied. Luis remembers violent protests that erupted on Christmas of 1970; within days, hundreds of holiday reservations were canceled. Euromar, once a beacon in a culinary world long left to operate in the darkness, shuttered in 1973.

The new generation of Basque chefs had never been better prepared to usher in a new age of gastronomy, but suddenly they didn't have the clients to cook for. To help fight the growing tide of isolation, and inspired by the young gunslingers of French nouvelle cuisine across the border, a group of fourteen chefs formed the pact of la Nueva Cocina Vasca, with Luis as the group's patriarch. During their weekly dinners members showcased new recipes and techniques as the group discussed the future of the food they loved so dearly. Groups of food critics, cooks, and favored clients were brought in to taste and evaluate these new creations, and together, they began to form the language of the New Basque Cuisine.

"Luis has always been our guru," says Juan Mari Arzak, chef of the eponymous Michelin three-star restaurant, long one of Spain's most famous and important outposts of innovation. "He was the master of traditional cuisine, and he offered his full support to this group of chefs. Whenever there was a problem, there was Luis to help solve it."

Armed with a new language to spread his message, Luis went on to open a series of restaurants that would unveil to the Spanish world some of the most sophisticated cuisine the country had ever seen. What he, Arzak, Subijana, and others created in the 1970s and 1980s didn't just form the basis of a new style of cooking in the Basque Country—one defined by a deep respect for classic technique but with an eye toward the future—but in all of Spain, eventually inspiring the likes of Ferran Adrià and other young chefs who would turn the country into the center of culinary innovation in the twenty-first century.

Today, the Basque Country is among the most Michelin-dense regions in the world, but every galaxy starts with a single star, and the Basque's first constellation belonged to Luis, who earned one in 1975 for his restaurant Gurutze-Berri.

In 1992, he and his daughters opened the Escuela de Cocina Luis Irizar, an intimate cooking school on the edge of the old part of San Sebastián, with a generous view of La Concha, San Sebastián's famous crescent-shaped beach. With the worst of the Basque Country's rocky past behind it, Luis and his family looked to pick up where they left off at Euromar.

As they began to equip a new generation of cooks with the lessons learned over a lifetime, the first wave of Irizar disciples spread out across the country, fomenting the revolution that Luis had sewn in 1967, winning their own loyal following, and earning for the man who had taught them a title still used by those that know the true history: *el maestro de maestros.*

The master of masters.

But it wasn't just the masters who passed through Luis's kitchen. In July of 2002, with the Basque culinary revolution already in high gear, he accepted an unlikely student into his summer course: a young, foolish, infatuated American looking to extend his lease in Spain.

I had come to Spain six months before to study at the University of Barcelona and promptly felt my world turned upside down. It wasn't just Spain that I fell in love with, but an entire culture dedicated to the earthly pleasures of food and drink. Those were heady days, skipping class to ride my skateboard to the Boqueria to fill my backpack with the cheapest ingredients possible, then transforming them into meals decent enough to fill our apartment with people. Our dinner parties had menus that, like the guests themselves, spanned the world: sushi night, fresh pasta feasts, mole-and-margarita fiestas. Every cook has that moment when he or she recognizes the power of food to bring people together, and this was mine. The lesson hit twice as hard in this foreign land, with foreign faces and foreign tastes; every night was proof of food's power to cut through color, creed, culture.

Up until then, I had taught myself to cook largely by reading my mom's magazines and watching endless hours of chefs like Mario Batali and Ming Tsai after school on the newly launched Food Network. I converted my parents' kitchen into a smoke-filled receptacle for my culinary failures, menacing Teflon and taste buds at every turn, but slowly I figured out how to sear a steak, fold an omelet, whisk a vinaigrette—just enough to impress my friends and woo a few love interests. But there were limits to my DIY approach to cooking, and I wanted to see what waited beyond a makeshift education. I went online and found a small but esteemed cooking school offering summer classes right next to the beach in the town of San Sebastián.

I had been to San Sebastián a few months earlier for spring break and fell hard for the convergence of soft sand beaches, shamrock mountainscapes, and dense clusters of bars and restaurants. I bodysurfed in the bracing pull of the Atlantic, drank wine in old plazas with pockets of young locals, tasted foods I didn't know existed from glorious bar spreads, and barely touched a pillow for forty-eight hours. As the train pulled out of the station, I scribbled a few words in my journal before passing out: *Come back soon. With a purpose.*

But I was broke. Six months of decadent dinner parties and all-night benders had depleted the meager funds I brought with me to Europe. My roommate David Klinker agreed to join me in the Basque Country, and together we hatched a multipronged plan to raise capital. We bought cheap European cell phones from departing American students and sold them to the new wave coming in for the summer at a steep markup. We recruited deep-pocketed tenants to rent out the extra rooms in our apartment. In a particularly desperate moment, we took jobs at La Ballena Azul, a new carwash on the outskirts of the city. After a month of suds and cells, we made the nut and headed north.

In a class of Spanish cooks looking to take their interest in food to the next level, I was the lone foreigner—outmatched in kitchen skills and language capabilities,

if not enthusiasm. My fellow classmates mostly seemed amused by my presence: by my marginal knife skills, by my Mexican-inflected Spanish, by the fact that David would wait outside the school entrance every evening with a bag of ice and a bottle of whiskey for sundowners. On one of the first days of class, we were left to clean piles of squid. Uninitiated in the finer points of cephalopod anatomy, I accidentally punctured the ink sack, turning my white jacket into a Rorschach test and the classroom into a laugh track.

But Luis went out of his way to make me feel at home in his school. When I'd show up for class, he'd announce my entrance— *"¡el californiano ha llegado!"*—and throw an arm around me. If he saw me mishandling a monkfish, he'd come by to gently correct my technique ("use the spine to guide your knife"). One day, after spending all night out in Pamplona drinking and all morning being chased by giant beasts down narrow streets, I walked into class late, disheveled, reeking of bull's blood and bad decisions. Luis stopped the class, looked up from his perch by the stovetop and smiled: "Let me guess, San Fermín?"

For a man of his towering stature, he cut a warm, inviting figure: soft eyes, bushy mustache, a smile that scarcely retreats from his round face. He's the grandpa you adored as a kid, the one with the bottomless supply of swashbuckling stories that left your mind racing for days. His desire to teach, to share with his students that great bank of knowledge he has accumulated over a lifetime of wandering the world, comes out in everything he does.

By the time I took up the toque, the day-to-day operations of the school were handled by three of Luis's four daughters: Virginia and Isabel in charge of enrollment and administration, and Visi, who ran all kitchen and classroom operations.

Born in London during the Hilton years, Visi grew up cooking at her father's side. Like her father, she spent her early years chasing the next lesson, cooking in London, then in Sevilla. Later, she joined him in the kitchen in Irizar Jatetxea, where Madrid's power class came to eat New

Basque Cuisine and debate the issues of the day.

I learned a lot that summer with Luis and Visi: that by adding olive oil in a slow, steady stream to a pan of cooked salt cod, swirling the pan in gentle circles, the fat will emulsify with the fish's natural collagen, forming a smooth sauce—*pilpil*—that is to Basques what hollandaise is to the French; that a squid's body (once carefully de-inked) can be cut into thin, ivory strips that look like rice noodles but taste purely of the ocean; that everything starts and stops at the market; that there are no recipes, only techniques and ideas; that certain contingents in the Basqueland may not have warm feelings for the central government, but their pride for the homeland creates some of the world's most hospitable hosts.

Above all, I learned that I was hungry. Until then, I spent most of my college years dreaming of penning salty novels in a tiny tropical beach shack, but suddenly, all I could think about was the next meal. Where would it come from? What would it taste like? What were the steps I would need to take to bring it to life?

I had never eaten in fancy restaurants before. In general, I had tasted very little of Spanish cuisine, spending the little money I had in Barcelona on cooking and drinking (the main meal I ate out in those days was Burger King's two-for-one Whopper special). The dishes we created in class, classics of the Basque canon, were the closest I had ever come to haute cuisine, and they quickly and irrevocably changed my idea about the alchemy at work in the kitchen: stubborn off-cuts of animals transformed into tender, gelatinous stews through slow, steady cooking; seasonal vegetables treated with the gentlest forms of heat and seasoning possible; fish and seafood of every imaginable permutation: salt cod tucked into weeping-soft omelets, squid bathed in puddles of its own ink, fat fillets of white fish blanketed in a warm sauce of roasted peppers.

The little I managed to eat outside of school opened my eyes even wider. A *pintxo* bar in full bloom is a creature of arresting beauty—where oil-slick anchovies and golden-fried *croquetas* and stuffed *piquillo* peppers like puckered red lips could arouse even the most prudish passerby. Spread out in the open, covering every square centimeter of bar space in a tapestry of plants and protein, they suggest a food world of infinite possibility. I could feel myself slipping ever deeper into its possibilities.

My mom, perhaps sensing I might never return, convinced a neighbor to hire me as a fry cook at his seafood institution in downtown Raleigh, a development which she shared via e-mail. (Subject: Good News!)

By the time I pulled myself out of San Sebastián, destined to spend the next few months frying catfish and hush puppies, the pioneering chefs who had passed through Luis's school were well on their way to transforming San Sebastián and the surrounding region into one of the most important food destinations in the world.

And I was well on the way to my own transformation.

Spoiler alert: I didn't turn out to be a chef. It wasn't for a lack of trying, though. I

FOR THE BASQUES, IT'S A BIRTHRIGHT TO EAT AND DRINK AS WELL AS POSSIBLE.

took the lessons of Luis and Visi back with me to North Carolina, where my family lives, tried to employ some of the savvy cooking that the father-daughter team imparted upon me in my new role as a grease jockey. But as it turned out, it's hard to find hake chin in Raleigh, and the eaters of the Deep South prefer red-eye gravy to squid ink. The old battery of cooks, most of them ex-convicts with cornbread hearts and buttermilk souls, took to calling me "tender hands," due to the fact that I was unable to reach directly into the fry basket and remove incinerating bits of fried shrimp and oysters with my uncallused mitts. I lasted a few months before heading West to finish my college career.

During my last year at UCLA, I helped open a café in Brentwood, the kind of earnest eatery that sells eighteen-dollar mixed green salads to rich Angelenos. Also the kind of place that packs two cups of heavy cream and four cups of sharp cheddar into a serving of "organic" mac and cheese. The first time I was left in charge of the kitchen, a well-intentioned young cook from Mexico tossed a handful of chilies into a massive pot of roasted vegetable soup, thinking they'd add a gentle glow. Turns out they were a mutant breed of habaneros, and the chef berated us both for days. I got tired of Los Angeles, tired of trudging back and forth between the library and the kitchen, tired of being tired.

I graduated, moved to Chile, lived in a cabana close to the beach north of Valparaiso smoking lots of pot and cooking elaborate meals for anyone who would come over. One guest was a young woman who cooked on a boat in Patagonia. Weeks later she called and offered me her job. The boat took small groups of passengers on week-long trips through the fjords and archipelagos of an impossibly lonely and beautiful stretch of earth. I cooked elaborate meals for them—mostly based around fish bought from the old fishermen who rowed those majestic fjords.

When summer drew to a close, the owner of the boat recommended me for a position running a kitchen at a resort being built nearby. For my tryout, I cooked the managers a fish dish I learned from Visi and they gave me the job. Seven miles of virgin Patagonian coastline fringed with old-growth forest, all part of a high-end eco resort years in the making. I signed on to run the kitchen, with a close friend growing the food and raising the animals I would cook. An incredible project, but one that would take years more to develop—years I didn't have to spend on a cold, wet coastline in Patagonia. (Years later, I'd watch in shock as Bourdain dined on the dishes of my replacement, overlooking the same wild beach I could see from my cabin, on an episode of *No Reservations*.)

All along the way, I wrote. Mostly bad poetry or hip-hop lyrics or tortured short fiction. But when I decided that maybe I wasn't cut out for a life behind the stovetop—that professional cooking demanded a level of physical exertion and geographical commitment I wasn't pre-pared to give—I needed a new source of income. The first publication to pay me for my words was a magazine distributed on college campuses called *Student Traveler*. I

wrote for them the most interesting story I knew: about being the only foreigner in a Basque cooking school.

Seeing my name in print felt better than seeing my face in the mirror after a long night of searing salmon and drinking Greyhounds. I also came to accept that I was better writing about food than actually cooking it. My career as an aspiring chef came to a sudden halt, and my career as an aspiring writer, while many years from being an actual career, lurched forward—both built on the back of that same half-moon slice of heaven, San Sebastián.

🌿 🐟 🐖

Somewhere shortly after my first paid writing gig, the food world exploded. The first decade of the new millennium saw a tidal wave of unprecedented interest that infiltrated every level of the culinary world. Chefs became the new rock stars, complete with tattoos and groupies. A new class of television and print media emerged to feed the growing appetites of the food-obsessed while online forums and bloggers cataloged every calorie consumed in pursuit of the perfect meal. And the travel world began to undergo its own transformation. Suddenly, the same people who once traveled to Spain to see the works of Gaudí now came to taste the works of Adrià.

In this delicious new world, the Basque Country was born to be a star. Towering restaurants of avant-garde adventurism, concentrations of bars proffering small bites and bonhomie, a reenergized class of old-world artisans now feeding a new-world audience—it had all the ingredients of a culinary uprising. In short order, the world's new class of gastronauts came pouring into the Basque Country.

I returned more than a few times myself over the years. With glossy magazines paying the way, suddenly I could afford the towering temples where once I only window-shopped. At Arzak, the first restaurant in Spain to receive three Michelin stars, father-daughter team Juan Mari and Elena served me bonbons of foie, packages of apple and pig's blood wrapped in seaweed, hunks of lobster scattered atop a video screen with a seaside scene on loop. At Mugaritz, I ate Andoni Luiz Aduriz's edible potato stones and braised cod tripe and charcoal-coated veal, dishes that combine the modernist techniques favored by Spain's new guard with a heavy dose of naturalism to create a cuisine that is both beautiful and befuddling. In Bilbao, which writers and chefs in this country correctly call Spain's most underrated food city (overlooked because it lies in the skirt folds of its sexier sister down the coast), I went on *pintxos* crawls that alternated bites of extraordinary imagination with ones of sublime simplicity.

Most remarkable of all is Etxebarri, in the mountain village of Axpe, where Bittor Arguinzoniz has created a restaurant like no other in this world—one fueled entirely by the flames of the hearth and his own relentless pursuit of perfection. Everything from the smoked goat butter to the just-cooked red shrimp stands as a resounding reminder that the beauty of Basque cuisine stretches well beyond pintxos and pyrotechnics. If forced to choose just one restaurant to eat at for the rest of my life, Etxebarri would be it.

At first glance, the lines between these modern meccas and the man I called maestro might not be so obvious. Ask the new guard of gastronauts who come to the Basque Country expressly to eat about the name Luis Irizar and they'll likely just keep chewing. Most Spaniards don't know the name either. Such is the nature of the teacher, bound to be forever overshadowed by his students. But Luis was more than just a talented teacher; he was a catalyst.

In the modern culinary world, the actions of a few powerful forces can have a profound impact over the years as the effects travel outward. In 1966, a rock landed in the center of the great Basque sea. Fifty years later, its ripples continue to work ever outward.

The first ripple, the one that set into motion dramatic changes in the world of Spanish fine dining, came from the mustachioed phenomenon named Pedro Subijana.

From his education at Euromar, he would go on to teach his own students: in the classroom, on television, and in the professional kitchen. Since taking the helm at Akelarre in 1975, it has been a constant presence on the list of the world's best restaurants—a perfect bridge between the classical, technically refined cuisine of Luis and the first wave of new Basque chefs and the more radical innovators who would come later on.

In Getaria, a small fisherman's town between San Sebastián and Bilbao, I encounter another ripple in the sea, Pablo Vicari, class of 2003. He now runs the kitchen at Elkano, a family-owned restaurant a few steps from the Atlantic. This is no small charge: Elkano is considered by some to be one of the world's finest seafood restaurants. Started in 1964 by Pedro Arregui and now run by his son Aitor, Elkano is best known for its heroic servings of whole turbot and sea bream grilled over oak.

Pablo hails from Argentina, but came to the Basque Country and fell in love with Luis and his school. "I learned every-

Karlos Arguiñano walks the vines at K5,
his txakoli vineyard above the Atlantic.

thing I know about being a cook from the Irizar family—not just how to do things well in the kitchen, but to do them with respect and humility that have characterized Luis's career." The recipes of Elkano come from the Arregui family, pioneers of the open flame, but you see in Pablo—in the way he works the fire, in the care he puts into plates of barnacles and anchovies and lobster—the other side of Basque brilliance, not a burning desire for innovation, but a religious respect for perfect product and perfect technique.

One of the ripples wasn't a ripple at all; it was a tidal wave, and its name was Karlos Arguiñano. One day I make my way up to the foothills of Zarautz to see the most famous student to pass through the School of Irizar.

For many people around the world, including millions in Latin America who watch Karlos every day, Basque cuisine, if not all of Spanish cuisine, begins right here. "When I started on television, I thought, okay, I'll give it six months until people get tired of me. But it was the opposite: every month more people were watching." Six thousand episodes, eight thousand recipes, and fifty-five books later, Arguiñano is one of the most influential chefs on the planet, responsible for inspiring the daily creations of countless home cooks.

Karlos shows me around the studio where he films all episodes of *Karlos Arguiñano en Tu Cocina*. He runs around the kitchen, playing with puppets, inspecting ingredients, dispensing one-liners with a comedian's ease and timing. Later, he takes me up to his vineyards, where he grows the most Basque product of all: txakoli, the dry, effervescent wine that lubricates a high percentage of the region's eating and socializing. We drink cold streams of K5, the only txakoli served in all of the Basque Country's three-star restaurants, while Karlos cooks us fried eggs with *jamón* and tells jokes about the guy who drowned in a cider tank. This is the Arguiñano that most of the Spanish-speaking world knows: frenetic, hilarious, unstoppable.

Not everything that Karlos cooks is

Basque—at some point, you exhaust the encyclopedia of dishes. And given the controversy surrounding the Basque Separatist movement, he's always been careful not to make Basque pride part of his television persona. But deep down, he bleeds for his homeland. "You have so many things that make this region so great. The climate, the sea, the proximity to France, to Navarra for vegetables, to the Rioja for wine. The hundreds of gastronomic societies scattered throughout the region. In a small space we have a lot of a gastronomic life. You know what they say? The Basques screw little but they eat a lot."

Karlos was sixteen and enrolled in a local cooking class ("forty women and me—they all thought I was gay") when he saw that a new culinary school had opened down the road, run by the ex-chef of the London Hilton. He didn't have the money for the school, but Luis accepted him anyway, an act of generosity that still visibly moves Karlos to this day. "It's hard to make money being one of the good guys.

You end up making it for everyone else. Luis has always been an example of that."

Karlos formed a part of the Triumphant Generation, the first class of Irizar students that would move on to reshape the Basque culinary landscape in the decades to follow. "He was an extraordinary professor, someone who transmitted everything he had seen and done to his students." Luis taught them not just how to clarify stocks and emulsify sauces, but how to handle themselves in the world. "Luis was a magnificent cook, a fantastic professor, but an even better person."

Back in the center of San Sebastián, I do a few laps around the city, eating at dozens of *pintxos* bars and restaurants. Some of these places—Astelena, Txubillo, the Michelin-starred Kokoktxa—are run by Irizar alums. Others are not, but wear the mark nonetheless. The terrines of foie, the seafood gelées, the plates of wild game all carry more than a few strands of Irizar DNA. The chefs behind these creations may not have trained down the street.

Some may not even know the name. That is how the ripple works. It hits you, whether or not you know it.

If you find yourself in the Parte Vieja of San Sebastián eating hake chin, or in the center of Bilbao feasting on fattened duck liver, or in a wine bar in SoHo sipping K5, it's safe to say the ripple has hit you too.

I've passed by the school countless times over the years, peeked through the windows into the sunken classroom to see a new wave of young students dressed in their crisp white jackets, boning turbot or braising oxtails or sweating out a pastry lesson. One day, I see a group out front smoking and I ask them how class is going. "Man, I love Visi, but she's tough. The other day I got in trouble for overcooking asparagus." How about Luis? "He comes by in the mornings and likes to watch us cook. Seems like good people."

But I can never bring myself to walk down those stairs. I was only there for part of a summer, and that was fourteen years ago. Will they remember me? Do they care? It's like meeting your favorite musician or author—someone who has impacted your life so deeply without them even knowing it. What do you say?

Instead, I take the easy way out. I send an e-mail from my rented apartment a few blocks down the road, tell the Irizar family who I am and that I'd love to say hello if they have a free moment. Virginia writes back immediately: "Of course we remember you. Luis would love to see you while you're in town. Come by tomorrow at eleven a.m."

The last time I saw Luis, I was twenty-one years old, on my way to an underwhelming four-year career as a wandering cook. He looks the same: same quiet elegance, same prodigious mustache, same endless smile.

We talk for a while downstairs in the school's office while students in the classroom behind us take in a lesson on fish fumets. The smell of monkfish and root vegetables fills the room.

"What have you been up to all these years?" he asks me. I give him a condensed rundown, tell him about my time as a fry jockey and a boat cook, that I married a Spaniard and am writing a book on his country. "You don't say. And that all started here?" He stares out the window, scanning something on the horizon. He's been a part of hundreds of genesis stories, but this one, admittedly, has a few unexpected twists.

Mostly, though, we talk about his life, about the years on the road, raising a family while accumulating an encyclopedic understanding of classic European cooking. When he tells me about those tough first years running contraband and scraping by in an industry threatened by famine, he lowers his voice and leans in—a habit you'll find with older Spaniards when they speak about the Franco years. But when it comes to the kitchen, he's as animated as I remember him: eyes wide, hands darting here and there, plucking anecdotes from the bookshelf of his mind. "All I ever wanted to do was share what I was fortunate enough to learn."

He doesn't get around like he used to, but he still loves to walk the old streets of his home city and pay his respects to the cooks he and his family helped shape. Luis and Visi take me to one of their favorites, Casa Urola, an institution in the old part with the typical two-pronged approach of good Basque restaurants: *pintxos* on the bar, ready for immediate consumption, and a longer menu of prepared dishes for those sitting down for a full meal. It's a place I've walked by a dozen times without ever noticing—a testament to the top-to-bottom potency of this eating town.

Visi goes back into the kitchen to have a word with the chef and soon the plates come rolling out. First, *guisantes lágrima*, teardrop spring peas studded with slices of raw wild mushrooms and a veil of acorn-fed *jamón*. The tiny peas pop like caviar against the roof of my mouth, releasing little depth charges of spring across the palate.

"The Basques take eating more seriously than anyone I've met in my travels. They believe it's their duty to eat as well as possible," says Luis. "And they never get tired of it. Even the old couples still go out on tapas crawls."

"Women set aside a night each week to go out with their friends," says Visi. "The men may have their societies, but we go out and eat and drink on our own too."

Years ago, on one of the early episodes of *No Reservations*, Visi took Bourdain out with her female posse and they all ate a ton and got pretty loaded. In a separate scene, Luis brought him to his local society, one of the 1,500 all-male gastronomic societies that dot the region, places where men gather to cook, drink, and sing homages to the Basqueland. Luis taught him how to make hake with *salsa verde*, a Basque classic, in the heavily accented English of his Hilton days.

"How is Anthony doing these days?" asks Luis.

The chef brings out a plate of farm eggs scrambled so softly they've barely coagulated, covered in thin shavings of St. George's mushrooms, one of the many foraged fungi that drive Basques wild in the spring and fall. They have the impact of truffles on the loose scramble, pulling us all in close to the plate with hunks of bread for mopping. Visi pours another round of txakoli.

We talk about the latest crop of students—a group that has started to skew more international as the Basque reputation has grown. (The school's waitlist swells with each passing year.) Visi has worked sensibly to evolve the school to fit the times, incorporating the types of lessons that the modern student wants to absorb before heading out into the restaurant world: how to thicken a sauce with xanthan, cooking sous vide, folding in flavors from the global pantry.

Luis, though, belongs steadfastly and proudly to a different era, one where everything starts with product, where surprise isn't an ingredient, where a bowl of peas sure as hell better look and taste like a bowl of peas. He can't tell you how the big names today spherify olives and turn liquids into powder, but come over for dinner and he'll make you a *liebre a la royale* that would make Escoffier weep. (About the time he made Arzak and a group of French chefs wild hare covered in blood sauce at Arzak's house, Luis says proudly: "They said it was the best they'd ever had.")

The master of the masters, with
an admiring student.

The chef plants a plate of *kokotxas*, hake chin, in the center of the table. Luis sits up. "This is one of the most important plates in Basque cooking."

Visi, the perennial professor, breaks it down: "You make it with olive oil and a pinch of chili and a splash of txakoli to temper the oil. You always make it with the skin side down with a pinch of salt. In just a minute the gelatin will start to release."

I ask them why you never find *kokotxas* outside of the Basque country. "Let's hope it stays that way," says Luis, growing increasingly animated with the wine. "We don't want the price to go up. It's like *jamón*. If the Americans ever find out about true Spanish ham, there won't be any left for us."

"We have an inferiority complex here in Spain," adds Visi. "We're possessed of this idea that other people's food is better than ours. We always stress to our students that they need to care about the local culture, they need to defend great producers and old traditions. Nobody wants to go to a city where the food doesn't have its own identity."

Listening to her talk brings me instantly back to the classroom: strong jaw and fixed eyes and sharp hand movements, with a gentle urgency that tractor beams you in and a generous smile, the same one that her father has, that opens you up to whatever message she's delivering. I can see it doesn't just work on me; whenever Visi talks, Luis closes his eyes and nods his head emphatically.

Subijana and Arguiñano and half a dozen other Irizar alumni may have gone on to be titans of the culinary world, but Visi will always be the most important student to emerge from the school of Luis. Of all the ripples Luis has left behind, none matters more than Visi, the one who carries on the Irizar name, who is responsible for teaching a new generation how to handle themselves inside the kitchen and out. "She's me. She's my daughter, but she's always been me."

A plate of candlestick white asparagus lands on the table, one of the region's most treasured ingredients, served with olive oil and bread crumbs. Luis sees the scantily clad plate and gives it a nod of approval.

"What matters most to me is that Basque cuisine remains Basque, that it doesn't fuse with Japanese or South American or anything else. That it remains ours."

Despite his loyalty to his home, as the conversation wanders across the Iberian landscape, Luis admits that he's worried about the future of Spanish food. "We've gone too far. There used to be an invisible line between the world of restaurant food and industrial food producers. These are the ingredients we use, these are the ones they use. Until one day someone crossed that line."

Visi sees him getting worked up and puts her hand on his forearm. "Come on, Pop. You shouldn't worry so much."

"What? You know it's true! One day soon you'll be eating a pill that tastes like a raspberry instead of an actual raspberry. I won't be around to see it, but when you taste it, think of me."

The last dish of the day comes out of the kitchen: *torrijas*, Spain's lavish take on French toast. Urola's version is stunning, so outrageously soaked with cream and egg that it tastes like flan.

I pass Luis a fork and gesture toward the dessert, but he waves me off. "You need it more than I do." By now, Luis has had his share of txakoli and his eyelids are slowly starting to shutter. He likes to head home in the afternoon, time enough to work in a nap before evening sets in.

He pays his respects to the chef. "Better than ever, my friend. Thank you for taking such incredible care of us."

He turns to me, sticks out his hand, shakes mine like he's shook so many before. "Best of luck to you, *californiano*."

The owner holds the front door open. Luis puts on his hat and grabs Visi by the arm and the two of them step out of the restaurant and into the orange light now bathing the narrow street, disappearing into the crowds that wander the old part of San Sebastián in search of the next bite.

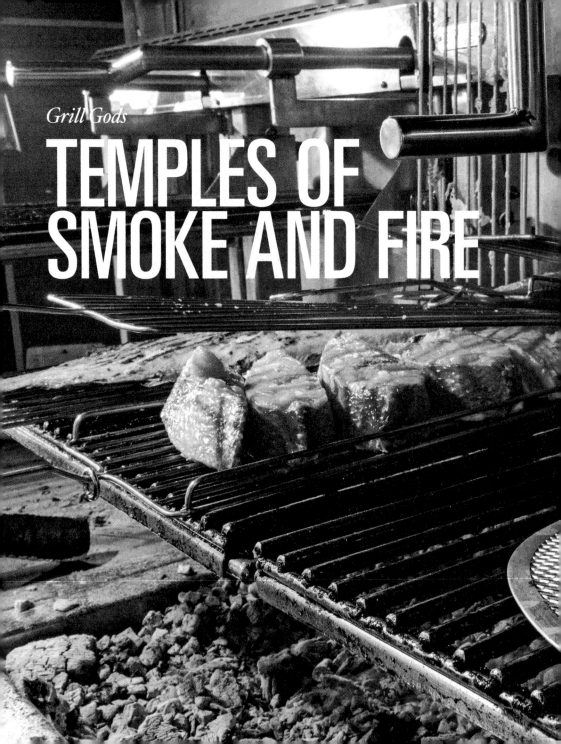

TEMPLES OF SMOKE AND FIRE

With all due respect to Argentina, Uruguay, and the Deep South, the grill culture of northern Spain may be the greatest on earth. From the mountain villages of the Basque Country to the coastal hamlets of Asturias, you'll find *asadores*, family-run restaurants powered by fire and protein, where meals consist of flame-grilled meat and fish, a token vegetable or two, and plenty of local vino. These four destinations are where world-class ingredients and unimpeachable technique conspire to ruin you for all other grilled food going forward.

Bodega El Capricho, León

RAISING THE STEAKS

Eating at Bodega El Capricho will be the most intense meat experience of your life. José Gordón is a man possessed by the pursuit of the perfect steak, a journey that starts by raising his own *bueyes* (oxen) on a special diet of grain and grass, then drying aging primal cuts of meat based on the age and race of the animal. A meal at El Capricho starts with ruby veils of raw aged ox loin, then moves on to *cecina* (dried beef cured and aged like *jamón*), ox blood *morcilla*, and an outrageously good tartare. But all of that is a minor prelude to the main event: *chuletón de buey*, massive rib steaks, cooked over oak with nothing but coarse salt until charred on the outside and barely warm throughout. The meat packs deep concentrations of umami and mineral intensity and a rim of dense, yellow fat that tastes like brown sugar. Warning: It will be hard to go back to regular beef after El Capricho.

Elkano, Getaria

THE TURBOT KINGS

Perched above the Atlantic in a small coastal village pinched between Bilbao and San Sebastián, Elkano is best known as an *asador de pescado*—a family-run restaurant with a hyper focus on grilled fish and seafood. The main attraction is *rodaballo*, wild turbot cooked whole over charcoal—a technique perfected by Elkano's founder Pedro Arregui in the 1950s and continued today by his son Aitor and chef de cuisine Pablo Vicari. After a heavy shower of coarse salt and a twelve-minute ride on the grill, the turbot is served whole at the table, then divided into its various constituents—dark, fatty back sections; light, meaty fillets; gelatin-rich ribs that leak juice down your forearms. The end product eats like an essay on the astounding potential of the sea, a range of tastes and textures you didn't think possible in a single fish.

Etxebarri, Axpe, Basque Country
MAN ON FIRE

"In the flames of the fire lives something that can help ingredients reach their fullest potential." These are the words of Bittor Arguinzoniz, high priest of the low flame who abandoned his job as a forester years ago to create one of the world's most astounding grill shrines. Everything—from the homemade goat butter to the caviar-sized spring peas to the grass-fed Galician beef to the apple tart—gets hit with smoke from wood the chef chops right outside the back door. But this isn't the hard smoke of a pitmaster; this is the delicate finesse of an artist in full control of every bite that passes into the dining room. Ask ten of the best chefs from around the world where they'd eat their last meal on earth, and half would tell you here, at the high-mountain altar of Etxebarri.

Güeyu Mar, Playa de Vega, Asturias

FISH TALES

On a quiet stretch of Asturian coastline, sandwiched between the Cantabrian Sea and the Camino de Santiago, Güeyu Mar at first blush looks like a *chiringuito*, a mellow seafood shack, but inside, nothing about husband and wife Abel and Luisa's work is the least bit laid-back—not the remarkable wine list or the specialized hand-cranked grills or the constantly rotating, individually sourced menu of fish and seafood. Depending on the day, your meal might begin with tiny, candy-sweet *quisquilla* shrimp and grilled oysters with caviar and conclude with any of half a dozen whole grilled fish: from the pull-apart flakes of grouper to big-bellied king fish rippled with fat and gelatin. Afterward, waddle your body down to the nearest stretch of sand for a siesta.

ANGULAS

THE LONG MIGRATION

Of all the rare, exceptional seafood pulled from the waters of northern Spain, baby eels may be the most revered. Born near Bermuda, they make the long, slow migration to Northern Spain in search of freshwater rivers along the Basque coast.

SPARE NO EXPENSE

Spaniards pay top euro for delicate marine treasures—the Basques most of all. Like many of Spain's lavish and rare foodstuffs, *angulas* are most popular during the Christmas season, when they command up to EUR 1,200 a kilo.

SWEET MEETS HEAT

Angulas are usually served *a la bilbaina*, cooked in crocks with olive oil, sliced garlic, and spicy *guindilla*—a foil to their delicate oceanic sweetness. A single serving, costing up to one hundred euros, could have more than three hundred baby eels.

SOCIETY'S EELS

You'll find the dish on high-end menus across the northern coast. There may be no better place to consume them, though, than in a Basque gastronomic society, where locals gather to drink and sing and cook rare delicacies from the sea.

Chapter Five

CADIZ

—

The Trap

The sun rises never the same. This is the Mediterranean, highway of wealth and wisdom, and beneath her surface stirs a silver storm of fish. A great migration, hunted.

With forty men on its way to forty more, the Bermudez cuts up the coast under the red roof of first light. Antonio González, hunched against the hull, takes a fisherman's breakfast of cigarettes and silence. Dressed for battle—camo jacket, camo hat—he has spent thirty-seven years of his life on this boat, one of a band of brothers that works these waters. Álvaro, Antonio, Miguel, Pepe, José: nearly two centuries of fishing between the brothers González.

"It always begins this way," Antonio says, "always with the silence and the smoke."

The engines whimper as the destination nears: a wall of nets, a maze of mesh and nylon meant to break the magnificent motion beneath. One arm of the trap stretches toward Africa, the other toward Spain. Zahara de los Atunes, its sunglass shops and mojito bars, stands starboard, motionless. The men begin to stir—stretching, stripping, shaking daybreak from their bones. A small flotilla bobs in the distance.

A crew of four, the youth of the Bermudez, step into their neoprene skins: the scuba team, the scouts, the ones who will take stock of what moves beneath.

As the boys go under, Captain Pepe surveys the sea. Fifth generation, sun on his skin, salt on his breath. A man of action, he of frosty mustache and granite jaw, wary of the foreign presence on his watch.

"Doesn't look good," Antonio whispers to himself. He's right: cloudless, light wind, but the sea swells and pitches the boats as the captain's jaw tightens like a guitar string.

The scouts resurface. The youngest, Gonzalo, beams. "They are there!" he says. "The tuna are all there, just waiting for us. Today, luck is on our side."

The boat's engines warm again, a raspy throat clearing. Antonio puts out his cigarette, the captain blows a whistle, and thus the almadraba, *one of the world's most ancient fishing traditions, begins.*

When the Phoenicians touched down in Cádiz over three thousand years ago, they found a small spit of land jutting out into the sea, a strategic commercial and military base at the mouth of the Mediterranean. In the millennia to follow, Romans and Greeks, pirates and pioneers, kings and conquistadores would impose their will on the peninsula, but Cádiz waited out each visitor like a batch of bad houseguests. Today, Cádiz is a city of 120,000 residents and the oldest continuously inhabited civilization in Western Europe.

On a clear day, you can see Africa from the tip of Cádiz. The province is the southernmost part of Spain, nearly as far south as Europe goes, and the city wears its mix of Moorish, Jewish, and Christian history conspicuously—in the maze of narrow, confounding streets that recall Marrakesh, on the smooth curves and sharp angles of mosques and churches, in the spices and dried fruits and nuts that adorn the food of the region. Despite its history and stature, Cádiz doesn't take itself too seriously. Its citizens possess a quiet confidence that recognizes they must have done something right to end up here. Indeed, it's the name that surfaces time and again when the rest of Spain debates its favorite corners of the country.

When people talk about Cádiz, though, they're not just talking about the city itself,

A crew of fisherman row into the teeth of the tuna trap.

but the constellation of coastal towns, hilltop villages, and inland islands that populate the peninsula. There is Jerez, where the dapper Andalusian gentleman shakes off his siesta with a glass of *fino* and a plate of *jamón*. In Sanlúcar de Barrameda, a sun-bleached city known best for its Manzanilla and the horse races on its beaches, you will find the finest fried dish in all of Spain, the *tortillita de camarones*, a lacy amoeba of tiny shrimp and olive-oil-crisped batter served in bars and *freidurías* around the region, but nowhere better than Casa Balbino. And if you make it to Vejer de la Frontera, a staircase of whitewashed houses and serpentine streets and quiet plazas of cinematic beauty, you risk never leaving.

This isn't exactly the southern Spain most people know—Sevilla, home of flamenco and matadors and oversized cathedrals, is an hour to the north—but it's not far off. Life moves slower down here than it does almost anywhere else in Spain. Beaches, among the finest in the country, cradle bronzed bodies in their soft sands six months a year. People sit for hours in

the amber afternoon light of the smooth tiled plazas, happy enough to feel the sun on their skin and the wine in their bellies. One afternoon, I stepped into a restaurant to ask directions and stayed for three hours, watching bullfights and bullshitting with the old men drinking beer at the bar.

As its oldest city and southernmost gateway, Cádiz has been on the front lines of Spain's food culture for millennia. This was one of Spain's earliest wine regions, started with grapes brought over by the Phoenicians in 1000 BC. Today, Palomino grapes for fortified wines, brandy, and sherry vinegar cover the hills and fill the bodegas around Jerez. The *gaditanos* (the people of Cádiz) have long been recognized as masters of fried food of all stripes, especially *pescaito frito*, small, oily fish eaten spine and all. And an entire culture of pastries and sweets developed in the convents of the province, nuns long a major driver of Spain's traditional food culture. The flan-like *tocino del cielo*, one of Spain's most enduring desserts, came about as a way for the nuns to use the egg yolks from sherry producers, who only needed the whites to clarify their wine.

But no food has done more to shape the history and the economy of the region than *Thunnus thynnus*, the Atlantic bluefin tuna, today considered the most valuable fish in the sea. Engravings and cave paintings of the bluefin date back to 4000 BC. Hippocrates wrote of the importance of bluefin, as did Aristotle and Pliny the Elder. Phoenician coins in early Hispania came with two tunas engraved on the face.

For most of tuna's long history in Spain, its principle value has been in by-products. The Phoenicians set up centers to make Spain's first *salazones*, salted and dried tuna products, which they exported to its colonies throughout the Mediterranean.

To catch the massive schools of tuna migrating from the Atlantic, where they fatten up in the winter, to the Mediterranean, where they spawn in warmer waters, the Phoenicians developed elaborate net traps and positioned men on top of towers along the coastline to spot the incoming schools. Later, the same technique would spread elsewhere in the Mediterranean—to Portugal, Morocco, Sicily.

The Romans continued the tuna-hunting traditions popularized by the Phoenicians. They still made salt-cured fish, but placed even greater importance on the oil extracted from tuna's fermented flesh, skin, and innards, called *garum*, one of the world's first fish sauces. Wheat, grapes, and olives, the heart of Spanish cuisine, have been at the center of its economy since before Christ, but it was *garum* that made the Iberian Peninsula the most valuable corner of the Roman empire. In the centuries to follow, the focus of the catch evolved with the times and tastes of those who did the fishing, but the tradition of trapping migrating bluefin in the spring has continued more or less uninterrupted for three thousand years.

Today, the *almadraba* takes place in four separate communities along the Costa de la Luz east of Cádiz: Barbate, Conil de la Frontera, Tarifa, and Zahara de los Atunes. It takes fishermen two months of work under water to set this elaborate trap, another two months to take it down. In between, six weeks to catch as many tuna as the year's quota will allow.

Phoenician fishermen would recognize the system used today by Spain's bluefin hunters: the wall of mesh net—ten thousand feet long, one hundred feet deep—set up to halt the massive migration; the labyrinth of narrow halls and holes and hard angles that lead the fish ever-closer to their captors; above all, they would recognize the *cuadro*, the grouping of boats in the final pool of this serpentine system, where each day's school of tuna meets its demise.

The Hunt

The fish don't see it coming. The females *swim on their sides, steely skin to the sky, sowing the water with millions of eggs. The Spaniards call the discharge a* fresa, *a strawberry, and the fruit grows best in these warm waters.*

Fat from the frigid tides of the Atlantic, they hurtle toward the Mediterranean like a clip of silver bullets. A wall breaks their migration, funneling the fish into the esophagus of a giant digestive system, churning them forward from one compartment to the next until they reach the final bowel. Panic takes over in this web of deceit, but the only way out is up.

The captain's men are all too happy to lend a hand. A small army clad in blue and orange stands at attention. A whistle signals the levantá *and the lifting of the final net begins. As the boats inch ever closer, the net grows ever smaller, the space between life and death collapsing on itself.*

The boats are one hundred meters away from each other with nothing but blue sea and frosted tips between. Men muscle the web and speak to each other in tongues. Cranes and metal hooks, the only modern flourish, reel in the nets like a giant fishing rod.

Seventy meters away and still nothing stirs. "You sure they're down there?" one says. "You sure it wasn't your shadow you saw?"

Forty and closing. "Let's go, let's go! Keep it coming!"

Thirty meters. Across the vanishing space a boat of Japanese men hold cell phones to their ears. Buyers, inspectors, arbiters of quality, the almost-invisible hand of the almadraba. *They don't set the trap, but they move the nets.*

Twenty. "Iza! Iza!"

And then, suddenly, the sea explodes. A great churn bubbles violently to the surface like a pot of milk boiling over. Colors change rapidly, from blue to white to silver, as a mass of bodies breaches the surface, frantic in the shrinking space, searching for a way out.

"Imagine a fire in a soccer stadium," a fisherman says, "and only one exit."

Now imagine it without an exit.

Bluefin tuna was not always the king of the sea. For the better part of the twentieth century, it was considered a trash fish, so dark and pregnant with fat that fishermen around the world would catch it for sport and throw it back into the water. Sasha Issenberg, in his exceptional book *The Sushi Economy*, writes about an annual deep-sea fishing competition off the coast of New England. At the end of the day, when the winner had been crowned, hundreds of tuna would be sold off to cat food companies or trucked out to holes in the earth and buried en masse.

Despite the importance of salted fish and fish sauce in the economies of early Spain, by the twentieth century, bluefin no longer carried the same value it once did. A 1933 documentary of the Barbate *almadraba* shows a process nearly identical to today's: the same network of nets, the same kind of hard-scrabble fishermen wrangling the catch by hand. It's not until the tuna reaches shore that the process diverges: the heads, fins, skin, and organs were sundried, then steamed, then pressed for oil used to make soaps. The flesh was salted and dried to make *mojama*, or boiled and packed into cans with olive oil and shipped across the Mediterranean to Italy. There is only so much value in canned tuna and fish soap: In 1933, a 150-kilogram tuna was worth about 150 pesetas, roughly half a cent per pound.

The Japanese changed all of that. Sushi culture took shape in the Meiji era, when cooks fermented fish in seasoned rice for months at a time, extending indefinitely the life of the country's primary source of protein. Modern sushi, Edo-style sushi, was born in the mid-nineteenth century, just as Tokyo was rising to prominence as

THE SPACE
BETWEEN
LIFE AND
DEATH
COLLAPSES
ON ITSELF

Japan's new capital. With fresh fish more readily available, cooks traded the deep funk of fermentation for freshly cooked rice, layering slices of the day's catch—eel, mackerel, halibut—over the top with a swipe of soy for seasoning and a dab of grated wasabi to kill off bacteria. Sushi was street food back then, a few bites of *nigiri* used to tide over passing pedestrians before they made it home for dinner.

Still, tuna was considered a lesser species by Japan's elite, a bluefish with too much fat for their refined palates. They left it for the lower classes, favoring lighter white fish instead. But as Japan's sushi culture deepened in the wake of World War II, the country's palate changed with it. Japan, long a nation of pescatarians, had developed a taste for meat, and not just any meat: deep-fried cutlets of pork, charcoal-grilled skewers of odd chicken parts, and, of course, wagyu, the magnificently marbled beef revered in the world's upper culinary circles. All have one thing in common: fat, an ever-increasing feature of a diet long considered to be among the world's healthiest. And nothing

in the sea has more fat than the big-bellied bluefin tuna.

By the 1960s, with domestic supplies dwindling, the Japanese began to scour the globe in search of bluefin. In the 1970s, Akira Okazaki, an executive for Japan Airlines, worked for the better part of the decade developing an advanced refrigeration system that allowed the Japanese to buy cheap bluefin in areas of abundance—Nova Scotia, New England, the South Pacific—and ship them back to Tokyo in near-perfect condition. The world's global food economy was born. Thirty years later, bluefin forms the heart of a sophisticated system of buying, dividing, auctioning, portioning, and distributing: Tunanomics.

The tiny coastal towns of Cádiz comprise a central cog in this sprawling tuna machinery. After reaching peak production in the 1930s, the *almadraba* suffered in the wake of the war, and factories in Barbate and beyond, vital to the coastal economy, began to shutter. But as the Japanese continued to search for ways to satisfy the country's growing appetite for fatty tuna, they found in the Costa de la Luz a seemingly inexhaustible supply of the fish they valued most. By 1990, emissaries for fish trading companies in Tokyo set up shop in Barbate, giving new life to an ancient culture that stood on the brink of extinction.

Spanish cooks might not have valued bluefin enough to pay top dollar for its meat, but the Japanese did. Between 1970 and 1990, fishing for Atlantic bluefin rose 2,000 percent, while the price for tuna exported to Japan rose a staggering 10,000 percent. A single large bluefin typically sells for anywhere between $2,000 and $20,000 in Tokyo, but occasionally an outlier will command an unthinkable price. In 2013, the owner of a sushi restaurant chain in Japan paid $1.76 million for the first bluefin of the New Year.

To give you a better idea of how Tunanomics works, let's follow the fish. On the morning of May 12, 2015, the Barbate crew netted 159 bluefin tuna from the morning session. Of those tuna, the Japanese bought 83, with their inspectors on hand to maintain quality control during every step of the process—from the decks of the boat during the *levantá* to the docks of the Barbate port during the butchering.

After being cleaned and quartered, the tuna go directly into a super freezer. Within eighteen hours, the day's haul will be frozen to -60°C, at which temperature they can survive without any discernible loss in quality for, well, forever, basically. All of this is overseen by Fuyuki Nakagawa, general manager in the marine products trading unit for Maruha Nichiro Corporation, one of the world's largest seafood traders, with more than $8 billion in revenue in 2014 (tagline: Bringing Delicious Delight to the World).

In the next step, the tuna are loaded into a special freezing container built to maintain the fish at -60°C and shipped off to Japan. (The Japanese abandoned air shipping for more affordable sea transport in the past decade.) Those eighty-three tuna join a conga line of bluefin dancing in cargo holds en route to Tokyo Harbor. If they arrive on a Tuesday, then by 4:00 A.M. Wednesday, they have gone from the harbor to Maruha's facilities on the outskirts of Tokyo to the Tsukiji tuna auction, the largest in the world. At 4:00 A.M. each day, the country's major tuna brokers gather around to inspect the catch, somewhere between two hundred and three hundred tuna of varying shapes and sizes shipped in from all corners of the globe: North Carolina, Zanzibar, Morocco, Libya. Tail sections are cut open, allowing for careful analysis of color, aroma, and fat content.

By 5:00 a.m., the morning's fierce round of tuna bidding draws to a close. The fish move from the auction floor to the buyers' stalls deeper in the market, where, using a mixture of band saw, katana blade, and fillet knife, the auctioned tuna will be reduced to over a dozen distinct cuts, based on fat content and muscle fibers: from lean pieces of loin to offcuts like collar and cheek. The most prized pieces, *chûtoro* and *otoro*, the expensive, fat-flush belly cuts, are reserved for the finest sushi restaurants in Tokyo and beyond—New York, London, even Spain. By the time the tuna make their final voyage from chopsticks to mouth, they will

have traveled thousands of miles and passed through a dozen different specialists.

What's the big deal with bluefin? It's just fish you say? The boats and the auctions and the prices may all be abstract, but if you've eaten a piece of *otoro* from the hands of a seasoned sushi master in Tokyo or Toronto or Toledo, if you've lost your composure over the mix of tender ocean protein and sweet, swaddling fat, you know a bit about what drives this economy. At its most visceral level, Tunanomics is driven by the endorphin-spiking pleasure of a single bite.

That bite has built a $6 billion annual industry that touches almost every part of the globe, and it's impossible to discuss bluefin without talking about the emptying of the oceans. In scientific and conservationist circles, the sudden surge in interest and the rapid decline in the species population has become the ultimate cautionary tale of what happens when human appetite goes wild. The Japanese have never been known for their restraint when it comes to plumbing the depths of the oceans in search of edible treasures, but the rise of *kaitenzushi*, conveyor sushi, has transformed tuna from an occasional indulgence into the country's most important protein.

That bluefin has quickly gone from a pauper to an ocean king responsible for sophisticated economies and multimillion-dollar investments from the world's largest fishery players underscores just how fragile the world below the water really is. Old-school fishing boats and subsistence fishermen have been subsumed by sophisticated sonar-enabled rigs run by the largest corporations ever to work the water. Careful capturing of the fish during the optimum breeding time has been replaced by a free-for-all fish grab backed by roving airplane spotters—omnipresent eyes in the sky who use their elevated vantage to spot the silver schools from above and relay their coordinates to ready vessels below. Savvy and shadowy maritime corporations have learned to subvert quotas, confounding the world's management agencies. Against such forces, no animal stands a chance.

More than 1,700 bluefin vessels work the Mediterranean alone. The more they catch,

the more prices go down, which means the more these massive boats must catch to meet their annual revenue goals—a vicious cycle with the power to decimate an entire species in a matter of decades. The Atlantic bluefin population has declined 90 percent since Japan Airlines developed its refrigerated shipping system.

Ocean management is tricky stuff— international maritime law, evolving technology, and, increasingly, global warming, all make the subsistence formula a constantly moving target. Perhaps the biggest hurdle for tuna sustainability, and the safeguarding of the oceans in general, starts with the consumer, who remains relatively indifferent to the impact of the fish choices he or she makes. Part of that stems from a basic education gap—a lack of understanding about just how fragile some of our favorite seafood staples really are—but at the most rudimentary level, we're blind to both the beauty and brutality that is the life and death of a tuna. Bluefin—elegant, sleek, heavy as a bull, swift as a cheetah—is every bit the beast that a lion is, but most of us

The fight to bring the tuna onboard begins.

can better identify a sesame-crusted tuna loin than the fish itself. Human outrage would never erupt over the killing of, say, Tony the Tuna the way it did over Cecil the Lion, shot dead in 2014 in Zimbabwe. Does the fact that we can't see fish change how we feel about eating them?

With tuna supplies so volatile and the economy so massive, farming is quickly overtaking the traditional *almadraba* practice as the preferred method along the Spanish coast. The tuna are still funneled into the nets, but instead of being lifted straight out of the water, they are put into pens and fattened for months before being killed. The taste of wild tuna versus farmed tuna is hard to distinguish, and the farming gives Japanese buyers more control over the age and fat content of the fish. But bluefin require an immense amount of food for fattening—ten times what farmed salmon need by body weight—which in turn means emptying the ocean of tuna's primary prey: herring, sardines, squid. Anytime we wrest authority from Mother Nature, bad things tend to happen.

Those at the heart of the *almadraba* are the first to complain about the recklessness of the global fishing industry. For Diego Crespo, fifth-generation tuna baron and president of the Almadrabas de Barbate, overseeing the fishing and distribution of hundreds of tons of bluefin annually, it stings to be roped into the same category as the goliaths of the water. "They're using airplanes and helicopters and multimillion-dollar tracking systems. We're using the same nets the Phoenicians used." Crespo is quick to point out that modern forces threaten both the tuna population and the livelihood of thousands of Spaniards around Cádiz. Bluefin quotas, once above 1,500 tons of tuna a year in these parts, dropped to 500 tons in 2008 and many fishermen, whose families have been catching tuna for centuries, were suddenly out of work. Even those who still had quota left to catch were increasingly coming up empty. "We'd pull up the nets and there would be nothing inside."

According to Crespo and the other major players behind Cádiz's tuna economy, the *almadraba* is the best way forward.

Unlike the massive purse seines that haul in a thousand tuna at a time, the *almadraba* produces very little bycatch, since the holes in the nets are specifically designed to let smaller fish—and young tuna— swim through. And if anyone needs proof of its sustainability, they say, consider its history as three thousand years of proof. There's a good deal of circular logic in this argument—the tuna will survive because they have always survived—but it's true that it wasn't the *almadraba* that brought the species to the brink of extinction in the early days of the twenty-first century.

Scientists and government agencies have sprung into action in recent years, slashing quotas and imposing strict timetables on when fish can be caught in their life cycle. After Japan scuttled a proposed global export ban on bluefin in 2010, top chefs around the world took unilateral action by banning bluefin from their menus; some fish purveyors still refuse to sell it. Thanks to these concerted efforts, Atlantic bluefin have begun to recover from the historic low hit in 2006 (though Pacific bluefin supplies continue to dwindle). As the fishery community shows signs of cautious optimism, Crespo and his team of fishermen believe it's time to loosen the quotas and let the fishermen do the work they've been doing since the dawn of Hispania.

The Catch

The engines whimper, the rumble replaced by the flapping of fishtails and the grunts of men. The boats surround the catch in the cuadro, *a coffin the size of a school bus; now it is man versus fish.*

Eight men take the plunge: toreros of the sea set loose to tussle with the thrashing bodies. The panic has left most belly-up, but a few still fight with fins and fishtails to fend off their aggressors. The Moorish meaning of almadraba—*a place for fighting—comes into focus.*

The mission: wrap a rope around each flapping fishtail, just below the bite of the dorsal fin. But the ample catch and the rising swells turn the cuadro into chaos. Screams and laughter, rage and rapture: the full spectrum of life trapped in a watery grave. "You're getting old, assholes!" the men shout from above.

A hook and crane lifts the tuna, two by two, from the water. In the piercing sun of midmorning, the colors stick with you: the bright orange slickers, the shimmering silver bodies twisting in the air, the crimson tide below. On board, a knife to the heart brings the ten-thousand-mile journey to an end.

When the water is still and silent, there is nothing left in the cuadro *but eight men and a soup of salt and iron. Above, 159 bodies fill the iced belly of the transport boat.*

The eight toreros wear the years of battles all over their bodies—dorsal scars, chest cuts, cracked ribs, tail tattoos.

"Protected we are not, son. A beast like this will kill you."

"I caught a tail to the neck once. Nearly bled out."

"It's dangerous, but we have a good time."

"I heard the Japanese paid a million for one of these a few years back."

"They should pay us more."

Pepe Melero doesn't look like a tuna man. Bald and short with a dense mustache and eyes that dart like goldfish, he looks more like a private detective, the kind of guy used to eating sandwiches in his car and living in the same wrinkled suit for days at a time. But as the head of the restaurant El Campero since 1978—as a chef, a powerful buyer, and one of the foremost bluefin experts in the world—he stands at the intersection of the sophisticated, multilayered tuna economy of southern Spain.

When the ships leave port, Melero knows about it. When the nets come up, he'll get a call or a text from the boat. If the boys bring in an especially impressive specimen, he'll be at the docks, waiting to inspect it.

If at first glance Melero seems like a man of few words, it is the tuna that teases out the poet in him. "The noble tuna comes in its natural state, captivated by the Siren song of the Mediterranean, to find peace and tranquility to reproduce in a place where it's happiest. This is the natural life of the tuna, and it sows its beautiful seed right here in our backyard."

Barbate is not where you'd expect to find tuna poetry. It feels like the shadow of a town past—the playgrounds are empty, the sidewalks chewed up by time and weather, the stores sell sunglasses and sofas under the specter of liquidation. But on the outskirts you'll find factories still making *salazones* and *conservas*, and on the beaches the same tuna towers used to spot the migrating schools for centuries, and in the center of it all, among an otherwise unremarkable block of apartment buildings, you'll find Pepe Melero and his shiny white restaurant. If tuna is a religion, then El Campero is the cathedral and Sr. Melero the supreme pontiff.

El Campero wasn't conceived as a church of tuna. The first iteration of El Campero was started by Melero's parents back in the 1960s—a casual bar in the center of Barbate where locals would come to drink and snack with friends. Melero was studying to be a pilot in the air force, but he would rise at 3:00 a.m. to be at the bar by the time the fishermen came in for a coffee or a glass of brandy to steel them for the morning ahead.

They buck and thrash and use fins like
knives to fend off their aggressors.

The tuna business was strong back then, but almost everything pulled out of the water went directly to the processing plants on the outskirts of Barbate that would can, cure, and package tuna for distribution around the country. The main tuna staple on the original El Campero menu was Mom's *atún encebollado*, chunks of fresh tuna smothered in onions caramelized in pork fat, one of the few fresh tuna dishes with deep history in Spain.

In the end, it was the Japanese who taught the Spaniards how to cook tuna—and, of course, how not to cook it at all. As they took up their exporting posts in Barbate in the early 1990s, the Japanese traders and fishermen would dine at El Campero, but they were distressed to find Barbate's best restaurant wasn't taking full advantage of Barbate's best ingredient. "We let the Japanese into our kitchen," says Melero, "and slowly they taught us all the different ways they like to eat tuna."

The only thing the Japanese take more seriously than the trafficking of tuna is the consumption of it. They have hundreds of ways of eating tuna—from broiled collar to stewed offal to fire-blitzed loin. *Mottainai*, nothing goes to waste, is an underlying Shinto principle with a huge influence on the way Japan eats. More than anything, the Japanese taught Melero and his crew that the tuna is a world of tastes and textures waiting to be explored.

The combination of Japanese guidance and Melero's persistence—not to mention super-freezer technology that made quality bluefin available year round—prevailed over the years, turning tuna from a one-dish homage to Melero's mother to the raison d'être for El Campero.

Today at El Campero, *mottainai* is something of a guiding ethos. You will find a handful of classic preparations along with half a dozen raw dishes that showcase the quality of the product and the reach of Barbate's tiny but influential Japanese population. But that is just the start of it. Melero and his team divide bluefin into twenty-four distinct pieces, and look at each cut as a different expression of the sea—a unique mixture of muscle, fat, and fibers that demands carefully customized treatment. Tough parts from neck and tail may be subjected to long cooking times; lean parts of the back and center sliced and served raw; and fat-rich specialty cuts may get nothing more than a shower of salt and a quick sear on the *plancha*, the flattop at the heart of so much Spanish cooking.

Every season brings new challenges and discoveries for the Campero team—new manifestations of the muse to bend to their culinary will. This year's obsession: *el paladar*, literally the palate of the tuna, a cut taken from around the lips with a tight texture and deep tuna flavor. They're also playing with tuna bone marrow, cooking chunks of spine in a thermal circulator, then braising it like *rabo de toro*, a classic Spanish dish of slow-cooked oxtail. "We haven't nailed it yet, but we're getting close."

I tell Melero I want to taste it all, and he doesn't disappoint. Lunch starts with a few burgundy slices of *mojama*, tuna loin salted and cured for three weeks. *Mojama* is the most famous of the range of tuna charcuterie, a world that includes *huevas* (pressed tuna roe) and various forms of salted, smoked, and oil-packed meat. It balances the sweetness and funk of the sea with the salt and umami of the curing process, and when made with fatty *almadraba* tuna like the one Melero serves, the results are extraordinary—the *jamón ibérico* of the sea.

From there, we move into a series of raw preparations: a rough-cut tartare made from the well-worked muscles of the tail; a ceviche charged with chili and anointed with lime foam; and a plate of dominoes cut from the *ventresca*, the belly, so densely marbled with fat there's barely any room left over for protein. In a nod to his Japanese sensei, Melero serves the belly like a plate of *otoro* sashimi, with nothing more than soy, wasabi, and a few slices of pickled ginger.

Things heat up from there. The *paladar*, the newest Campero creation, comes atop a bed of lightly mashed potatoes spiked with pork fat and smoked paprika. The meat itself is braised, dark, collapsing—a dead ringer for a beef stew with just the faintest suggestion of the sea. It's common chefspeak that the creative process starts with the ingredient itself, that the product drives the conversation and the rest falls in line. But that's not what I see here: at El Campero, Melero imagines a dish he'd like to eat, and then finds the appropriate cut to make it possible.

Next come two plates that transport me a few thousand miles and a few decades back to my days as a meat-and-potatoes poster child: First, tuna "ribs"—thick and substantial bone-in pieces cut from the spine, slow roasted and glazed in a spicy barbecue sauce. The tuna peels off the bone in juicy chunks, the way it used to off my dad's Weber. The second, perhaps Melero's most famous creation, the McAlmadraba, is a mini burger made with ground tuna belly spiced with cumin and black pepper and goosed with foie gras and Dijon. All the details are right: the cardboard box, the sesame bun, the drippy special sauce—a Big Mac gone overboard.

The anatomy lesson continues. The deeper I go into the meal, the deeper we travel into the tuna itself.

NECK: Melero's favorite cut, found just behind the brain, *morillo* is the apotheosis of all that is great and good about the noble tuna: dense, meaty muscles, rich deposits of fat that swaddle the meat as they warm up. Cooked hard and fast on the *plancha* with a shower of salt and served with a few sauces on the side that should be studiously ignored.

HEART: Cut in thick planks, marked on the *plancha*, and served with raw onion and sherry vinegar to rein in the ocean offal.

BLOOD: Cooked and caked and heavily spiced, then stuffed into casing to make maritime *morcilla*, a convincing riff on Spain's famous blood sausage.

SKIN: Vacuum-sealed and slow-cooked into gelatinous sheaths meant to recall tripe, Spain's favorite viscera. To deepen the comparison, they come served in a bowl of braised garbanzos, a riff on *callos a la andaluza*, the famous tripe stew of the region.

SPERM: The strawberry seed of the migrating tuna, skewered into a lollipop and dressed with onion jam and ginger-peach compote to hammer home the sweetness.

He talks about the Japanese-style creations with reverence and appreciation, but in the end it's the Spanish-inspired inventions, the voyage into uncharted territory, that moves Melero most. After thirty-eight years of exploration, he has hundreds of recipes in his memory bank, and a few dozen more waiting to be filed. Still, when it comes time to eat, Melero takes his tuna two ways: griddled or smothered in onions, just like Mom used to make it. "I don't care for raw tuna. I just don't come from that culture."

The Breakdown

Giant claws bring the bodies, two at a time, from the bowels of the boat to the floor of the fábrica de despiece, the butchering room of the Barbate tuna factory.

Thirty men with hooks and blades break the bodies into pieces. Chain saws for the head, swords for the loins, kitchen knives for carving out the imperfections. Heads and tails in one bin, organs in another. These were gold once, pressed into service to season an empire. Now they await a less delicious fate.

Beyond the blood, bones, and brawn, the day's prize: four quarters of flesh, long purple planks placed on metal trays stacked ten feet high.

In the sea of Andalusians, three Japanese: two quartering fish, another talking to Tokyo. All of them look anxious.

The room sings with cracking bones and grinding gears, a disassembly line of fantastic efficiency. With every minute the tuna loses what the world values most. Forklifts push thousands of pounds into powerful blast machines. Super freeze they call it, from cool to

The largest tuna weigh up to 1,200 pounds, roughly the size of a bull.

cryogenic in fourteen hours, the ideal state for the long road ahead.

But not all tuna will travel. Some have a home in Barbate, others farther north with chefs who know just what to do with it.

The butchers wash the blood from their hands, trade rubber for denim, and step into the daylight. Some set off to Ca Reventa to settle bets and share stories. Others go straight to lunch: steak or stew or maybe another sandwich. Almost no one eats tuna.

Mr. Nakagawa of Maruha Nichiro Corporation doesn't bother changing. "It was a good day," he says in between drags in the parking lot. "Too good, maybe. Too many fish in the cuadro. *Fear can compromise the meat."*

In six months, at a hinoki countertop in Ginza, no one will taste the fear.

If Barbate is the town that tuna built, Zahara de los Atunes is the town that tuna is building—a thicket of restaurants, bars, and souvenir shops with the coastal mascot at the center of it all. Stores sell novelty cans of tuna with fish heads peaking out; signs and shirts show smiling bluefin

drinking beers and singing songs; restaurants bear the name of the most famous citizen—Thunnus, Hotel Almadraba, Cervecería El Atún. Everywhere you turn, menus run long on seared fillets, sashimi, onion-slathered loins.

The centerpiece of this burgeoning tuna economy is the annual Ruta del Atún, a coordinated effort by the local government to turn the fatty flesh of the *almadraba* into an enduring PR machine for the hospitality industry. Forty odd restaurants participate in the five-day event in May, each offering a single taste of tuna. Up and down the coast, Barbate, Tarifa, and Conil de la Frontera, towns with their own *almadrabas*, also have their own Rutas. When it first started in 2010 in Zahara, the offerings were what you might expect from a southern Spanish town easing its way into a tuna culture—seared belly, tartare with Japanese whispers. But the ambitions of the event have grown substantially in five years. Now, it's not just tuna tapas, but tuna butchery demos, tuna conferences and panels, tuna sculptures, tuna poetry, tuna documentary screenings.

At 1:00 p.m. on a Thursday in May the coastal town is electric with the hunger of prowling tunaheads. Part of it, no doubt, stems from the fact that every tuna creation comes with a beer or wine chaser, but everyone, from the servers to the line cooks to the mix of Spaniards and foreigners, seem genuinely caught up in the revelry. Diners carry elaborate maps with glossy color photos of every dish and passports ("*tunaportes*" one server jokes) for stamping at every stop they make.

I get my first passport stamp at Thunnus, a small fusion spot off the main drag: fillets of tuna marinated in sesame, soy, and sake, wrapped in thin sheaths of shaved shiitake and sauced with thickened dashi. Japan makes for a fitting start to today's journey.

Vaguely Japanese touches—wakame, wasabi, sesame—show up everywhere, but many restaurants have abandoned the safe shores of the Far East and sailed into deeper waters. Hotel Antonio, a longtime tuna haunt and winner of the best tapa in two of the first four events, calls 2015's dish Red Hot Tuna Peppers: a squid body stained red with beet juice and chili and stuffed with raw tuna. At Taramanta the tuna comes in a tube of toothpaste to be squeezed over a cracker studded with sunflower seeds. La Tasca calls its creation Canta Atún, a mini record player with a tipsy fish on the record and a microphone to the side. The vinyl is real, but the microphone is fashioned from phyllo dough, stuffed with tartare, and covered with dark sesame seeds to complete the effect.

Taking a cue from El Campero, the restaurants of Zahara have turned the local catch into both canvas and paint: stuffed into tacos, ground into meatballs, suspended in fondue, sandwiched with swipes of dark chocolate. The question isn't whether these dishes are delicious or not (many of them are); what matters is that they exist, and that people are here, filling out the streets of this tiny coastal town on a Thursday afternoon, brushing their teeth with tuna toothpaste and biting down on marine microphones.

The fact that a single ingredient can essentially elevate the creative and technical prowess of an entire town's restaurant industry is a testament to the excellence of the tuna itself—something that can be seared, stewed, cured, ceviched, carpaccio-ed, taco-ed, pattied, planked, liquefied, emulsified, and stuffed into everything from plastic tubes to cephalopods. But it also testifies to a coastline of industrious souls, Spain's first civilization, who have shown it's never too late to adapt. When the week is out, Zahara and its visitors will have consumed ninety-nine thousand tuna tapas, many of which will move on to become staples of the local restaurant scene.

The last stamp in my passport comes from La Malvaloca. They serve a small bowl of *cocido*, the most traditional dish in all of Spain, fashioned entirely from tuna. The traditional chunk of chorizo is made with tuna tartare stained bright red with the same flavors of the pork version: smoked paprika and roasted red pepper. The *morcilla* is fashioned from ground tuna heart and tuna blood. A few toothsome garbanzo beans and a puddle of clear tuna broth tie the dish together.

The flavors are as powerful as they are perplexing: it tastes both entirely of *cocido* and of the sea, a magical bridge between land and water, past and present. It's not the taste of Japan, not the flavor of fusion or fashion or a passing interest. It is the taste of a culture, still in its infancy, three millennia in the making.

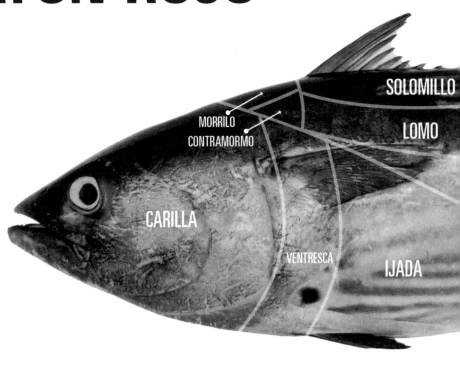

Best Cuts
ATÚN ROJO

SOLOMILLO

MORRILO
CONTRAMORMO

LOMO

CARILLA

VENTRESCA

IJADA

COLA AZUL

ANTELO

COLA BLANCA

TUNA TACTICS

For many years, Spain's tuna culture was based largely on dried and canned products. But bluefin's star turn in the Spanish kitchen has created a culture of specialization, where every cut has a different taste and texture to be teased out by fire and finesse.

PEOPLE

GONZALO SÁNCHEZ
Fisherman,
Cádiz

—

"Every year it seems to
get a bit harder. Less
fish, less money. But I'll
still be here. I can't get
enough of the sea."

SISTER CONSOLACIÓN
Nun and Baker,
Medina-Sidonia

—

"Spanish nuns have
always made sweets.
Eating sweets isn't a sin,
but you need to eat
them after a meal."

OF SPAIN

PATRI MANES
Flamenco dancer,
Madrid

—

"Flamenco is an expression of
the soul. It gives voice and
movement to your deepest
feelings. When I don't dance,
a part of me dies."

SALEM KHABBAZ
Shawarma master,
Barcelona

—

"Making good shawarma
is like making poetry.
You say as much as
possible with as little as
possible."

ANATOMY *of a dish*

SALMOREJO

KINGDOM OF COLD SOUPS

No country on earth can top Spain's cold soup game. The desert climes of Andalusia birthed a trinity of *sopas frías*: gazpacho: *ajoblanco*, a dreamy puree of garlic and almond: and *salmorejo*, hailing from Córdoba but found in bars across the region.

FROM SCRAPS TO SOUP

Cold soups accomplished two objectives: providing cooling nourishment for shepherds and manual laborers working under the sun, and utilizing cheap, abundant ingredients (old bread, garlic, olive oil, tomato) to fill bellies in one of Spain's poorest regions.

SUPER SUAVE

Like most of Spain's best dishes, *salmorejo*'s ingredient list is short. The beauty lies in the velvety smooth texture created by blending ripe tomatoes, stale bread, garlic, sherry vinegar, plus enough extra virgin olive oil to achieve a brilliant orange color.

DRESSED TO IMPRESS

The fun stuff goes on top, not inside, a *salmorejo*. Chopped boiled eggs, chunks of *jamón*, and a final swirl of olive oil complete a complex picture: salty, savory, sweet, and sharp—a world of tastes in a clay terrine of cold soup.

Chapter Eight

ASTURIAS

—

What is the Spain you see when you close your eyes? Do you see rolling hills of glowing wheat? Creaky windmills that look like giants? A perfect-circle plaza, a cloud of dust, the hot, heaving breath of a bleeding bull? You see oranges bobbing in purple wine, no doubt, and pans like sewer caps paved in grains of golden rice. Salted legs of fattened pig dangle from the ceiling of your Spanish dreams. Dresses that move like apparitions, skin that shimmers like an autumn sunset.

Arches and crescents, corridors and steeples, a land of everlasting sun and sand: this is no doubt the Spain tattooed on the inside of your eyelids.

That is the Spain that Spain wants you to see. It has been projected onto your imagination through decades of board meetings and magazine spreads. It exists, to be sure, in puzzle pieces scattered across the Iberian Peninsula. But that is not the Spain you are about to see. That is not the Spain that José Andrés sees when he closes his eyes at night—at least not all of it.

When he shuts his eyes, he sees a land of arresting beauty—of snaking rivers pink with running salmon, mountain lakes like water bowls for wild horses, towering peaks that tumble into the ocean; of heavy rains that stain the geography fifty shades of green, from the shamrock carpets of

ASTURIAS,
THE NORTHERN
KINGDOM,
THE SPAIN BEYOND
YOUR IMAGINATION.

coastal grass to the broccoli-floret forests that cling to mountain crags. He sees a house on stilts, a flock of sheep, an iron pot of beans bubbling over an open fire. He sees a hissing ocean instead of a silent sea, apple orchards in place of rolling vineyards, a cool platinum mist instead of a thousand splendid suns.

He sees Asturias, the northern kingdom, the Spain beyond your imagination.

Thursday, 6:48 p.m., Mieres, Asturias
¡Qué bonito es Asturias! You see! You see! It's absolutely magnificent. There's no place like this in Spain. Look at those peaks. Look at that coast. Look at those farms. Look at those cows that won't move off the goddamn road and let us pass! There's everything you want in Asturias. Okay, so maybe I didn't spend that much time here. Maybe I'm more Catalan than I am Asturian. But there's no place in Spain that makes me feel so hungry, so thirsty, so alive! Maybe for everyone it's not love at first sight. The first time I brought my wife here we had our two young daughters and it rained the whole time and finally one night we ran out of gas and

we were stuck on the side of the road and it was pouring and the girls were crying because they had crapped their diapers and my wife looks at me and she says, "This is your precious Asturias!" She is from Cádiz, where clouds go to die, so she can't understand how magical this place is. It's funny, people say, "I love Asturias, it's so beautiful! It's so green! But does it have to rain so much?" Ha! People can be so silly.

So what was I saying? Ah yes, qué bonito es Asturias . . .

"Hey, you're that chef aren't you? You're José Andrés!"

Do you know José Andrés? Surely, if this eighteen-year-old punk kid with purple hair and a neck tattoo on a backstreet of this mountain town knows José Andrés, you must too. Right?

No? Well, where to begin? Let's start at the end and work our way backward.

José Andrés owns twenty-one restaurants in the United States. A traditional tapas bar, a modern tapas bar, a hypermodern twenty-second-century tapas bar serving food in tiny bites to people who wait many months for the luxury of tasting cotton candy foie gras and olive oil bonbons. A Greek restaurant. A Mexican restaurant. A Mexican-Chinese restaurant. A Chinese-Peruvian-Japanese restaurant. A fast-food restaurant serving boiled vegetables. A sandwich truck. By the time you finish reading this story, José Andrés will operate an Italian dim sum cart on the moon.

Most of these restaurants are in Washington, a place he has called home for twenty-four years. He has made quite a life for himself in the nation's capital. He plays golf with politicians. He cooks dinner at the White House. He leads foundations and pushes policy and gives lectures at universities on the molecular structure of olives. He once greeted the news of a $20 million lawsuit from Donald Trump with a round of Monday-afternoon salt-air margaritas. He's what you would call in Spanish *un personaje*, a character.

José Andrés lives large in every sense of the word. His company, ThinkFoodGroup, employs two thousand people and brings in $100 million a year in revenue. He has

a library with many leather-bound cookbooks, enough awards to fill a wing of his modernist Maryland palace, potato chips and olive oil and canned sea urchin with his face on the packaging. A three-hundred-foot billboard towers over Las Vegas of José Andrés holding a ham.

Before the meetings with Michelle and the show on PBS, before the soup kitchens in Washington and the solar kitchens in Haiti, before the lovely Andalusian wife and three bright-eyed girls, there was just a young Spanish cook from the mountains of Asturias shipwrecked on the stone shores of Manhattan. With little more than the fire in his belly, he set out to translate his Spanish Identity into an American Dream. He started cooking for his family when he was twelve; at fifteen, he attended culinary school in Catalunya. Later, he cooked omelets and rice aboard the *Juan Sebastián Elcano* as a corporal in the Spanish Navy. At nineteen, he found his way to Cala Montjoi on a rugged stretch of the Catalan coast where a young man named Ferran Adrià was planting the seeds for a culinary revolution. José was one of the first employees at El Bulli, a restaurant that would serve as a sacred classroom for the greatest chefs of the twenty-first century, and there he learned the lessons that would come to define the food he brought to America: not just the fancy techniques and the cavalier spirit of the modernist chef, but a profound respect for the core tenets of Spanish cuisine.

A million meals later, he is a human bridge to the Iberian Peninsula, with stars and stripes on his chest and cold-pressed olive oil in his veins. The man most responsible for bringing the tastes and traditions of Spain to America. And for José, Spain starts here, in Asturias, in the mining town of Mieres, where he spent the first chapter of his life.

José would prefer that I not tell you about our first trip to Asturias together seven years ago, but I can't not tell you about the first trip. I'll skip most of the seventy-two-hour romp—the cheese festival where country farmers read poetry about unpasteurized milk, the ocean of cider and islands of Cabrales, the 3:00 a.m. gin-fueled exis-

tential arguments—and just say that the trip ended with a smoking car smashed into a cement column in an underground parking lot. An angry security guard. An escape taxi. A governmental pardon.

José is a busy man. At this very moment, he is driving, talking to a reporter on speakerphone about his love of American basketball, dictating an Instagram post to his assistant, and explaining to me the history of corn in northern Spain. But he's made time out of his crazy schedule to take me back to Asturias to see all of the things we missed the first time. I have been back since and done well enough on my own—eating wild boar *fabada* and raw-milk cheeses in tiny mountain villages, undertaking meandering, cider-fueled feasts through the old streets of Oviedo and Avilés. Or so I thought. "You know nothing about Asturias," José told me sweetly on the phone a few weeks ago.

We've broken a lot of bread in Spain together since that first Asturias trip—snails and sparkling wine in the Catalan countryside, twenty-course tasting menus in Madrid, wood-fired suckling lamb off the highway on the way up here a few hours ago. His boundless enthusiasm for everything Spanish, especially the parts that most people miss—the sound of *socarrat*, the magic of Spain's rural inns, Asturias itself—has been a fundamental part of my own courtship with his country.

Asturias may be gorgeous, but Mieres is not. It is a mining town, a mountain outpost for coal collection that stands sentinel over the region like a lonely lighthouse. Mining and metallurgy made Asturias one of Spain's wealthiest regions for much of the twentieth century, but one by one the mines and steel factories have shuttered over the past thirty years, and communities like this one have felt it most.

Mieres, like most towns in Asturias, is a cider town. As a region, Asturias produces less wine than any other in Spain, opting instead to ferment its immense haul of apples into *sidra*, a heavily carbonated, aromatic, lightly alcoholic brew. More than the soccer stadium and the Catholic Church, the *sidrería* may be the most sacred

institution in Asturias, the place where friends and family gather to fill their bellies and make sense of the world. Fittingly, the central plaza of Mieres is little more than a collection of *sidrerías*, and on a wet and cold Thursday night, it's packed with people eating shellfish and cured pork and washing it all down with spirited swigs of the national beverage.

We settle on Casa Fulgencio at the base of the plaza, and, one by one, members of José's tribe—cousins, distant aunts and uncles, former neighbors—arrive to welcome him home. Word gets out and soon the town of Mieres lines up for photos with its most famous son. José makes jokes, shakes hands, kisses cheeks. At one point he signs the photograph of a nervous man's baby girl. He does it with an inside-the-Beltway skill and savvy, but with the intimacy and sincerity of someone who never forgets where he comes from.

The table fills out with classic cider food: plates of local cheeses, slices of boiled octopus, chorizo simmered in *sidra*. As the group begins to snack, the waiter assumes his position at the head of the table and commences the intricate ritual of Asturian cider consumption. José's cousin Covadonga, named for the region's most postcard-perfect town, walks me through the cider house rules.

1. DON'T POUR YOUR OWN. That is, not unless you know how to land a thin stream of cider just under the lip of a tilted glass held at full-arm extension with minimal spillage, all while looking as nonchalant as possible. Best to leave it to the professionals. These servers—predominantly middle-aged men with serious faces—hover around the cider house, pouring rounds for tables as soon as they go dry. You'll have a chance to practice, no doubt, often with a plastic pouring spout that allows for easier control of the cascading juice, but it's their job to keep you and your crew lubricated, and they do it with a very specific skill set honed over years of errant cider streams.

2. DRINK. Not in five minutes, not in one. Now! Cider is poured from great

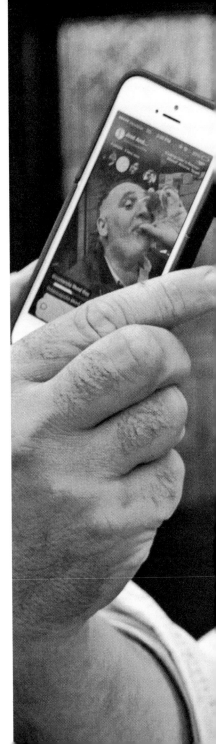

José Andrés, unstoppable force of nature, broadcasting his first sip of cider to his fans.

heights in order to introduce air into the brew. It is not to be sipped, quaffed, nor carefully and thoughtfully consumed. It is to be absorbed in one swift gulp, the better for savoring the aromas teased out by the elevated pouring. A glass of cider left idly on the table is not just an insult to the servers, but also a social faux pas that will immediately brand you as an outsider to anyone within splashing distance.

3. NEVER FINISH THE FULL GLASS OF CIDER. Instead, leave half a finger of liquid in the base of the glass, then, with just enough casual cool, pour that lingering juice back out over the same area of the rim where you drank from, an entirely ineffective but obligatory way of cleansing the glass and preparing it for the next thirsty soul.

4. DO NOT TRY TO GET DRUNK ON CIDER. At least not at first. The mix of pork fat and shellfish and fermented fruit will make for an unsettling stew in your stomach. Ease into the cider world,

and by the second or third day, you'll be drinking it like water.

Asturias has its own fragrance—of smoke and fermentation, crushed apples and crisp mountain air—and as we slurp the ocean from clamshells and soak heels of bread in pools of cider shimmering red with chorizo fat, I fill my lungs with it all.

Friday, 2:57 p.m., Casa Gerardo, Prendes

Asturias es España; lo demás es tierra conquistada. Asturias is Spain; the rest is conquered territory. This adage has echoed across the region for centuries, a reminder that while the rest of the country suffered the slings and arrows of invaders and imperialists, Asturians remained resistant to anyone who would threaten their home or their way of life.

The Romans were the first to feel the full force of Asturian resistance. After conquering all of Hispania, only Asturias and Cantabria remained to complete the Iberian conquest. But in 29 BC, the outnumbered Asturians employed an ancient form of guerrilla warfare, taking advantage of the unique terrain to coordinate devastating surprise attacks that kept the empire at bay. So serious and embarrassing was the Romans' inability to subdue Asturias that the emperor himself, Caesar Augustus, took up residence in northern Spain to oversee the campaign. Ten years and fifty thousand soldiers later, the Romans finally had their last piece of Hispania, though they had to station two legions of soldiers in the region for the next eighty years just to hold on to it.

Later, when the Moors took control of Spain in the eighth century, Asturias once again held its ground. Christians from around the peninsula who resisted the new Islamic rule fled north, to higher, colder climes, hoping to find protection in a land known for defending its own. Led by the Visigoth nobleman Don Pelayo, in a page torn from the playbook of the ancient Spartans, three hundred men funneled the sprawling forces of the Moors into a narrow valley in the Picos de Europa, forcing them to retreat and abandon their northern ambitions. In 722, in the wake of this impossible victory, the Kingdom of Asturias was officially established, with Pelayo as its first king. For seven hundred years, Asturias remained the only part of Spain not to fall under Moorish rule.

That this land contrasts so sharply with the popular imagination of Spain only strengthens the Asturians belief in their exceptionalism. More than anywhere else in Spain, Asturias is a place where history and culture are defined by the landscape itself—the towering peaks and verdant valleys, twisting rivers and rugged coastline that confounded would-be conquerors and forged a community and a cuisine unlike any other in the country.

José wants me to understand this, so he takes me to see Pedro and Marcos Morán, the father and son behind Casa Gerardo, one of the oldest and most revered restaurants in the region. Casa Gerardo opened its doors on a quiet country road in 1888 as a simple *casa de comida*, a place where travelers and locals could stop in for a piece of fish or a bowl of stew. Pedro and Marcos make up the fourth and fifth generation in the Gerardo culinary line, and together, the two have done as much for Asturian cuisine as anyone in the region. They work as a unit: Pedro standing guard over the traditions of *la cocina asturiana*; Marcos, like most young chefs in this country, always looking for new ways to build on top of those traditions. They share a gift for quick-witted humor, heroic hospitality, and an infectious passion for their *país*— virtues you'll find again and again in the people of this region.

My first memorable meal in Asturias came at this table, when Pedro and Marcos gave me a twenty-five-course lesson on the connection between landscape and cuisine—an edible and emotional journey through its orchards, cheese caves, pastures, and coastline. I still remember a dish of barely cooked razor clams laid gently atop a swipe of salty-sweet sesame paste, a rich, heady puree of Asturian cheese pinched between two caramelized pieces of pastry. I have lost hours to the memory of Casa Gerardo's *arroz con leche*, a rice pudding of impossible deliciousness encased in a shattering cloak of burnt sugar. Before we

sat down that afternoon, José told me that Casa Gerardo was the most underrated restaurant in Spain, if not all of Europe; by the time they wheelbarrowed us to the parking lot five hours later, I believed him.

Today what makes the place so special is how seamlessly it packs all of Asturias into a single meal—the mom-and-pop restaurants in the Picos de Europa, the cider houses of the rural villages, the modernist restaurants popping up in the big cities like Oviedo and Gijón. It takes a deft hand to follow up a plate of braised leeks bathed in pine nut butter and caviar with a naked filet of red mullet, or a plate of poached cod throat in an emerald broth of thistle and plankton with a single *albóndiga* crafted from grandma's recipe, but these guys do it, and you'll be left wondering which you like more: the wit and ingenuity of a fish adrift in a sea of fish food, or the overwhelming endorphin-spiking pleasure of a single tender meatball cloaked in a dark and delicious gravy.

We sit at a long, smooth glass chef's table in a private room next to the kitchen—one of the few modern touches in a restaurant that feels like somebody's home (it once was). At our table is a distinguished crew of dining companions: a wine producer, a cheese maker, a Catalan chef covered in tattoos, and an Asturian doctor named Francis Vega. Vega is in many ways the archetype of the Spanish intellectual, the kind of crisp character you might expect to find in a Woody Allen film: simply but elegantly dressed, with a deep vocabulary and the ability to speak intelligently and seamlessly about film, medicine, art, and, above all, food. Together with José, he keeps the conversation at the table nearly as impressive as the cuisine.

Sobremesa is a Spanish word that doesn't translate well into English. Literally, it means *on the table*, but really it refers to the tradition of lingering around for hours after the last bite of ice cream has been spooned and the last snifter of brandy sipped in order to soak up each other's company and push the boundaries of family, friends, and fellowship.

Sobremesa is a reminder that the Spanish dinner table is more than a table: it is a podium, a panel, a mirror, a microphone. This is where you discuss the problems of the country, lament the corrupt souls of politicians, share stories of your childhood, trade barbs with dining mates, wax nostalgically about paradises lost, and submit your world views to the scrutiny of the sated mob. This is not the coerced prattle of an American dinner table, where Dad asks Son how his day in school went and Mom tries to fill the ensuing silence; this is where bonds are formed, decisions are made, happiness is secured, and dissidence fomented.

Granted, most of the dissidence fomenting at our table revolves around decidedly first-world problems like the tyranny of the Maillard reaction, the post-Bulli trajectory of Spanish cuisine, and, just as the meal marches into its fourth hour, the proper length for a high-end tasting menu.

The most animated debate comes with the final savory course of the meal, the famed *fabada* of Casa Gerardo, a staple of the menu for more than one hundred thirty years. *Fabada* is a key constituent of Spain's *cocido* class, hearty stews of legumes and pork that bind this country's regional cuisine like the spine of a book. Beyond *cocido madrileño*, the king of all Spanish stews, *fabada* is the slow-simmered dish Spaniards dream of most when the temperatures start to drop.

José has long proclaimed his deep affection for Casa Gerardo's *fabada*—"maybe the greatest version of Asturias's most important dish." *Fabada* is normally made by stewing fat, dried white beans (called *fabes* in Asturian) with cuts of cured pork until the beans become soft and suffused with the smoke and fat of their porcine partners. But the Morán family revolutionized the *fabada* years back by making one simple but radical change: they use fresh beans instead of dried ones, creating a modernized version with the soul-warming flavors of the original, but cleaner, lighter, more immediate. It's a stellar rendition, a candidate for José's short list of last-supper dishes, but he has one major issue with the Casa Gerardo *fabada*: By the time it arrives to the table, ladled out from a giant porcelain chafing dish twenty courses into the meal, you're too full to truly appreciate it.

"It's beautiful, every bit as good as I dream of when I'm stuck in Washington a million miles away from *fabada*. But I can't eat oysters and tuna and cheese and fifteen other things, then be expected to enjoy this." Both father and son look on, mystified, as José's voice grows louder. "You need to serve the *fabada* at the beginning of the meal, when people are most hungry, but you'll never do it because you don't have the balls!"

Notionally, he's not wrong about the inverted pyramid of high-end meals. You sit down to a four-hour feast with wide eyes and an empty stomach. Slowly, steadily, you fill up, and just as you're ready to wave your white linen napkin in surrender, the largest plate of food with the most assertive flavors arrives: a braised lamb neck, a plank of lavishly marbled Japanese beef, a slow-simmered stew of giant white beans laced with three kinds of pork. High-end restaurants all over the world fall into this trap.

The entire table erupts at José's suggestion, some calling him blasphemous, others reluctantly accepting his logic. Pedro and

Marcos, for their part, look apoplectic; *fabada* won't be a first course at Casa Gerardo anytime soon. Another round of gin tonics—the official lubricant of the Spanish *sobremesa*—and a new round of controversies for debate. Our plans to hike along the coastline will have to wait for another day. Nobody in Spain is in a rush to leave the dining room table, least of all the Asturians.

Saturday, 11:45 p.m., Casa Kilo, Villaviciosa

José Andrés feasts with relish on the inner organs of crabs, lobsters, urchins, and other sea creatures. He likes slurping the ocean brine off tiny clams, plumbing the savory punch of boiled crab innards, sucking the dark, mysterious pleasures from the brains of giant red shrimp. Most of all, he likes to excavate the meat from gooseneck barnacles, with a twist of his wrist separating the rough, inedible skin from the phallic-shaped appendage of prized ocean protein.

We've already eaten two lunches, the first at Güeyu Mar, a restaurant in the tiny coastal town of Playa de Vega with views of the breaking surf from its terrace, where chef Abel Álvarez and his wife, Luisa, devote tremendous energy and skill to one thing: fish and seafood cooked over oak embers and seasoned with little more than salt and a lifetime's dedication to the fusion of fire and flesh. The meal begins with smoked oysters and caviar and finishes with a kingfish large enough to feed the Spanish royal family; every bite is a reminder of northern Spain's inimitable grill culture.

The second lunch—billed by José as "just a little tapa" at La Huertona in Ribadesella—turned into a ten-course, three-hour scuba dive through the Cantabrian Sea: anchovies, octopus, hake, clams, and a superlative *salpicón* of lobster, fat chunks of just-cooked tail and claw meat laced with a crunchy mince of onion and green pepper and bathed in a pitch-perfect blend of olive oil and sherry vinegar. The final dish, a whole turbot grilled over a wood fire, a full-fish exploration of the varying levels of fat, muscle, and gelatin in one of the ocean's most elegant creatures, pushed our bellies to the bursting point and the concept of lunch even beyond the decidedly liberal definition held by the Spaniards.

Fabada, the king of the northern stews.

For dinner, I'd love nothing more than a fistful of antacids and a soft feather pillow, but José has other plans. We pull into Casa Kilo just before closing time and the owner—like most owners I've found in restaurants across Spain, gripped by a mixture of excitement and fear to have José Andrés eating at his restaurant—takes us back to the kitchen to the live tanks and begins to show José today's catch: small, dark-shelled lobsters called *langosta*; large, sweet lobster called *bogavante*; barnacles; three kinds of clams; and a cadre of crabs of varying size and spunk—from small, sweet *nécoras* to the monster spider crab known as *centollo*. José rolls up his sleeves and begins to pluck two of everything from the water, like Noah, only the ark is his prodigious belly.

He calls over the cook—a large, sweet-faced woman with a sagging toque and a look of mild terror in her eyes—and begins to discuss in extraordinary detail the cooking of each individual piece of seafood. (In less experienced, less charismatic hands,

this maneuver—invading a chef's kitchen and asking difficult questions—would be a deeply dickish thing to do, but José has a special talent at making indiscreet behavior genuinely charming.)

"I want half a kilo of *percebes* brought in three separate batches, spaced out three minutes between each. As soon as the first batch goes out, go ahead and drop the second batch. Later, let's do the *nécoras* for three minutes and the spider crab for eight."

The lobster is the biggest I've seen—north of five pounds—and José is already salivating over the prospect of excavating its various deposits of oceanic intensity. "How long would you cook this?" he asks the woman. "About thirty minutes," she says, more a question than a statement. "No! Not a minute over eighteen."

Falstaff, Louis XIV, Joey Chestnut: history's greatest eaters have nothing on José. I've seen him down a dozen pork belly tacos, scrape one hundred fifty individual sea urchins clean from their spiky purple shells, follow up a meal of tripe and frogs' legs with five hyper-aged tomahawk steaks. To conserve space, José bans bread from the table, which doesn't sit well with our rotating cast of dining partners throughout the trip. But he enforces it with sergeant-like discipline. "Bread is for mediocre people."

When the first round of *percebes* comes out, I keep my distance and let him go to work. Two minutes later, they're gone and sixty seconds after, right on schedule, the second round arrives and the barnacle bonanza continues.

Later comes the rest of the Asturian aquarium: *nécoras* so sweet and briny we suck the shells, clams that release a warm burst of umami the second I bite down, the mutant eighteen-minute lobster that takes up half the table. Galicia is regarded as the capital of Spain's seafood industry, but Asturias shares that same strip of cold, deep-water ocean, and the haul here is every bit as delicious as it is sixty miles west. Asturias overflows with places like Casa Kilo, family-run restaurants serving little beyond pristine seafood cooked as simply as possible.

Everything that we eat tonight is boiled, following José's detailed instructions, and arrives on the table with no other discernible sign of human interference. "Chefs love to talk about respecting the product," says José. "In Spain they actually mean it. Most of what we've eaten this trip has been two ingredients: product and salt. No umami this or spicy that. No sauces or weird spices."

Despite Spain's reputation as a haven of post-modern culinary experimentation, the real cuisine of this country—and especially of Asturias—works with this very simple formula. The tapas bar that builds its menu around the morning market. The grill spot that uses smoke as its only condiment. The family seafood shack with a two-item pantry: salt and olive oil. In this world, not only are sauces superfluous, but even lemon and black pepper are deemed aggressive affronts to the purity of product.

But sometimes, for even the most restrained eater, reverence can be boring. When the spider crab comes out of the kitchen, José abandons his love of Spanish restraint and begins to tweak at the table. He fills the underside of the crab shell with its brains and guts while I pick out the tiny shreds of sweet meat from its legs. He folds those in, along with the juice of two lemons and a plate of chopped hard-boiled egg that he orders from the kitchen. The final touch: a splash of *sidra*, like a good Asturian.

Though I barely have the strength to bring my spoon to the spontaneous stew in the crab shell, I have to admit that it's the best thing we've eaten all night.

Sunday, 12:47 p.m., three thousand feet up in the Picos de Europa

These are mythic mountains we are climbing. Our jagged ascent through the sharp angles of the Picos passes by Covadonga, a tiny village with a fairy-tale church that holds a special place in the Asturian psyche. Legend has it that Don Pelayo founded the Kingdom of Asturias and the entire Spanish Reconquista that would eventually wrest the country back from Islamic rule in a cave carved into the side of this mountain. The *Chronicle of Albelda* of 881, one of the few surviving texts from that period, paints a heroic scene:

Pelayo and his three hundred men versus the 187,000 soldiers of General Alqama's feared Moorish army. At the last moment, the Virgin Mary appeared before Pelayo and assured him that his troops would prevail, and when Alqama's soldiers broke on the rocks of the Asturian mountains, they did.

The entrance to Covadonga today, like most days, is clogged with cars looking to catch a glimpse of the country's most famous cave. But this morning, we are in search of a different kind of cave entirely.

When people in France talk about a cheese cave, you think of a dark, damp room where a variety of *fromage* is carefully matured in a controlled environment. When people in Asturias talk about a cheese cave, they mean actual caves—stalagmites and tufas, torches and head scars—where they age cheese. The mission we're on this morning, more spelunking than cheese tasting, would be dangerous under any circumstances; on four hours' sleep, four gin tonics, and two foot-long hot dogs—we stumbled onto a summer festival last night—it seems downright negligent.

Luckily we're in the callused hands of Juan Sobrecueva, a man that looks to be chiseled from the mountain itself—cement shoulders, barrel chest, a beard as white and wild as a winter blizzard. He didn't sleep last night, kept awake by one of his cows giving birth, but even in his seventies, he shows no signs of wear for the worse. The fact that his last name means "above a cave" somehow puts me at ease.

"The mountain makes people strong because you have to defend yourself," he says, handing out walking sticks and headlamps.

To get to Sobrecueva's cheese stash, we hike nearly a mile off the road, through a flock of grazing mountain goats, over a handful of rocky ridges, along patches of grass slick with mist, past a stone shepherd's refuge, and finally, through the jagged mouth of a cave and down into the belly of the mountain, where Sobrecueva ages his supply of raw-milk cheese.

He chose this spot not for its remote location, but because it stays cool and damp year round, perfect for breeding the delicious bacteria that will turn a blend of animals' milk into a product of extraordinary depth and nuance. That transformation is on full display once we hit the bottom of the cave: hundreds of wheels of cheese, weighing between three and eight kilograms, lined up like a battalion, their exterior a psychedelic swirl of blues and reds and yellows.

After cider and *fabada*, cheese is what Asturias does best. Spain's cheese game is strong from top to bottom, but whereas most regions specialize in a single style of cheese, Asturias's tableau of topographies makes for a diverse culture of crumbly aged goat cheeses, creamy cow's milks, and spicy, stinky blues. It's in the latter category where Sobrecueva plies his trade, specializing in *queso de* Gamonéu, along with Cabrales and Valdeón, part of the great trinity of blues birthed in the caves of the Picos de Europa.

We had spent the first hours of the day in the cheese market of Cangas de Onís, one of the oldest markets in all of Spain, where wheels, wedges, and triangles of lactic excellence share table space with other Asturian staples: smoky coils of chorizo, bottles of cloudy homemade cider, a rainbow of dried beans. But Sobrecueva isn't impressed. "They lost their soul a long time ago down there, abandoning the way we've always made cheese to sell a cheaper product."

Sobrecueva's approach to making cheese is like a jam band's approach to making music: all finesse and instinct. "The formula is to make little, but make it really well. That's the Asturian way." I ask Sobrecueva about the makeup of his cheese. "Forty percent cow, fifty percent goat, thirty percent sheep. Does that make one hundred percent?"

He calls his thirty years as a cheesemaker a "journey through the desert," but slowly he has refined his technique through trial and error. "The hardest part is getting good raw material. If I buy my milk from where everyone else buys it, how will my cheese be much better?" Instead, he raises his own animals—nine cows, forty goats, seventy sheep—at his farm at the bottom of the mountain, where he makes the cheese before bringing it up to the cave, a few wheels at a time, in an old black backpack.

"The work in the cave is all movement. I change the cheese's position, I change the direction, constantly trying to expose it to the best bacteria."

He digs a small cheese knife into the top of one of his wheels and hacks out a few chunks for us. He's right: It's nothing like what we tasted at the market. The rind shocks the tongue like a live wire, the firm cheese sending currents of salt and spice, funk and acidity across the palate. The most confounding part is the taste of smoke, pervasive despite the cheese being entirely smoke-free. "That's what you get in the cave," says Sobrecuevas, "this incredible bacteria creating complex flavors."

The cave doesn't come without its challenges—that is, even beyond the extraordinary expenditure of time and energy it takes to haul thousands of pounds of cheese up and down the mountain each year. "A fox came down here once and tipped the entire production over. One thousand kilograms of cheese on the floor. I salvaged some of it, but the damn thing took bites out of a bunch of the wheels."

Animals aren't the only unwanted visitors, but humans prove to be a little more thoughtful in their plundering. "Someone found the cave once and took a wheel. But they left thirty euros behind."

Throughout all of this, José hikes, tastes, and listens in complete silence. He doesn't normally have the time or the patience for silence, or for nostalgia, but it's clear that he finds something down in the cave that moves him deeply. Later, on the climb back down the mountain, he puts his hand on my shoulder: "*Qué bonito es Asturias.*"

Sunday, 2:35 p.m., Casa Marcial, Parres

Traveling east to west in Asturias is like driving anywhere else in Spain: wide highways run along the region's biggest urban centers: Gijón, the rough and rowdy port town; Avilés, with the lunar architecture of the Oscar Niemeyer Center; and Oviedo, the capital, just inland.

But traveling north to south is another matter entirely. Three-lane highways shrink to one-lane country roads that wind up mountains at oblique angles. Covering ten kilometers could take ten minutes or two hours, depending on the weather and the number of cows and sheep sharing the road. This is where you want to be: among the rolling apple orchards and the staircase gardens; near the mountain villages with the wild horses and the houses on stilts; in the vast green expanse beyond the reach of GPS, where you're always one wrong turn away from a deep discovery.

Casa Marcial is what you find when you get lost in Asturias—the kind of place where you'd stop for an accidental lunch and luck into the meal of your life. The only restaurant in Asturias with two Michelin stars is found at the nexus of five tiny country roads, each one leading to a different bubble of pastoral beauty.

We find Casa Marcial after a few wrong turns of our own and settle into our reservation an hour late. The first dish comes flying out of the kitchen almost immediately: a steaming bowl of *fabada*. Someone has been talking.

"You see? Finally someone listens to me!" says José to the grinning server.

Juan Sobrecueva and his magical cheese cave.

"What's next? Bring it on!" And so they bring it, plate after plate:

Crunchy salt-cod skin: fish and chips.

Late-spring vegetables—raw, pickled, boiled—with melting cylinders of bone marrow: beauty and the beast.

Pigeon and sardine: surf and turf under a weather advisory.

Strawberry mousse and kimchi puree: a Craigslist Missed Connections played out on the plate: *I saw you that one time in the refrigerator section of Grand Asia and thought we should hang out.*

Nacho Manzano is the composer of this Asturian ballad of soil and sea. Born and raised in this restaurant, at the same stoves he dominates today, he knows every contour of this region's layered landscape, and how to employ its most impressive means to hair-raising ends. One by one, the stars of our road trip resurface in various states of undress: cold-water creatures, garden legumes, cave-aged cheeses, house cider.

The meal is filled with sophisticated compositions and challenging conceits—a fillet of red mullet cooked on a hot stone lined with kelp and coarse salt, a melting wedge of eggplant suspended between the bitter bite of coffee and the fermented sweetness of black garlic—but it's the simplest dish of all that hits me hardest: the *torto*, a crunchy corn cake topped with a loose scramble of farm eggs and deeply caramelized onions. It's unabashedly Asturian, a reminder of corn's prominence in the northern kingdom. "It's the first thing I ever learned to cook," says Nacho, whose grandma taught him how to make *tortos* when he was three.

Of course, Nacho's corn cakes aren't the same as his grandma's: they're thin and shattering and puff up like *pommes* soufflé. I have eaten thousands of meals in Spain, but I've never come across this flavor before, both totally foreign but disarmingly familiar, like the childhood you were meant to have. The taste of pure discovery on a winding country road in Asturias.

· · ·

Monday, 10:24 a.m., Hotel Imperial, Oviedo

I wake up to a hammering headache and the vague memory of barnacles and blood sausage and a statue of Woody Allen without glasses. I call José from the lobby and tell him to pack his bag.

It's time to go. Like a couple of junkies on a Vegas bender, we've been pushing our luck too long. It's not just the five marathon meals a day, the sweaty seafood sessions, the great rivers of fermented fruit juice. We're getting sloppy. José has taken to leaving our car rental wherever he damn well pleases. Last night, he parked it on the steps of the Imperial, the most august hotel in all of Asturias, a pleasure palace for kings and queens and diplomats. When we step out to survey the day, an old man in a bellhop's outfit comes running up to us.

"This is yours, sir? We didn't know whose car this was. You left it here all night with the windows open."

"Did I really leave the windows open?"

"I'm afraid so, señor. And it rained."

And so we load up our soggy chariot and reluctantly head south. Before us is a long, winding road up into the mountains and back out through the front door, where the rest of Spain—conquered territory—awaits. There are aged ox steaks to try near León, and a new yakitori joint in Madrid with two seats tonight at 8:00 p.m. But not even the promise of the next great meal has José prepared to leave home.

We can't go yet. We've only scratched the surface! We have so much left to do. I know a woman who collects razor clams. I haven't taken you to the little restaurant with the ocean views and the best fucking monkfish you'll ever taste. Did I tell you about the place in the mountains run by an old woman who only serves fabada *and the only way to get there is to take a funicular? Baby eels should be coming into season any day now. We could go salmon fishing. We could make cheese. We could drink cider. We can't leave, we're just getting warmed up! Look at that shepherd climbing the rocks with his sheep. Look at that woman with an armful of apples. Look around you. Every path is a painting. Every turn is an opportunity. Look!* ¡Qué bonito es Asturias!

The Big
CHEESE

Spain's cheese culture doesn't have the fame of its Mediterranean neighbors, but it has every bit the game. Raw and pasteurized, fresh and aged, made with cow, sheep, and goat's milk: This is but a small sampling of the Spanish cheese dominion.

03

04

05

01 **IDIAZÁBAL**

Sheep / Basque Country

02 **TORTA DEL CASAR**

Sheep / Extremadura

03 **TETILLA**

Cow / Galicia

04 **GARROTXA**

Goat / Catalunya

05 **CABRALES**

Cow + Sheep + Goat / Asturias

06 **MANCHEGO**

Sheep / La Mancha

Amazing Shit

IN THE MIDDLE OF NOWHERE

From the grill shrines along the Atlantic coast to the far-flung rice meccas of Valencia and Alicante, the backroads of Spain have long been a place for culinary enlightenment. These are places that exist beyond the reach of passing fads and urban excesses (not to mention GPS)—places where the food is as honest as the people serving it. Places you'll be happy to get lost for.

Picos de Europa
STONE MOUNTAIN STEW

The Picos de Europa, home to Spain's most dramatic mountain terrain, are a setting for hearty people and hearty fare. No restaurant proves that better than Casa Juanín, in the tiny village of Pendones, where both are on the daily menu. You'll find Juanín out front pouring drinks and telling stories to a thick pack of locals while his daughter Isabel works magic behind the burners. Here, fifteen euros will get you a feast fit for an Asturian coal miner: braised goat, venison *picadillo*, bottomless bowls of wild boar *fabada*, and a flan and a rice pudding that will make your knees buckle. The only thing you need to worry about is how to get back down the mountain.

CLANDESTINE COCKTAILS

Just beyond the apple orchards of Villaviciosa, down a winding country road, you'll find an unassuming tobacco shop. Make your way past the packs of Camels and rolling papers and into Soda 917, a low-lit bar lined with leather couches where one of Spain's legendary bartenders plies his trade. Kike once ran Negroni, one of Barcelona's top cocktail outfits, before retiring to this clandestine countryside spot. But the slower lifestyle hasn't dulled his ambition: He stocks more than one hundred gins and an arsenal of artisanal vermouth and bitter liqueurs. Whether the crew of old barflies perched on the stools know they're in the presence of greatness matters not; they're here for the beer and cigarettes, anyways.

Cádiz
DREAM EGGS AND HAM

Mesón del Toro, in the shadow of the whitewashed hilltop village of Vejer de la Frontera outside Cádiz, doesn't serve much—sliced meat and cheese, a rotating daily vegetable dish, and, above all, fried eggs served over fried potatoes. Not just any eggs and potatoes, though: Both are cooked slowly in an abundance of olive oil until soft and outlandishly savory. The sunset yolk becomes the sauce, while the *jamón*, should you opt for it (you should), lifts the creation to dizzying heights. It could take an hour for your order to come, but you'll be kept company by packs of beer- and sherry-drinking locals who know how good they have it down in these parts.

Northern Catalunya
FARMHOUSE FEAST

The rural reaches of northern Catalunya play host to some of Spain's most powerful country cooking—none more so than Els Casals, where, from your bedroom in the refurbished farmhouse, you'll see farm animals through the window and smell amazing things through the floorboards. What waits below is a dinner as honest as it is astonishing: oven-roasted local game, rice studded with truffles and young pigeon, and, best of all, thick rounds of smoky *sobrassada* made from their own pigs, covered in honey and roasted until bubbling. The best part about staying the night? You get to wake up and do it all over again for breakfast.

Valladolid
WOOD-FIRED FANTASY

An hour north of Madrid, on the same plains where Don Quixote once did battle with windmills, you'll find a sterling example of Spain's obsession with oven-roasted meat. At Mannix, you can eat everything from tiny, juicy sweetbreads to inch-thick steaks, but you're really here for one thing: *cordero lechal*, baby milk-fed lamb, slow-roasted in a traditional wood-burning oven until the point of collapse, then hit over a final blast of intense heat. As the skin shatters like a fallen wineglass, and the meat below pulls apart in tender, juicy ropes, all you can do is laugh at the genius of the Spaniards, and at your good fortune for eating among them.

FABADA

CLASS OF THE *COCIDOS*

No dish better represents Asturias
than this slow-simmered pot of
pork and beans. Born sometime
in the late nineteenth century,
it forms a vital part of Spain's
cocido class, the slow-simmered
stews found in every region
around the country.

ALL ABOUT THE BEANS

As the name suggests, the star of
the dish is the *fabe*, the large,
creamy white beans that swell
with the flavor of the braising
liquid. Like a good plate of pasta,
the integrity of the bean is
everything: It should be toothsome, creamy, and fully intact.

THE PORCINE TRINITY

Fabada is an expression of Spain's deep dedication to cured pork. This holy trinity comes with its own name: *compango*, the mix of heavily smoked chorizo, blood sausage, and pork belly that give *fabada* its bulk, aroma, and color.

THE RED TIDE

That shiny layer of red resting on top of the stew? A mixture of fat and smoked paprika leached from the slow-simmered cuts of pork. Classy restaurants will de-fat the stew to keep the flavors light and clean, but *fabada* is meant to keep you full, not thin.

Chapter Seven

GALICIA

—

Xosé Lorenzo is in the middle of explaining how he got the seven stitches on his scalp and the eight on his leg when a call rings out from the other side of the rocks. A pack of men and women in wet suits aim a chorus of shouts and whistles and waving arms at the bald, bearded game warden, who squints into the light and cups his right hand to his ear. Waves crash wildly against the coastline, a wall of white noise that muffles the panic bubbling over in the distance. Finally, a single voice rises up above the churn of the Atlantic: A man is down and he's being swept out to sea.

Xosé holsters his binoculars and takes off at full speed toward the source of the commotion. He moves quickly, but the arms wave ever more wildly, and between him and the emergency, an obstacle course of jagged rocks, slippery stones, pools of seawater. Everyone, a dozen people at least, have dropped their gear and are making their way down the coast as quickly as possible, which isn't nearly quick enough. Suddenly, on the inside track, bounding from one rocky precipice to the next like a pair of mountain goats, two women in wet suits break away from the pack: one short, compact, with a bouncing blond ponytail, the other large and solid with a bob of crinkled red hair. Without breaking stride, the larger woman pulls a rope from her pack and ties a loop at the end. Twenty meters beyond, in a rough channel of ocean churn, a portly fisherman in a checkered shirt is clinging to a triangle of quickly vanishing stone. Even from this far away, you can see his arms shaking, struggling to hold on as the force of the ocean sucks him out toward the horizon.

The women loop the rope around a rocky appendage and take off swimming toward the man and his diminishing island. Another man joins them, and together, the three lasso the fisherman, wrap him in their arms, and begin to swim him slowly back across the channel.

A dozen hands wait on the other side. An ambulance arrives to take away the man, who will live to fish another day. Spearing for octopus on a rough outcropping of rocks, a rogue wave came in and washed him off his feet. Had he been alone this morning, the taller woman says, picking up her gear and getting back to work, he would be dead.

Then the shorter one flashes a little smile. "He's famous around here for being a *machista*," she says. "Imagine that: A raging chauvinist saved by a couple of women. It will be a long time before he lives this down."

But Susana and Isabel González are not just a couple of women. They are *percebeiras*, hunters and gatherers of the gooseneck barnacle of the Spanish Atlantic.

Tucked into the northwest corner of the Iberian Peninsula, Galicia has long been shorthand for Spanish seafood supremacy, a distribution center as much as a destination, a fountain from which flows the most sterling examples of rockfish and razor clams, oysters and urchins, monkfish and mussels. Anything from Galicia commands premium prices in Spain and beyond, but the king of the ocean here, at least by the time it lands on the ice beds of wet markets across the country, is the gooseneck barnacle, known in Spanish as the *percebe*.

Galician barnacles are short and slender, with a hard, rocky base and a dark, leathery sheath hiding a single finger of ocean meat

Isabel and Susana González, at dawn, in search of *percebes*.

that drives Spaniards wild. Boiled briefly and seasoned with nothing but the essence of the ocean, *percebes* combine the same wave of umami and undertow of sweetness particular to all great seafood, only in a dense package with a taut, snappy texture. In a country where people are willing to invest an imprudent percentage of their income on ocean treasure—Catalonian red shrimp, Asturian spider crabs, Cantabrian anchovies—*percebes* can fetch up to two hundred euros per kilo, nearly half of which is inedible, making it one of the most expensive delicacies in the world.

The elevated price reflects a confluence of both market and organic factors: the unpredictability of supply, the uncontrollable elements that create quality barnacles, the massive seasonal swings in demand. And, above all, the danger of being a *percebeiro*. Barnacles grow in very specific places: namely, clinging to the sides of sharp rocks with full exposure to ocean swells. To be a successful *percebes* hunter, you must negotiate a series of natural challenges—frigid water temperatures, the fierce Galician weather, and the force and unpredictability of the ocean at its angriest. Almost everyone living in these coastal towns has lost a friend or a family member to the Atlantic.

The González sisters have the barnacle business in their blood. Both of their grandmothers were *percebeiras*, women who scratched out a living from the cracks and crevices of the Atlantic coast. Their maternal grandfather was called on to fight with Franco in the Spanish Civil War, and though he made it home alive, he never fully returned. With eight children and a local economy driven exclusively by farming and fishing, his wife took to the rocks to feed the family. After collecting a cache of *percebes*, she would travel thirty kilometers up the coast to Vigo with baskets of barnacles on her head to sell at the city market.

Her only daughter Palmira, the González sisters' mother, took up barnacle hunting at a young age. Palmira would ride her bicycle down the coastline with her mother packed on the back in search of a decent living. She spent so much time between the spokes and the stones, riding up and down the coast in search of barnacles, that she lost her first baby to a miscarriage. The doctors implored her to give up *percebes* hunting the next time she got pregnant.

In 1963 Palmira married Eduardo, one of Bayona's most famous *percebeiros*, a man known for his bravery in tough conditions, his intuition, and for a rare skill among the *percebes* hunters of his day: He knew how to swim. "There was one rock along the coastline that was known to be covered with the best barnacles in the area," says Isabel. "No one could get to it—nobody except my dad. He was a water buffalo, fearless, immovable. When his friends came back with ten kilos, he'd come back with twenty." But it wasn't just his skill that earned him repute: Eduardo was known for his humility, for his unwavering support of his fellow *percebeiros*, for risking his life in the name of others. "He saved a lot of lives, but he also saw a lot of friends die."

Eduardo always said he wanted to have a son so that he could raise a respected *percebeiro* in his image. Instead, he had four daughters. "We were all born at home," says Isabel. "When the wet nurse came in to announce the last birth, he nearly dropped his coffee. 'Wow, another one!' "

Lala, Isabel, Susana, and Belén: The González sisters of Galicia, born with the ocean in their eyes. But the barnacle world wasn't a preordained destination. Each sister set out on a different career path. Lala owned a food market, then worked as a pastry chef in a local bakery. Isabel sweated out years as a line cook at a small tapas bar in Bayona. Susana was an administrator for a pharmaceutical company.

But the siren call of the sea proved too much to resist, and by the time Belén left her job working retail at a local market, all four of the sisters had gone the way of their grandmothers. They embraced an unspoken pact: to always work the rocks together, to watch over each other in the way that only family members can. Together, they would form a team stronger than the sum of its parts. And in that way, they'd stay safe. "The first thing we've always done when leaving the water is call our mom to tell her we're safe," says Susana.

But turns out their biggest challenge wasn't the whims of the sea, but the colleagues they worked alongside. The plump octopus fisherman was not the first *machista* the sisters have wrapped their arms around. Barnacle diving, like the fishing industry the world over, is a male-dominated profession, even if this southern corner of Galicia has a long tradition of women working the rocks.

For as long as barnacle sales have been regulated by the government, women and men have been treated differently: For many years, men were allowed a quota of five kilograms of *percebes* per day, while women were allowed just three. And when it came time to sell the barnacles in the afternoon auction, the two groups were separated, with women only allowed to sell their catch once the men had off-loaded theirs.

We're not talking about the 1920s or the 1950s or even the last few decades of the twentieth century. This practice persisted until 2003, when Susana decided to run for president of Bayona's *percebes* association. This is no idle role: The president works to implement new rules, enforce quotas, serves as a conduit between the *percebeiros* and the Galicia government. Needless to say, her candidacy was not well received by the old male guard on the docks of Bayona, many still possessed by the same laws of machismo that prevail in many corners of Spain. Protests formed, threats followed. Even many of the women divers, long accustomed to the established hierarchy, viewed Susana's ambitions as an unnecessary challenge to the status quo.

As her sisters and parents and pretty much anyone in this town of three thousand inhabitants will tell you, Susana does not back down from a challenge. When she was eleven years old, she canvassed middle school administrators to change the lunch rules so that boys and girls could all eat together. "I don't have more rights than anyone. But I don't have less, either." She's let that conviction carry her from one cause in life to the next. When she left her job to work the rocks, she fell instantly in love with almost everything about her new profession: the open air, the ever-changing office space, the sisterly camaraderie. But she didn't love the way she and her fellow women were treated.

"Imagine, most of these guys go home, slam their hands on the table, and watch their wives obey their commands. They wanted us to do the same, but that wasn't going to happen."

The campaign was tough on the family, on all of Bayona, really, because Bayona is the kind of small Spanish town where individual pains are felt as communal wounds, but Susana prevailed, winning sixty-five votes to her opponent's fifty-five on the back of a late tide of support from Bayona's female divers. The tensions stirred up during the elections, though, died hard.

"During the first meetings, the national police force had to send out a patrol unit to keep the peace. The men would insult us, threaten us, try to intimidate us."

The breaking point came when Susana announced that men and women would have equal quotas. "Tables were turned over. Chairs flew. They said that we were stealing their livelihood. That as women,

we didn't need to provide for our families—only they did. We came to the *percebes* world to bankroll our vices, to buy makeup and creams. Those were a rough three or four years."

Susana wasn't done, though. In 2014 she ran a successful campaign to become president of the Cofradía de Bayona, overseeing all fishing—crab, octopus, sea urchin—in the town's twenty-kilometer stretch of coastline.

In an extra blow to the old guard, Susana's vacated seat as the president of the *percebeiros* was soon filled by another González—her older sister, Isabel.

Galicia, depending on how you look at it, is either where Spain ends or where it begins. A postage stamp region tucked into the northwest pocket of Spain, the *gallegos* share a border with Portugal, a bloodline with the Celts, and a twisted coastline that makes for a rough welcome mat for the rest of the world.

Along the fringes of Galicia, clusters of tiny islands block the mouths of the region's fabled *rías*, massive estuaries that carve watery arms into the coastline. (On the outskirts, the grandest of Galician islands, the Islas Cíes, play host to the types of baking-powder beaches that countries can build entire economies around.) Inland, along the rolling valleys and steep river slopes around Ourense, you'll find one of Europe's most underrated wine regions, where the cool temperatures and heavy rainfall creates white wines—Albariño, Godello—of steely complexity. Deeper still into Galicia, dramatic sierras hide tiny villages that shrink with each passing season. In Cuera, population forty-seven, a child was born in 2014, the first new face this dwindling community has seen in twenty-five years. The town rejoices, but life is slowly slipping away from Galicia's farthest reaches.

Galicia's has long been a surf-and-turf economy, but increasingly the farmers have traded their hoes and tractors for nets and rods and moved toward the coast, where the heart of the Galician economy sur-vives. These aren't the lonely seascapes of Asturias and Cantabria. In Vigo, $100 million ships equipped for months out at sea loom large in one of Spain's largest ports. Everywhere you turn, you see the gears of the ocean economy turn: from the ubiquitous *rías*, where men at work with shovels and wheelbarrows dredge for clams and mussels, to the tableau of canning factories big and small, where nimble-fingered women Tetris everything from baby squid to bluefin tuna into aluminum cans for Spain's formidable *conservas* culture.

It was here, in the Bay of Bayona, where Christopher Columbus and a band of scurvy-riddled men made landfall after making history's most devastating detour en route to India. Along with the news of a brave new world to the west, Columbus and his men carried in the cargo holding an ecosystem of new plants and animals that would come to dramatically redefine the way Spain and the rest of Europe eats—unleashing on the world the building blocks for cuisine as we know it today, from the chili-laced curries of Thailand to the corn-studded stews of Africa to the potato-dense *tortillas* found in every bar across Spain.

Today an exact replica of the *Pinta* can be seen from the damp cement floor of the Cofradía de Bayona, where the principle products of the southern Galician coastline gather under one roof. Sea urchin season just opened yesterday, and mountains of purple spikes trade spaces with buckets of octopus and bags of barnacles. Outside, two sunburned fishermen trade stories in the singsongy cadence of *gallego*, sucking the seawater off barnacles like salt off of sunflower seeds to fill the long silences.

All of the association's 120 licensed *percebes* hunters must bring their haul here every day to be sorted, sold, and taxed by the Galician government. The González sisters have had a decent morning of *percebes* picking, and they spend twenty minutes sorting through the catch, removing shells and rocks and any barnacles that don't meet the minimum legal size for commercial sale.

A new regulation has gone into place today, banning *percebeiros* from touching their catch after submitting their barnacles to be weighed and set aside for the auction—a small, but significant change that will keep people from manipulating their lots to look attractive to potential buyers. Nobody is happy about it, not the woman who gives Susana and Isabel the stink eye, not the two guys boring holes through their heads from across the room, and certainly not the burly gentleman who corners Susana by the coolers. But if the sisters are concerned about the delicate tempers of their colleagues, they don't show it.

The lively spoken auction of the past has been swapped out for a silent, automated version involving a series of electronic devices and a barnacle stock ticker that looks like a high school basketball scoreboard. Most members mull nervously about, adjusting to another tiny new reality, wondering if a single straw will ever break the camel's back.

The auction does not go well for most of the hunters. The auctioneer sets the

As barnacle supplies diminish
over the years, so do the quotas.

opening price at one hundred eighty euros a kilo, but it plummets to fifty-nine before the first buyer buzzes in on his electronic device. He surveys the lots one by one, probing and smelling the little piles of barnacles, then decides to pass entirely, convinced that the price will continue to drop.

All around, the *percebeiros* of Bayona wait to see what they'll take home today. It's a motley crew of seafaring souls, a perfect cross section of the *gallego* demographic: muscle-bound young men, veterans who wear their years in belly folds and nose wrinkles, husbands and wives who work wordlessly through their catch, grandmas putting in their last few years before retirement.

A buyer from Madrid bids forty-five euros on a good-looking lot, but the *percebeiro* isn't having it. "I'll take my chances elsewhere," he says to no one in particular. To underscore his indignation, he plucks a few fat barnacles from his collection and flings them over his shoulder onto the auction floor. Maybe he has a restaurant waiting to buy them for more; maybe he just can't stomach the idea of letting them go for so little.

The *percebes* market is highly volatile, due to the fact that Spaniards eat barnacles at very specific times of the year. Summer attracts people to the coast and barnacles to the plate; the Christmas season brings about the most radical price surges, the market value tripling nearly overnight and provoking risky behavior from the region's barnacle hunters. The surging economy of the 1990s and early 2000s helped change those habits, making it easier to shoulder the cost of barnacles year round for consumers, but when the bottom fell out and *la crisis* set in, the value of *percebes* outside of Christmas and summertime plummeted.

Adding to the anxiety on the floor today is a general sense of concern surrounding the future of this industry. Five years ago, the quota in these parts was five kilograms per diver; today, it's down to three. Nobody is happy about earning 40 percent less money for the same high-risk job, but like everything else in this great wet world, supplies are capricious, sporadic, dwindling. Academics and experts don't know why barnacle supplies are disappearing. The best guess is global warming and the resulting rise in the ocean water's salinity, which makes it difficult for delicate barnacle larvae to survive and thrive in rough conditions.

"I don't know if *percebe* culture is sustainable. I really don't," says Susana. "But we're trying our best to make it so."

Those attempts are embraced by some who recognize in Susana and Isabel's efforts a sober strategy geared toward the future. The opposition, fierce and persistent, comes from those who view reduced quotas and increased regulations as a direct threat to their immediate survival.

Gallegos are known throughout Spain for their special disposition—direct, emotional, capable of swinging from good-natured to punishing in a flash—and those traits spill out constantly onto the auction floor, the meeting hall, the ocean-battered rocks.

When I ask Isabel about the *gallego* character, she doesn't hesitate: "Courageous and spontaneous and unpredictable. Like the sea."

What do you do when the well dries up? What do you do when you've lived your entire life off the ocean, off octopus in the winter and rockfish in the summer and tiny juicy barnacles year round, then one day, when you're out hunting down dinner along the same stretch of coast you've been working since your dad took you out and gave you a stick and a sack and taught you how to probe the dark underbellies of rocks until you felt the taught flesh of an octopus, how to scrape the mussel shells for worms for luring bottom-feeding fish, how the best barnacles are the ones that grow in the parts of the rocks where the elements—sun, rain, sea—are most extreme, and you've followed and refined that advice over the course of decades, during lean times and fat ones, until one morning, when you're out looking for your next meal, someone in a uniform with a whistle in his pocket stops you and asks to see your license. *License for what?* You say. *See that shack right there? That's where I live. See that boy with the stick and the sack? That's my blood. If you think I need a license to feed my family, you've got something coming to you.*

Hunger will push a man to do dangerous things. Just ask Xosé Lorenzo. He has spent the past twelve years patrolling these shores. Part of his salary is paid by the government, but most of it comes from the *percebeiros* themselves, who pay him to keep eyes on both the licensed hunters and the ever-expanding mass of *furtivos*, poachers who work the rocks when they think no one is watching. Most of them aren't fathers bringing home dinner for their families, but experienced hunters looking to cash in on the coastline without the cost of a license and the limitations of a quota or a schedule.

"You don't want to know all of the threats they've made over the years. More than one hundred to me and my family and my children. Outrageous shit."

I ask him for a sampling.

"Let's see: 'I'll kill you.' 'I'll cut your throat in your sleep.' 'I'll burn your car.' 'I'll shoot you in the leg.' 'I'll go to your house and fuck your wife while you watch me.' 'I'll kill your family first and make you watch and then I'll kill you.' 'I'll call a drug

THE BEST
BARNACLES GROW
WHERE THE
ELEMENTS ARE
MOST EXTREME.

addict friend from Vigo who's going to take a needle and inject you with AIDS.' That last one was pretty interesting, I thought. I said, 'Tell your friend where I live. You'll see who ends up with the needle in his balls!'"

Xosé rattles these off with a mix of clinical precision and quizzical detachment, like a public defender running through a list of charges. But unfortunately, they're not always empty threats. A year ago, he set out on his routine nighttime patrol route ("The poachers prefer to work under a blanket of stars," he says) when he came upon the car of a well-known poacher. He pursued, following him down the coastline toward the Portuguese border. Suddenly, the car put on the breaks and two men in wet suits stepped out. "I thought they just wanted to talk. Then I saw the *raspa*."

One slice to the head, another to the leg, and the poachers sped off, leaving Xosé bleeding on the side of the highway. He shows me the marks, pulls up pictures; later in the day, he sends me a video of him on the local news, undaunted by the vicious attack. "If they think that's going to slow me down, they're wrong."

It's one thing to come down to the sea to find something to eat for your family, Susana tells me. "It's another to be selling *percebes* illegally to restaurants and jeopardizing our livelihood." This is a small community, and everybody knows who the poachers are: Many are former licensed *percebeiros* who grew tired of paying fees; some are current members of the Bayona's barnacle association who sell their quotas legally, shoulder-to-shoulder with their dues-paying colleagues, then sneak back out to collect barnacles to sell on the black market.

Despite the best efforts of guys like Xosé, one of six wardens hired by the Cofradía de Bayona to patrol the coastline, poaching has run rampant in recent years, thanks to a struggling national economy that has left more than a quarter of the country jobless. Unsurprisingly, a high percentage of the deaths and injuries in the *percebes* business come from poachers, who are forced to work in the most dangerous conditions to evade the wardens. The only

tool of enforcement, beyond physical al-
tercation, has been issuing fines, which go
largely ignored by the bands of poachers. "I
know a guy with a million euros worth of
fines against him," says Xosé. "You think
that's stopped him? There's nothing to stop
these guys from taking one thousand kilos
of *percebes* whenever they feel like."

That, everyone hopes, will change with
the introduction of a new law this past
summer, allowing the government to im-
prison poachers who don't pay up. "Once
we stick one or two of these assholes in jail,
then we'll see what the rest do."

But anyone who slips out into the night
with a wet suit and a headlamp to battle
with the ocean and a labyrinth of serrated
rocks isn't thinking about tomorrow; he's
thinking about right now.

🍇 🐚 🐖

"How do you see it?" asks Isabel. "Do
you think we can work the rock today?"

"Right now it looks good," says Susana.

"But?"

"But I'm not sure we've seen what the
sea can really do yet."

"Yesterday was fine."

"Yes, but today's not yesterday."

"True enough. So what do we do?"

"We wait. We watch."

"For how long?"

"As long as we need to. Until we see one
of those rogue waves crash and make sure
there's a place for us to hide on the rock."

"I see a few good places. I know where
we'll be safe."

"We all know the safe places. But until
we see the big ones crash, we won't know if
they're safe anymore."

"You remember what happened to
Belén. It was a day just like this."

"Of course I remember. How could I
forget?"

"That's why it's best to wait. I don't
trust this rock."

"I don't trust it either. The rock is a trai-
tor."

Today is not yesterday. Not even
close. Yesterday, a bright, windless, warm
autumn day, the González sisters worked
this section of Zona 3 ten kilometers south
of Bayona in relative calm. They had their

choice of a stretch of rock untouched in months, allowing them to cherry-pick the biggest, fattest barnacles and leave behind the smaller ones that fetch lower prices in the afternoon auction. They did surprisingly well on the selling block, fetching about forty-five euros per kilo from a variety of buyers on a day when most of the barnacles went for thirty. That's EUR 135 pretax in each sisters' pocket—not bad for a morning's work. But when you do well in the auction, word gets out, and today, a group of fifteen *percebeiros* are already combing the coastline by the time the sun comes up. Wrapped tight in black neoprene, poking and probing with long, pointed sticks, they look like a futuristic crew cleaning up the dregs of some violent environmental fallout.

But it's not the new company that has Susana and her sisters concerned; it's the rising swells rolling in from the horizon. It's clear and unseasonably warm, but the offshore winds have picked up, and with them, the waves that come slamming into the rocks where the best barnacles live. These are exactly the kinds of conditions you have to be most afraid of, says Isabel. Everything looks beautiful and easy, but beneath the surface, something bigger may be brewing.

They've brought a wet suit for me today—like their own, shot through with holes from years of use—and together we plunge into the water and cross the narrow ocean channel to the pointed rock island peaking just above the tide. Thirty meters long and ten meters deep, it's a small space for a dozen to share.

The workplace is a constantly morphing topography. As the tide shifts, so does the assortment of peaks and valleys, cracks and crevices you have to negotiate. It takes time to learn each venue, to understand how the currents pull, how the ocean vacuums, how one surface can diffuse the oncoming crush of seawater while another can amplify it. The good *percebeiros* know every rock on this coastline. Which ones will accept their feet under any circumstance, which ones will always do their best to pitch you into the Atlantic. For the *percebeiros* of Bayona, there are forty-seven distinct venues in their territory—places like Lover's Point, with its narrow slashes of stone cutting through the water; Cow Shit, a chocolate-chip dusting of dark rocky points poking out of the white ocean froth; the Women's Rock, large and flat and sturdy as a truck bed—and it takes years, if not an entire lifetime, to understand them all.

Complicating matters, barnacles grow best where the elements—sun, rain, wind, sea—converge, which means the best places for picking are also the most treacherous: slippery surfaces; sheer rock faces; dark, hard shelves that are swallowed whole with each ocean swell. Two hours to the north, where the biggest barnacles grow, *percebeiros* hang from cliffs attached to ropes, scraping barnacles as waves smash them into the razor-edged rocks. The most important technique of *percebeiros* everywhere is the pick-and-run: to collect a handful of barnacles from the edges of the rocks as the tide ebbs, and escape before the next wave rolls in. "If you fall into the ocean and it spits you back out onto land, then you're one of the lucky ones," says Susana.

In the summer of 2014, Belén, the youngest González sister, was executing this exact maneuver when she hit a patch of seaweed and went tumbling down, falling head first onto a pointed rock that shattered her shoulder instantly. It was a perfectly normal day, sunny and blue and breezy like today, but one wrong step brought a changed life. She had a prosthetic shoulder put in place, and doctors told her she would never regain full control of her right arm. The Spanish government forced her into early retirement, and you can see in her face that sitting on the sidelines while her sisters continue the family business will be her life's greatest challenge.

The sisters start slowly, working together in a tight formation in the relative safety of the center of the island. Eventually, they fan out, working their way toward the more perilous parts where the good stuff hides. Even then, they have an ingrained system of collective vigilance, one sister watching the sea swells as the other two work with their heads down. When she sees something forming that she doesn't like, she'll give an advanced warning. As a swell picks up steam, her verbal cues grow accordingly—from forecast to suggestion to pointed demand. "Isabel, get the hell out of there now!"

The gear itself proves a persistent dilemma—finding the happy middle between something that keeps you warm and protected without restricting your movement. Susana, for example, wears a three-milimeter wet suit, even in the dead of winter when the water temperatures are near freezing, to allow for maximum mobility. And only in the most extreme conditions will the sisters put on the hoods of their wet suits, since covering your ears means eliminating one of your most valuable warning systems.

The *raspa* is the one absolutely indispensible tool of the *percebeiro*, a thick wooden stick with an iron knife at the end that allows the hunters to scrape the barnacles cleanly from the rocks. The *raspa* gets so much use that the sisters take theirs to a local sharpener for a tune-up every five days.

The thick groupings of *percebes* may look the most appealing, tucked in tight and resembling a wall of prehistoric toenails, but those go mostly untouched by the sisters. When I excitedly point out to Isabel what I think is the discovery of a cache of juicy barnacles, she quickly curbs my enthusiasm. "Those won't work. You can't pull them off with the base intact, so as soon as you pick them, they begin to lose water and wrinkle. Good *percebes* last for a week; within a day, these'll be dead."

Isabel explains that the best barnacles are short and stout, not necessarily the longest or the loveliest, but with a solid base and a generous circumference. The flavor from one barnacle to the next doesn't change dramatically, she says, what people pay for is texture. At its best, this edible appendage should snap like an ocean hot dog, releasing a flood of warm umami to the enraptured eater.

An hour into the excavation, the swells start picking up. A wave knocks one of the men onto his back before two partners pull him out of the tide. Another sweeps a man off his feet as he's trying to jump from one rock to another. I can feel my heart suddenly beating in my throat, as the imagined danger of a barnacle hunter suddenly becomes very real.

Susana looks at her watch: 10:46 a.m. Low tide today is 11:19, meaning we're in the danger zone, the thirty minutes before the ocean bottoms out, when the swells are most savage. Suddenly I look around and see that we're alone, the sisters and me, on what's left of the vanishing island.

They talk rapidly among themselves, shifting their eyes from the horizon to the coast behind us, where the others have fled for higher ground. The *gallego* they speak, with its Portuguese cadence, the pinched-cheek pronunciation that turns the hard edges of Spanish syllables into soft, rounded corners, belies the severity of the situation at hand.

Finally, Susana sees me and switches back to Spanish.

"We need to get off this rock. Now."

Try as we might, we cannot tame the ocean. Over thousands of years of evolu-tion, we've learned to subdue nearly every other part of nature: leveling forests, damming rivers, dynamiting mountains down to molehills. Converting patches of inhospitable desert sands into spectacular oases of sin. But no amount of determination or technology or accumulated understanding can weaken the ocean's resolve.

It's not for lack of trying. Trapped in its tides is the answer to our most pressing questions, an inexhaustible supply of energy this planet will need to survive. We flirt constantly with its potential; there's a reason why the world's most dangerous jobs—from king crab fishing to underwater welding to barnacle hunting—take place in or on the ocean. In Spain, in Galicia above all, people refer to the ocean in two ways: *el mar or la mar*. Masculine and feminine. One gives us life, the other takes it away. It's up to you to decide which is which.

The danger of the barnacle hunter is the knowledge that even the slightest edge—a learned intuition, a measured bravery, an extra bit of resistance in the legs—means a better life for you and yours. For them, the ocean is both an open invitation and a standing threat. Ask Susana about the most important skill in a *percebeiro*'s tool kit and she won't hesitate: respect. Deny the ocean the respect it demands and it will drag it out of you, one way or another.

Just ask the plump octopus fisherman trembling on the rocks.

As we vacate our vanishing island, swim back across the water in between swells, drag ourselves onto higher, dryer ground, he stands stubbornly on the edge of the rocks, his long bamboo stick probing beneath the water. One of the women warns him about the waves, but he tells her to leave him alone.

Twenty minutes later, after the González sisters drag his trembling body from the ocean and leave him in the hands of his pan-icked wife and a group of paramedics, they are back on the rocks, scraping up a living.

Only when they hit their quota do they relax. Isabel grabs a sea urchin, cracks it open, scoops out its soft orange innards and eats it with her fingers, seasoned with nothing but seawater. She passes one to Susana, another to me.

"People ask me if I ever think of finding a different profession," says Isabel, picking through her bag of barnacles, doing rough calculations of what she might expect to fetch at today's auction. "Are you kidding me? You think I want to work at a desk? This is my office: the ocean, the coastline. I'm out in the open air, the wind in my face, my sisters by my side. What could be better than this?"

"The first thing we do when leaving the water is call

The Majesty of Spanish
CONSERVAS

Northern Spain reserves its most pristine seafood for canning, turning *conservas* into one of the most popular and extravagant delicacies in this seafood-obsessed country.

 **MEJILLONES EN ESCABECHE**
Marinated mussels

 **ERIZOS DE MAR AL NATURAL**
Sea urchin in water

01 SARDINILLAS EN ACEITE
Olive oil–packed sardines

02 VENTRESCA EN ACEITE
Olive oil–packed tuna belly

05 ALMEJAS AL NATURAL
White clams in water

06 SARDINILLAS EN ESCABECHE
Marinated sardines

PEOPLE

ESPERANZA FUENTE MUÑOZ
*Churro maker, Huéscar,
Andalusia*

—

"Business is booming. With
the financial crisis, more
people eat breakfast out than
lunch or dinner. It's more
accesible."

EDUARDO MIGUEL IGLESIAS
*Sanitation worker,
Bilbao*

—

"The kids drink in the plazas
on the weekend and totally
trash them. But I don't mind
cleaning up. I used to trash
these same plazas."

OF SPAIN

ARMANDO JALEO
Owner, Bodega Armando,
Barcelona

—

"I work here sixteen hours a
day. I need to look for a woman.
Or maybe a rich man. Anybody
to give me a break."

ALEJANDRO MONTES
Cheese shop owner,
Vigo, Galicia

—

"Every cheese has a personal
history that it tells through
its flavor. Selling artisanal
cheese is first and foremost
an education."

ANATOMY
of a dish

PULPO A

OCTO-VORES

Spaniards consume more cephalopods than anyone in the world, thanks in large part to Galicia, where *pulperias*, dedicated octopus restaurants, take advantage of the nearly eight million pounds of octopus pulled from the Spanish Atlantic each year.

FIGHTING THE FIBERS

Octopus cooks the world over have long been vexed by one dilemma: how to make it tender. The traditional Galician tactic is to "scare" it three times: lowering the octopus into a copper pot for fifteen seconds each round. Only then is it ready to cook.

LA GALLEGA

FAIR FOOD

This dish, one of the most beloved and ubiquitous in all of Spain, was developed around the cattle fairs of Galicia in the nineteenth century (hence the alternative name: *pulpo a la feria*). Curiously, the inland areas of Ourense and Lugo are ground zero for *pulpo* culture.

THE *GALLEGO* WAY

The octopus is cooked until just tender, then served atop boiled skin-on *cachelos* (the famous *gallego* potatoes), and dressed with olive oil, spicy paprika, and coarse salt. Legend has it that drinking water makes the octopus expand, so the *gallegos* eat octopus with young red wine.

Chapter Eight

MADRID

When I travel to a city, I come with two simple objectives: to walk a lot and to eat a lot, goals with a certain symbiotic kinship. I've dedicated many days to doing both in Madrid: as a cerveza-soaked teenager first on the loose in Spain, as a young journalist eating elaborate feasts of fish and fowl on someone else's dime, as a new husband looking for nothing more than a weekend of memories with my Spanish bride. The longer I spend in the capital, the more I come to realize: Madrid isn't a place you want to take sitting down.

Hemingway had it wrong: He spent most of his time here holed up in Sobrino de Botín, where Jake and Brett sought refuge in the final pages of the *The Sun Also Rises*, bathing himself and his loyalists in wine and nostalgia for hours at a time, saving the peripatetic pleasures for the cafés of Paris. Now more than ever, Madrid is a movable feast.

And Madrid looks pretty damn good when it moves; it would give Milan a run for its money as the world's best-dressed city. Walk the streets midday and find yourself in a sea of soft fabrics and custom-cut suits that conform to Spanish bodies in ways they will never conform to yours or mine—an animate expression of the word you most often hear other Spaniards use to describe Madrid: *señorial*. Stately,

273

like those wide avenues and smooth stone columns; regal, like the gold trim and the horse-and-chariot fountains. Those Italian loafers look good beneath the red and gold of the Spanish flag; that confident step, the one that leads with the chest, marches perfectly to the rhythm of the capital's traffic.

Don't be fooled by the good looks and svelte figures—these suits eat more, drink better, and stay out later than the rest of Spain. You'd be wise to follow them. If you do, you're likely to end up in Ibiza, in a few-block section just to the northwest of Retiro Park known for the density of its quality, polished restaurants and tapas bars.

One o'clock is the *hora de aperitivo*, the warm-up ritual observed by the better part of Madrid's workforce—a bridge between the grind of the morning and the slow pleasures of lunch ahead. Any good wolf pack of suits will start with a *caña*—say at Arzábal, where a well-poured beer (does anybody in Spain know how to pour a beer better than a *madrileño?*) and a plate of anchovies from Cantabria make for a bracing transition to the more serious eating that lies ahead.

Laredo is where the well-heeled form like Voltron Vutton—a loud, lively mass united by their dedication to good food and navy blue. Men with ties slung over their shoulders excavate the protein from mountains of shellfish; groups of stunning women—who may or may not be returning to work, depending on whether Rosio orders a glass or a bottle—nibble on the ribs of rabbits, fried and dipped into puddles of aioli.

I survey the room and have what everyone else is having. The *salmorejo*, the satiny orange union of blended tomato and fruity olive oil, thickened with bread and garlic, further proves that Spain is the king of cold soups. A loose scramble of blood sausage and baby fava beans—sweet and funky with a gentle undertow of iron. And the star of the bar: fried shrimp and asparagus bound in a cloak of Japanese mayonnaise, a plate nestled on every table I see (two next to Rosio and her crew, now on their second bottle of Albariño).

A few blocks down on Calle Ibiza, you'll find one of the newer kids on the block, Taberna Pedraza, owned by Santiago and Josefina Pedraza—husband works the floor while wife holds down the kitchen. If Madrid is a quilt of regional Spanish food culture, Taberna Pedraza is where it all comes together.

The couple both lost their jobs during Spain's economic downturn and decided to bend the crisis into an opportunity. They spent a year traveling around the country, eating their way deeper into the DNA of Spain's regional cuisine. They ate *fabadas* and cava-aged cheeses in Asturias, fried fish and stuffed mussels in Cádiz, *migas* and acorn ham in Extremadura. Taberna Pedraza presents the diner with the greatest hits of their travels—not just the recipes, but the ingredients they found along the way: the thin, lightly spiced *chistorra* of Lasarte, the poetic olive oil of Casas de Hualdo, the finest I've tasted.

The *croquetas* have earned a dedicated following around town (they won best in the city at Madrid Fusion in 2014): a shattering crust just barely contains a lava flow of béchamel that tastes like a *jamón* milkshake. Some say the *tortilla* is even more of a category killer, made with eggs from pampered hens and thinly sliced Galician potatoes that Josefina fries to order in individual batches. As if she was making a good French omelet, she works the eggs over a low flame, and it arrives to the table soft and pale, jiggling like a waterbed; slice into it and it exhales across the plate. (So popular is the *tortilla* that a ticker counts off the number ordered since the restaurant's inception; mine, number 11,421, is a fine specimen, if not a little shy with the salt.)

"The more history you have, the less liberty you have to play," Santiago tells me. "We have better products, better techniques. If we can improve a classic recipe in a meaningful way, why wouldn't we?"

Move down the menu and move across the peninsula: boiled artichokes peeled open like blossoming flowers and drizzled with olive oil, *tigres*, mussels stuffed with *sofrito* and a prick of spicy smoked paprika, funky aged beef from Galicia kissed on the *plancha* and served black and blue. And back to Madrid with a plate of *callos*, the offal obsession of the capital. Finish in Cantabria with *quesada pasiega*, the preco-

Santiago Pedraza, slicing tortilla number 11,421.

cious love child of flan and cheesecake, a wish that all Spanish meals ended along the northern coast.

Everywhere you eat and drink in this part of town will leave you wondering if the guy on the stool next to you shoots elephants with the king. Another day takes me to Ave, a restaurant dedicated to creatures of flight. The food is fine, but the clientele is better. I run into the cabinet of the Real Academia de Gastronomía, a distinguished body of men and women whose official charge is to "positively influence the gastronomic offer of Spain and improve the quality of life of Spaniards." The median age of today's crew hovers somewhere north of the Warren Buffett neighborhood. Some wear suits with the group's emblem emblazoned on the right breast.

We exchange business cards like a Japanese boardroom, stopping to admire each other's rank and purpose. The oldest in the group, Pedro Aznar, presses a card into my palm with a number scribbled on the back.

"Here you go, young man. That's my personal number. Anytime you're near Logroño, you're welcome to stay and drink with me." Later, I discover he owns Marqués de Riscal, one of Spain's largest wineries, and the accompanying hotel, designed by Frank Gehry. I put the card in a safe place.

Say what you want about the affectations of a governing body of gastronomy, these guys know how to eat better than you and me combined. They leave me with a list of first-rate bars and restaurants that I work my way through over the coming days, until I'm ready to pledge my allegiance to this august gathering of gastrocrats.

My favorite place on the list is Asturianos, an unsuspecting restaurant in Vallehermoso serving superlative versions of Asturias's soul-soothing cuisine: plump sardines swimming in an emerald stream of olive oil, golden nuggets of potatoes bathed in a sharp Cabrales cheese sauce, *fabada*, the iconic pork and white bean stew, that would make an Asturian coal miner weep.

I eat here with Victor de la Serna, an old-school scribe with a big appetite, strong opinions, and a crop of loyal readers who feed off of both. He forms part of a tradition of writers—critics, essayists, reporters, novelists—who have played an outsize role in shaping the culinary landscape of Spain. With biting critiques and challenging think pieces and stirring love letters, guys like Néstor Luján, Josep Pla, and Manuel Vázquez Montalbán—and Victor—imbued cuisine with an academic and cultural gravity, laying the foundation for generations of thoughtful cooks and eaters.

Born in Cantabria, Victor has been writing about food and wine in the capital for the past fifty years. "Madrid, more than anything, is a collection of regions. This is the city that migration built, one that attracted the Galicians and Andalusians and Asturians." What do immigrants do when they come to a new land? They open restaurants.

As I drop the last sardine in my mouth like a cartoon cat, the chef, doña Julia Bombín, comes out of the kitchen to ask how much more we're prepared to eat. We tell her that we have a long night of eating in front of us, but she won't let us leave before

tasting her *arroz con leche*—tender rice cloaked in Asturian cream and crowned with cinnamon and caramelized sugar, so staggeringly delicious I am tempted to cancel my other eating plans and pitch a tent in the dining room.

As we knife through the backstreets of Malasaña and Chueca on our way to the next destination, Victor finds something to celebrate on every block. "They have the best *pescaito* you can imagine here. Better than the fry joints in Cádiz. . . . I wish we had time to try this Galician restaurant. Incredible seafood. . . . My sources tell me this new Murcian place is doing fine work."

In the hands of a guy like Victor, you get the sense that the feast in Madrid knows no bounds. You could happily spend a lifetime eating your way around Spain without ever leaving the capital, Victor insists, and in many cases, doing so better here than you would on native terrain. But I am not after the flavors of Spain at large; I want the pure taste of Madrid, and Victor knows where to find it. Tomorrow, we will not eat *marmitako* from Bilbao or *migas* from

Cáceres or *arroz negro* from Alicante, but the one dish that represents Madrid and its cuisine better than any other.

"Spain is the strongest country in the world. Century after century trying to destroy herself and still no success." Keep in mind that Otto von Bismarck, the engineer of a unified Germany, said this in the late nineteenth century, more than fifty years before the Spanish Civil War and the decades of internal turmoil and national soul-searching that followed.

Even in the nineteenth century, though, Spain had more than 1,500 years of internal strife behind it. The Visigoths versus the Moors. Catholics versus Moors. Catholics versus Jews. Catholics versus everyone, including themselves. The Reconquista, the Inquisition, the Civil War: in some form or another, all involved one group of Spaniards violently questioning the legitimacy of another.

The subtext behind the constant infighting, political maneuvering, and at times naked violence employed by the various factions vying for supremacy was the same question Italy, France, Greece, and others across the Mediterranean were struggling to answer: What makes a country? A political decree and a national army? Shared language and culture? A collection of lines on a map?

In 1469, Isabella of Castile married Ferdinand of Aragon, thus uniting the two largest and most contentious factions of Christians on the Iberian Peninsula. Together, in 1492, they drove the Moors from Granada, ending 781 years of Islamic rule and uniting Spain as one country for the first time. The Catholic monarchs went on the march, undertaking two hundred years of empire-building at a breadth and scope the world had never seen. Columbus cracked open the New World for the Spanish crown, and two men from a dusty corner of Extremadura in western Spain gathered their horses and their men and crossed the Atlantic in search of gold and glory.

What followed were two of the most impossible stories of empire expansion in human history. Hernán Cortés, with a crew of 500 men and a plague of European diseases riding shotgun, toppled the Aztec empire, one of the largest and most sophisticated civilizations of its age. Inspired by his distant cousin's success, Francisco Pizarro set sail to Peru in 1531 with 180 men and 27 horses and, over the next few years, brought the two-million-strong Incan empire to its knees. With the spoils of the New World, the Spanish crown had the resources needed to expand its empire across Europe and into Africa and Asia. Three hundred years before British rule reached its peak, the sun never set on the Spanish empire.

The Siglo de Oro, Spain's golden age, wasn't just about territorial expansion, but a flourishing of art, literature, music, and architecture that would dramatically reshape intellectual thought around Europe and beyond. These were the years Cervantes and Lope de Vega transformed literature and drama, when Velázquez and El Greco developed a new language on the canvas. But for all the remarkable political and intellectual achievements of the Siglo de Oro, it failed to create a coherent vision for a unified country.

Over the seventeenth and eighteenth centuries, Spain lost its territories to revolts, piracy, military defeats, and fractured internal politics. By the time King Amadeus of the House of Savoy was tasked with uniting the country in 1870, he proclaimed the people of Spain ungovernable and beat a trail across the Mediterranean to Italy.

Today, a not-insignificant part of Spain would rather not be a part of Spain at all. The Basque separatist campaign dates back to the late nineteenth century, fomented in the wake of the Carlist Wars. By the 1950s, the most extreme faction of nationalists began to wage war on central Spain, a campaign that resulted in a red tide of car bombings, kidnappings, and political assassinations. ETA's reign of terror subsided at the dawn of the twenty-first century, even if the Basque dream of secession has not.

Catalunya has been trying to escape this country since 1714, the year it became part of it. Catalans have always viewed themselves as an independent body, with their own language, culture, and national identity. In recent years, with the residue of Franco finally dissipating and the collapse of Spain's economy exposing a new set of regional grievances, that belief has taken on a new momentum. The forceful Catalan campaign, based not on violence, but on popular uprising and savvy political maneuvering, has positioned the region a few steps from independence. (At this rate, I could be living in a separate country by the time you read this book.)

But it's not just the two most visible separatists that dream of independence. In Galicia, the *gallegos* still have their own language, their own cuisine, their own temperament. You'll find pockets of radical independent factions scattered throughout Asturias, as I did one morning at 2:00 a.m. in Avilés, when a local friend pinned an Asturian flag to my jacket before we walked into a bar: "Trust me, we need these to drink here." Even Andalusia—home to so many of the toasted brown stereotypes of

Spanish culture—has its strains of nationalism; southern factions have been trying to separate from Spain on and off since the Duke of Medina Sidonia attempted secession in 1641.

So what holds this nation of nations together? King and constitution? Catholicism and *castellano*? Perhaps, but they do little to explain what it means to be a Spaniard—to live and eat and drink like a Spaniard. More than anything, it might be food that connects the disparate peoples of this country in some meaningful way: a common pantry, a shared palate, a handful of emblematic dishes that surface in bars, restaurants, and markets across the country. *Tortilla*, gazpacho, paella—these may be the country's most famous culinary creations, but if one dish represents a centralized Spain, a Spain connected by history, culture, and circumstance, it is *cocido*.

Cocido started off as a Jewish dish dating back to the Middle Ages, known then as *olla podrida*—a collection of meat, beans, and vegetables gathered in a clay pot on Friday nights and left to simmer in the embers of the fire for eating on the Sabbath. When Catholics reclaimed the country, pork went into the pot, an edible litmus of sorts to test your allegiance to the Holy Roman Emperor. If your stew didn't have swine, then you must have been a Jew or a Muslim in disguise.

Like the other great peasant stews of Europe—pot-au-feu from southern France, *bollito misto* from central Italy—*cocido* is a simmering pot of necessity, crisis turned into opportunity through patience and ingenuity. What Néstor Luján called "the peak of the cuisine of evaporation." None less than Sancho Panza, one of the world's great fictional gastronomes, was an avowed enthusiast: "This great steaming plate that I believe to be *olla podrida*, because of the diversity of things it contains, I won't stop bumping into ones that I like."

Cocido madrileño, with its garbanzo base and mixture of pork, chicken, and beef, is the mother of all *cocidos*, but every region of Spain has its version. In Murcia, the garden of Spain, *cocido* comes filled with plant matter. Asturians replace garbanzos with fat white beans in their smoky, pork-heavy *fabadas*. In Catalunya, *escudella i carn d'olla* unites meat and vegetables and a giant *pilota*, a meatball made from ground pork, breadcrumbs, and egg. The *puchero valenciano, bullit mallorquín, berza gitana, cocido montañés*—the list goes on and on. "If there's a meeting place for Spanish cuisine, it's *cocido*," Victor de la Serna tells me.

Many *madrileños* insist that *cocido* needs to be eaten at home—like our family friend Rosa, who has been making the same fantastic version for forty years, and who carries gallons of Madrid water to make *cocido* whenever she travels. But you'll find restaurants across Madrid serving up perfectly solid versions of the staple, especially on Wednesdays, *cocido* day in the capital.

For the best *cocido*, though, you'll need to travel outside the city, to El Escorial, the great granite monastery and royal retreat erected by Philip II in the seventeenth century, tucked into the foot of the Sierra de Guadarrama. There, a few blocks from the magnificent stone structure, you'll find Charolés, opened in 1977 by the Minguez family.

Cocido comes in three stages, called *vuelcos*, a staggered meal meant to stretch the bounty of boiled meat and vegetables and the very limits of human digestion across a few hours of exaggerated feasting. Things begin innocently enough; the first pass, like a good bouillabaisse, is simply a bowl of the *caldo*, the rich, complex cooking liquid, usually with a drift of short noodles floating on the surface. In the second *vuelco* comes the ostensible star, the garbanzos, cut from the mesh sack they're simmered in and drizzled with olive oil. Unless you live in the Middle East, and even if you do, these are likely to be the best garbanzos you'll ever eat. And finally, the third *vuelco*: the meat from the simmering cauldron.

That's the basic blueprint, but Charolés takes the whole production to ludicrous extremes: stewing hen from Santa María; plates of bone marrow with tiny spoons for excavating the semi-solid innards; two types of *tocino*, back fat so rich and luscious it eats like goose liver; pink chunks of salted ham; snappy red coils of smoky chorizo; muted brown beef ribs meant to be played like harmonicas.

Along with the protein procession comes a tour of the garden: boiled Galician potatoes dressed with olive oil, stewed cabbage lashed with smoked paprika, spinach and chard studded with chunks of *jamón*, whole simmered carrots that owner Manuel Minguez assures us have been out of the ground for less than forty-eight hours. By the time the tuxedoed servers nestle the last plate onto our enormous table, there is not a square of visible tablecloth remaining.

Minguez, justifiably proud of his restaurant's Herculean creation, comes out frequently to offer us new parts of beasts plumbed from the depths of the pot. He straightens his suit and tie, rubs his hands like a traveling salesman, asks if we might like to hear a story—about the provenance of the pork, the secret to the garbanzos, the history of the bowl itself.

"I come from a humble family and we ate *cocido* every day growing up—not this *cocido* you're eating, but one with a few garbanzos, a bit of chorizo, maybe a piece of hen." You'll hear that same sentiment echoed from the older generation across Spain—*cocido* being less of a recipe and more a manner of making the most of what you had on hand. Once upon a time, when Spain was starving, owls, eagles, and rats found their way into *cocido*.

"It used to be a serious plate, an important plate, the kind of meal you ate once or twice a week," says Victor, wistfully. "Now with the modern diets, it's no longer the same. It's a niche plate. Maybe eight or ten good places in Madrid still serve it."

Chief among restaurants still dedicated to *cocido* is Lhardy, located a few steps from the Plaza del Sol.

Ask a *madrileño* where to eat a good *cocido* in the city and odds are they'll say Lhardy. By some accounts, Lhardy was Spain's first fine dining restaurant, in operation since 1847. Milagros Novo, the great-granddaughter of Emilio Lhardy, the restaurant's founder, makes a lovely hostess. Before lunch, she shows me the rooms where heads of state dine, the favorite tables of kings and kingmakers. The wooden floors groan with history. "This was the only place the queen could eat—either the palace or Lhardy's. Since then, it's been a meeting place for the most important artists and politicians of Madrid."

Beyond *cocido*, people come here to eat Madrid's other most iconic dish: *callos*, tripe simmered into submission with aromatics and chunks of chorizo and blood sausage, a potent bowl of texture and substance that dates back to the late sixteenth century. Both *cocido* and *callos* have been humble cuisine for most of their history—of cuts sold cheap and worked long and slow until they give up the ghost and take on some other incarnation. The story has it that the founder's son used to bring his Bohemian friends to eat at Lhardy's, and they introduced *callos* and *cocido* as soul food for the free thinkers of old Madrid. "The bohemians are always hungry," says Milagros.

Something of the soul-warming essence is lost in the pageantry. Men in suits are fed by men in suits who serve soup from silver chaffing dishes. It feels like eating lunch in the Prado. The *cocido* is a perfectly fine

Tuxedoed *cocido* service at Lhardy, Spain's oldest fine-dining restaurant.

specimen: the quality of the individual components—from the lighter broth to the less-precisely cooked proteins—can't compare with Charolés, but it gets the message across forcefully enough. Surrounded by suits and suit pants, it's impossible to imagine that anybody eating here has afternoon ambitions. After a bowl of tripe, a three-course *cocido*, and Lhardy's take on a baked Alaska, I barely have the strength to make it back to bed.

Lhardy doesn't fit in the way it once did. It feels like a character from a Goya painting wandered off the canvas and is looking for his place in a city he no longer recognizes. "My son told me we should go for something a little more minimalist," says Milagros. "I just about died."

This is old Madrid, *la España castiza*, ripe with history and majesty—the culinary equivalent of Neptune fountains and royal portraits—and long may it live.

🐑 🐂 🐖

Sacha Hormaechea is short and spacious, with a wide nose and salt-and-pepper hair that long ago migrated from his head to his cheeks and chin. He speaks with a soft but commanding voice, filled with delicate details and tantalizing turns of phrase—the poet laureate of the Madrid kitchen.

In a way, Sacha's story is the story of Madrid: His father, Carlos Hormaechea, was Basque, his wife, Pitila, Galician. They opened a restaurant in the northern part of the city, just beyond the Bernabéu soccer stadium, in 1972, and named it after their son. Over the years, Sacha developed a reputation for serving simple but sophisticated fair to a mix of politicians, thinkers, writers, and artists.

If Lhardy is old Madrid, Sacha is middle-aged Madrid—mature, self-assured, equal parts classic and contemporary.

Sacha took over the restaurant in 1996 and has created a rare species of supper club, with old paintings on the walls and flickering candles at the tables. Madrid's elite feel at home here, as do off-duty chefs—precisely because Sacha cooks the kind of food he himself loves to eat. When I ate here years ago with a crew of international chefs, Morgan Freeman and a Spanish film director sat across from us, chewing on steaks. We ate a wild mushroom tortilla that seemed to melt onto the plate, a pile of briny-sweet sea urchins, and a microwaved potato that years later I still talk about every few weeks.

I catch Sacha outside before service on a warm spring day and he offers me a fishbowl gin tonic. His reservoir of knowledge for Madrid is deep and his mind is restless, so conversations turn into slow-migrating monologues, as if he were playing a game of telephone with himself.

"Madrid is an island of lambs. It's totally absurd. You have a city built on a mesa with nothing but lamb grazing around, and inside you have the second largest fish market in the world. We auction off a greater variety of seafood than anyone else in the world. You won't find a barrio in Madrid without shrimp, without barnacles."

Catalans and Basques have a reputation for regional chauvinism, but *madrileños* know a thing or two about pride too. "The most important thing to know is that be-sides San Sebastián, Madrid is the best place to eat in all of Spain—thanks to the migrants, who have brought all of the best of Spanish food together in one place."

In Sacha you will find a flood of fascinating table talk—that the original sauce for *patatas bravas*, Spain's most famous fried potatoes, comes from the leftover cooking liquid from *cocido*, that there were no kitchens in the Alhambra, that the concept of clandestine restaurants was born in Madrid during the time of Cervantes. Occasionally, the man goes overboard, like when he calls the *pepita de ternera*, the *madrileño* steak sandwich, the greatest sandwich in the world. But all the great ones go overboard, because that is how they show the world how much they care.

At the table, though, there is no questioning Sacha's taste. First, a single lightly cooked red shrimp, head separated from the body and placed beside a granite mortar filled with roasted garlic, grassy olive oil, and a battery of leafy herbs. Sacha instructs us to squeeze the shrimp head, extracting its brains into the mortar, then use the tail

287

meat to stir it all together and eat. Genius.

Next, a spring gazpacho made from wild asparagus, radish, and dill, a complex convergence of bittersweet notes and soft and snappy textures—a bracing reminder that gazpacho is an idea, not a recipe. Sea cucumber can be an expensive mistake in most hands, but Sacha's team teases from it a supple elegance that makes you question if you've ever truly tasted it before. For dessert, a jiggling cylinder of *tocino del cielo*, basically a pork flan, a totem of Spain to slide your spoon into.

There's a strange comfort in the restaurant's confidence: The server might not have a clue what went into the dish, but he'll stir you the coldest fucking martini of your life, the kind where a thin shelf of ice forms on the surface. I'm told by some that not everyone is treated the same here, that important *madrileños* are the ones being feted with table-side truffles and regaled with stories of the city's underbelly. If Madrid had a mafia, they might find a fitting home in a low-lit corner of Sacha, working over a femur of bone marrow.

After dinner, we sit around drinking mezcal with a group of young actors and academics—the kind of scene Vargas Llosa might paint with his pen. There is no shortage of intellect or opinion among them, but we are in Sacha's house; he pours the liquor, he sets the table. As the agave takes gentle hold, he returns to Spain's Siglo de Oro.

"What we've never done well is we've never explained to the world that it all began here: Pizarro brought the first tomato plant to the port of Vigo. Ceviche wouldn't exist without lemon. Fish and chips don't exist if we don't bring back the potato. After Spain, you didn't need to go out looking for spices. We were the ones who changed the history of the world."

If much of Madrid seems content to celebrate the glories of the past, others occupy themselves with the triumphs of the future. David Muñoz is the apostle of New Madrid, sent down from the heavens to give the finger to conformity and rescue Madrid from the long shadow cast by the more famous kitchens to the north.

Dubbed an enfant terrible by the Spanish press, his Mohawk, his model wife, and his fuck-'em-all attitude form a vital component of his personal brand. He has a penchant for picking fights with culinary heavyweights both here and abroad. In this way, Muñoz has positioned himself as the wunderkind outsider in a world too rigid to understand his brand of radicalism.

Muñoz comes from humble roots. Born in 1980 in a working-class barrio of Madrid, he took to the kitchen at a young age; some of his earliest culinary adventures include baking squid and seaweed cakes in the microwave. After years cooking high-end Asian food in London, he returned to Madrid to open DiverXO in 2007, and quickly gained a following for his brash style and discordant combinations. By 2010, it had its first Michelin star; two years later came the second. When Michelin anointed DiverXO as Spain's newest three-star restaurant in 2013, the country went nuts. Yes, there were already seven gods and goddesses atop Mount Michelin, but all but one resided in Catalunya and

the Basque Country. The Basques had the Arzaks and Andoni, the Catalans had the Adriàs and the Rocas. In Muñoz, Madrid finally had its homegrown hero. (A hero with a powerful sidekick; in 2015 he married Cristina Pedroche, a television personality whose fame in households across Spain dwarfs her husband's.)

With all of this in mind, I sat down to dinner at DiverXO with trembling anticipation—ready to taste the latest iteration of the Spanish revolution. The restaurant announces its ambitions to disrupt at the doorway: spinning circles of psychedelia, black butterflies fluttering on the wall, and everywhere, the famous flying pigs that Muñoz has chosen as his spirit animal. Servers wear monochrome jumpsuits, a cross between a posse of break-dancers and a chocolate factory of Oompa Loompas.

On the plate, Muñoz deploys flavors that haven't commonly been harnessed at the upper echelons of Spanish fine dining: miso, chilies, hoisin, XO sauce. On the fork, he concentrates energy like a black hole: a corn and lychee soup that will make you question whether you've ever tasted either before, duck hearts wearing a cloak of warm Indian spices that override your brainwaves like a hallucinogen, or a play on pad thai that will make you forget the millions of mediocre Asian fusion dishes clogging up the world's fancy restaurants. The so-called show reads stronger as an aesthetic and an attitude than as groundbreaking cooking, but it's still outrageously delicious.

DiverXO remains the most difficult reservation in Spain, but Muñoz has taken his brand of audacious dining to the top floor of an El Corte Inglés department store. This is an area more in need of a shake-up in Spain: the midlevel restaurant. Not just modern tapas bars, which grow on olive trees in these parts, but casual, outward-looking, well-priced restaurants that take their food more seriously than they take themselves. And that's exactly what StreetXO is: loud, arresting, the kitchen a kinetic mass of cooks grilling proteins, wok-frying noodles and plating dishes with a street fighter's intensity. If

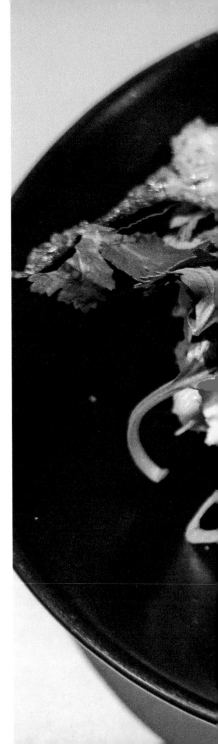

David Muñoz's food concentrates energy like a black hole. Here, Street XO's club sandwich.

the team—rocking the tattoo/bandanna/ scowl uniform of the modern line cook— has inherited the swagger of its leader, they channel most of it onto the plate. The "club sandwich"—a soft, saucy amalgam of pork jowl, shrimp paste, and quail egg—detonates across the palate in waves of sugar, salt, and fat. Pork dumplings come enhanced by the sweetness of strawberry hoisin, the funk and crunch of braised pig ears, and the explosive visuals of a Pollock plating. It's stoner food with a PhD.

From my perch at the bar, I watch a rotating cast of chefs assemble the famous Korean lasagna: an Asian-inflected ragù made with forty-five-day-aged Galician ox, layered over sheets of pasta, and goosed with a cardamom-spiked béchamel, kimchitomato puree, and coconut powder. (They call it Korean, but I count at least six flags planted on the plate.) One sweaty chef in a bandanna turns it into an MMA demonstration, arm-barring and hammerfisting his way through the saucy mass. The young Asian woman who takes over uses tight, precise movements to build this geologic pasta

invention, more sculpture than collision. It's the kind of counter spectacle I want in every restaurant. A flotilla of effervescent, citrus-forward cocktails perfectly matched for the occasion makes the food and the scene down all the easier.

StreetXO is an important restaurant in Spain, reinforcing a decade-long groundswell of international restaurants to hit the capital: Punto MX, Kabuki, Soy Kitchen. You won't find this diversity of riches anywhere in the country, not even cosmopolitan Barcelona. If you want good Thai or Chinese or KoreViet-JapaMexi, you come to the capital.

🐖 🍶 🐷

Sometimes Old Madrid and New Madrid make surprisingly good bedfellows—like the tangle of businessmen I spot drinking jalapeño-infused gin tonics at 4:00 p.m. on a Friday at Macera, a beautiful new cocktail lab in Malasaña where Narciso Bermejo infuses hundreds of spirits with flavors of the season—wild fennel, chestnut, asparagus. Taken by the owner's artistry and hospitality, the group vows not to leave until they've tried the entire fall lineup.

Other times, strange things can happen when the two worlds combine. One afternoon, I find myself in a windowless locker room with the chef José Andrés and eleven men (and one woman), captains of industry gathered to discuss a business deal that could alter the fate of the free world. One of the suits, a sharp and serious eater who takes great pride in his insider knowledge of Madrid's sprawling culinary scene, has invited us to the Academia del Despiece, "one of the hottest new places in Madrid. It's going to blow your mind."

Javier Bonet, the son of Mallorcan butchers, earned a name for himself at the Sala de Despiece next door, a long marble bar with a reputation for fool]d that strikes the right balance between pleasure and playfulness. The Academia is the next iteration of the Despiece, a three-hour interactive meal served to a single group of diners.

"Chefs from Madrid used to go to Barcelona to look for inspiration," Bonet tells me, behind him a chalkboard with formulations for mysterious infusions and extractions. "Now it's the other way around.

For the past three or four years, the young chefs in Madrid have been driving the creative conversation in Spain."

Apparently, that conversation involves uniforms for the diner. Staff pass out rubber aprons for us to wear, and the suits begrudgingly slip them over their Massimo Dutti jackets. Bonet tells us to surrender our cell phones and personal belongings in little safes before entering the dining room. The room tenses up. People look at the boss man. "Why would we do that?" he asks, mildly annoyed. José, sensing mutiny, drops his phone into the safe. "¡*Vámonos!*"

We sit at a single long white table in a room made to look like the inside of a meat locker. Everyone is given a set of tools: knives, spatula, metal chopsticks, a mini kitchen torch. The concept starts to take shape: The *sala de despiece* is the room where animals are butchered, and we are now temporarily enrolled as students in the academy.

Before each course, the lights dim, sounds come pumped in from hidden speakers, and instructional videos are projected onto the table. Students must use their tools and their wits to add the finishing touches to the day's dishes—sometimes it's as simple as adding clipped herbs to a vegetable composition, other dishes require more finesse, like toasting a scallop "marshmallow" over an open fire.

Somewhere near course three of twelve, the suits start to stir.

"I didn't know I was going to have to kill my own lunch."

"It's just not comfortable."

"Would it kill them to put a couple of pillows out?"

"We can't talk. You can only talk about the food."

"I love to eat, but I don't want to talk about food for three hours."

Everything is meant to be interactive, expansive, genre-bending, but the food falls short—underseasoned, mismatched flavors, a puzzling progression of dishes. Bonet's creative drive is hugely admirable, but the shortcomings reflect a larger problem in post-Bulli Spain, one where the rabid search for culinary innovation often outweighs the objective to serve paying customers delicious food in a comfortable setting. You can only eat so many spherified *tortillas* and deconstructed *patatas bravas* before you pine for the real thing.

Ferran and Albert Adrià's pioneering work at El Bulli freed Spanish chefs from the shackles of tradition and the formalities of haute cuisine, but it also created an arms race of innovation that doesn't always make for great dining. Chefs do R&D in laboratories and forge esoteric interdisciplinary collaborations—with structural engineers and marine scientists and Parisian perfumists—and share the discoveries ad nauseam at culinary conferences around the country.

Sometimes the results are stunning, but often they can be punishing. At Sublimotion in Ibiza, Paco Roncero charges diners $1,800 per person for a theatrical meal filled with holograms and self-mixing cocktails—a dinner which he has called "the cheapest life-changing experience anyone can have." This type of attitude has long threatened certain unhinged strains of Spanish gastronomy. Serving seafood on top of an iPad with a loop of the ocean playing isn't innovative; piping in music of rustling leaves while you eat some autumnal composition doesn't make the squash soufflé taste more like squash. You can't eat smoke and mirrors.

As the chef at Lhardy told me as we discussed my eating itinerary: "You have young chefs leaving culinary school playing with siphons and nitrogen and they can't even cook lentils."

Dessert arrives for the disgruntled students: a painter's palette of matcha tea powder, Pop Rocks, fruity sauces. The room perks up. Soon cuff links clank and ties swing as the class excitedly paints, sculpts, and shapes edible works of art. And right before we are about to devour our creations, we are instructed to pass our plates to the left. The whole room sighs in unison.

You can feast for hours at a single table in Madrid and linger over coffee and *digestivos* until the sun goes down and rises again, but I always come back to that same formula: walking and eating, movement to maximize the feast for all the senses. And the more I move about Madrid, the more I begin to see it not as a sprawling metropolis but as one endless pastiche of pueblos.

In Chueca, Madrid's gay district, bearded bears drink wine and listen to jazz in cozy cafés. Next door, in hip Malasaña, the wine is traded for Negronis, the Coltrane for Kendrick Lamar, the soft pillows for distressed folding chairs. The upwardly mobile slurp oysters and champagne at the stands of the San Miguel market; the downtrodden take shelter in Vallecas and Villaverde, the outskirts of the city where a beer still buys you a free bite. Occasionally these frames in the comic strip of Madrid converge, like on Sundays at El Rastro, where princes and prostitutes and the penniless pluck what they can from Spain's largest flea market. (Beyond *cocido*, maybe it's the love of a bargain that binds Spain most convincingly.)

Maybe that's been my problem all along—looking for the soul of the city as if it were Waldo, occupying some hidden part of the urban landscape. Or the fact that

Madrid doesn't conform to some easily articulated identity, one that I can describe in a few sentences to friends when they ask me about my trip. The great cities of the world are both canvas and palette; it's up to us to figure out the picture we want to paint.

I like to paint mine on the other side of Retiro, in Lavapiés, a web of narrow, hilly streets where a colorful coalition of students, young professionals, and immigrants converge—nearly all of them adopted citizens of Madrid. The neighborhood trades in *cortados* and curry, punk rock and pawnshops, ignorant of the whims of the more self-conscious corners of the city.

Here, you don't follow suits; you follow dark jeans and plumes of hash smoke. Tonight, that smoke and those jeans belong to Liliana López Sánchez and Sergio Fanjul, a hard-puffing young couple who have been living in the neighborhood for the past seven years. We are on the hunt for a particular breed of bar, according to Sergio an animal threatened with extinction in the twenty-first century: the *grasabar*.

GRASABAR (def): A dive bar whose decided lack of ambiance is overshadowed by cheap booze and fatty food. Common characteristics: waxy napkins, hospital lighting, surly bartenders, the acrid aroma of reused oil. *See also* Bar Manolo, Bar Paco, *bareto, bar de toda la vida.*

Sergio is Asturian, born and raised in Oviedo, but has lived in Madrid for years, working as a journalist for *El País*. Like most Spaniards his age, he's quick with a joke or to light up your smoke—exactly the guy you want leading a *grasabar* offensive.

"A lot of the *grasabares* in the neighborhood have been bought in recent years by young entrepreneurs. They change the bright lights for lower wattage, make a few other small adaptations, and raise the prices. The real thing is a dying breed."

We start a few steps from the Lavapiés metro stop, at a place called Bar Madroña. Tube lights, gurgling oil, bad pictures of the menu items out front: textbook.

Once the neighborhood fishmonger,

the space was transformed into a family-run bar back in the 1960s. The menu on the wall reads like a greatest hits of Spanish bar food: fried potatoes, anchovies, *ensaladilla rusa*, stewed tripe, fried calamari, *bocadillos* packed with every pig part conceivable.

Two Chinese guys play *pai gow* and chew on chicharrones. Back on the *plancha*, the wife renders a mountain of bacon with a giant spatula.

A drink gets you a free bite—in this case wedges of fried potatoes, reheated in the microwave and covered in squiggles of an unidentifiable sauce. A second drink brings a plate of chicken wings, sweating out fat and gelatin onto the plate. But we're here for the *albóndigas*, the springy pork meatballs, which come bathed in a dark yellow sauce with hints of curry spices—a nod to the neighborhood's constantly evolving demographic.

"Sometimes it feels like nobody in Madrid is actually from Madrid," says Sergio. "They adapt to the city and make it theirs, but the idea of a native Madrid culture isn't as clear here as it is elsewhere in Spain. Maybe that's why Madrid doesn't sell itself as well as Barcelona." I tell him about my pueblo posit—that Madrid is a patchwork of little villages—and he nods his head: "*Madrid es un pueblo sin fin.*" An endless town.

Liliana is from Barcelona, but moved to the capital in 1998 to work in television. "My first year was rough. I missed the sea and the mountains and the whole Mediterranean vibe. But Madrid grew on me, especially the social life. In Catalunya, nobody goes out during the week, and when they do go out, groups don't mix." Everywhere you turn in Madrid, you see large groups moving about the city, splintering and reforming throughout the evening, a constantly evolving force of eaters and drinkers who wouldn't think of going from the office to home without a beer and a tapa.

We move up the street to Café Melo's, a Lavapiés institution—stampeded from the moment the metal shutter comes up at 8:00 p.m. The place is loosely Galician, and the entire menu—all eight dishes—is built around four key ingredients from the region: Padrón peppers, blood sausage, *tetilla* (a cow's milk cheese shaped like a woman's breast), and *lacón*, salted and dried pork shoulder—sweeter and less intense than traditional Spanish *jamón*.

Presiding over the chaos of abandoned plates and cries for more is Ramón, captain of this sweaty closet of a bar since 1979. "He's famous in the neighborhood for his prodigious memory," says Txema. "He never writes anything down, and always remembers exactly what you ate and drank."

You can eat fried Padrón peppers or a convincing *croqueta* roughly twice the size of every other *croqueta* in Spain, but the real star of the menu, the reason why the place buckles at the knees at any given hour, is the *zapatilla*, a melted ham and cheese sandwich of Flintstonian dimensions. A young woman works a large griddle paved with thick slices of ham and melting blankets of *tetilla*. It looks like she has enough protein to make four or five sandwiches for the hungry crowds, but all of this material

is stacked and wedged between two massive slices of toasted bread and served as a single *zapatilla*. The name, meaning slipper, must be ironic; the three of us struggle to put down one among us. It's equal parts art and science: the art in the layered beauty of the melted beast; the science in its place as a preemptive strike against tomorrow's hangover.

We ask for the bill and Mr. Memory doesn't blink. "Six beers, two wines, two *croquetas* and a *zapatilla*. Twenty-eight euros." It's only as we waddle out that I spot the sign: PORTIONS HERE ARE ABUNDANT. PLEASE, ORDER WITH MODERATION.

We end the crawl in El Chiscón, a *grasabar* covered in thirty-six posters, each one announcing the same message in a different language: No smoking joints inside. We order *calimochos*, the drunkmaker of the Spanish youth: box wine mixed with off-brand cola, served over ice in one-liter glasses. A party in a plastic bathtub.

Liliana surveys the scene, smiles like someone half her age. "Now it's hard for me to go back to Barcelona." I can't promise that it will be the same for me, but I can start to see her dilemma.

Outside, everyone smokes and rails against the assholes in government in a flurry of accents: the clipped-consonant patter of Andalusia brushes up against the melodic rise and fall of Galicia, which gives way to the sun-soaked syllables of the Canarias. Txema tells me that before I board the train tomorrow, I must eat the *gallinejas* on Calle de Embajadores—fried lamb ventricles, a sacred weekend ritual, he assures me. (Nine hours later, as I chew through the gristle, I will curse this parting advice.)

As I wobble home at 2:30 a.m., the neighborhood shows no signs of slowing down. The kebab kings slice their spicy towers of spinning meat; the hash dealers do brisk business on the dark street corners. Inside the bars that dot these hills, most have traded beer and wine for gin tonics and whiskey colas. Beneath the curtain of a half-shuttered storefront, the man of Melo's with the prodigious memory scrapes the last of the caramelized cheese scraps from his battle-tested griddle.

Somewhere out there, in the never-ending pueblo of Madrid, a man with a mohawk shows his cooks how to turn a cocktail into a salad, a mezcal-soaked restaurant owner captivates clients with tales of the greatness of Spain, a pot of simmering bones give up their marrow for tomorrow, and a group of suits still crisp from the workday decide there's enough time for one last round.

301

Small Plates

TAPAS
TAXONOMY

What began as an inventive way to cover drinks in the fly-infested heat of southern Spain has turned into a style of eating that has fundamentally altered dining in this country and beyond. Tapas may have been born in Andalusia, but small plates reign all over the Iberian Peninsula. From Basque *pintxos* to Galician seafood to Andalusian fry bars, regional styles abound, but the following represent a tasty (if incomplete) snapshot of the titans of the Spanish tapas world.

PATATAS BRAVAS
Fried potatoes with spicy paprika sauce

ALBÓNDIGAS
Braised pork meatballs

CHIPIS A LA ANDALUZA
Fried baby squid or calamari

ALMEJAS A LA MARINERA
Clams cooked with garlic and white wine

SETAS AL AJILLO
Garlic-heavy sautéed mushrooms

ANCHOAS
Cured anchovies from Cantabria

BOQUERONES
Marinated white anchovies

ALCACHOFAS FRITAS
Artichokes fried in olive oil

PIMIENTOS DE PADRÓN
Fried Padrón peppers with coarse salt

NAVAJAS A LA PLANCHA
Razor clams cooked on the flattop

CROQUETAS DE JAMÓN
Cured ham croquettes

ACEITUNAS
Marinated olives

SARDINAS EN ESCABECHE
Sardines in garlic, herbs, and vinegar

RULES OF THE CRAWL:

01 Find the balance. For every crispy croqueta you'll want a briny clam to keep your palate primed for more.

02 Keep moving. The point is to work your way from one bar to the next, sampling the best of each.

03 Fill it up. Tapas culture is as much about drinking as eating. Not getting drunk, but enjoying good wine, sherry, or your poison of choice.

TORTILLA DE PATATAS
Potato omelet

GAMBAS AL AJILLO
Shrimp sautéed in spicy garlic oil

One night at a
THREE-STAR RESTAURANT

9:00 p.m.

STAY LOOSE

This ain't Paris circa 1968. Enjoyment and cost should have a direct relationship in the dining world, so let loose. Dress casual (anything beyond a T-shirt and jeans will do), make jokes, tell stories, get drunk. Have a big night. The service staff and the chefs will thank you for it.

9:30 p.m.

SMOKE AND MIRRORS

The meal starts with a flurry of small bites that deliver bursts of taste, texture, and surprise. (That stone ain't a stone. It's a potato!) The bait and switch is a well-worn Spanish conceit. Delightful when it's delicious; a buzzkill when it leaves you missing the genuine article.

10:05 p.m.

BANISH THE BREAD

The bread basket looks like a box of crayons, colored with everything from tomatoes to saffron to squid ink. Don't be fooled: You have three hours and twenty courses in front of you, and even the best bread is still your foe. There's nothing worse than being too full for the finale.

11:20 p.m.

DIVE DEEP

Spanish chefs value the quality of their seafood above all, and tasting menus typically play out like a marine geography lesson: Galician razor clams, Catalan red shrimp, tuna from Cádiz. Most meals will end with a single plate of pristine protein—suckling pig or lamb or even game.

12:15 a.m.

HALF-WINE IS FINE

Do a wine pairing and you'll end up with a dozen vintages on your table, which can be thrilling or overwhelming, depending on how you roll. A more restrained option is a half-wine pairing, or sharing a few bottles. The best restaurants go beyond wine and play with sake, beer, and spirits.

1:00 a.m.

TOUR THE TEMPLE

Why yes, the chef would be happy to show you the kitchen. Expect to find a silent, sparkling, lab-like environment. What's that crazy device, you ask? (One of so many!) It's the machine responsible for all those distillations you didn't know you were enjoying. Score one for science!

NOT INVENTED, JUST PERFECTED

Gin and tonic may have been born in India in the nineteenth century, but "gin tonic" is a uniquely Spanish culture, one that began to take shape in the early 2000s in corners of Madrid and Barcelona. Now, it's common to find even dive bars selling dozens of customized creations.

SIZE MATTERS

No highball or rocks glasses, a Spanish gin tonic must be made in a big-bellied wineglass, like the ones used for powerful reds. Same goes for the ice: normal ice means instant dilution. Good bars serve two to three massive cubes that will hold the cold.

MIX AND MATCH

Bars stock up to fifty gins, half a dozen tonics, and an arsenal of garnishes: citrus peel, fresh herbs (thyme, rosemary, basil), whole spices (cardamom, peppercorns, juniper), and fresh produce (cucumber, ginger, chile). You want harmony between gin, tonic, and garnish.

DRINK IT LIKE A SPANIARD

Spaniards don't drink gin tonics (or any hard liquor) before a meal (just one of these on an empty stomach will get you going). Gin tonics are most commonly consumed as a *digestivo* after a big meal, or at the bar in the early-morning hours.

Chapter Nine

GRANADA

To make *migas de harina* the proper way, you must first build a fire. When you have a glowing bed of embers, fill a pan—black iron, wide-mouthed, and heavy-bottomed like a wok—with water and place it over the fire. Once little bubbles break the surface, season the water with salt—a fistful should do—then add the flour: a kilo for every liter you have boiling. The primary technique for *migas* is stirring, which you do with a long metal spatula without pause until the pan is removed from the fire. At first, the union of liquid and solid forms a large, shapeless mass—a lumpy primordial stew—but after a few minutes carving long, swooping arcs through the sludge, the mass will begin to multiply, from two pieces to four to sixteen to sixty-four to god knows how many—a single-cell organism splitting over and over again. Life takes shape.

Soon the stirring becomes slashing as you use the sharp edge of the spatula to chop the dough into increasingly smaller pieces. Run the instrument against the hot belly of the pan, scraping and rolling to give the *migas* equal share of the cooking surface. Now you are ready to add the fourth and final ingredient: olive oil, boiling yellow like the desert sun outside. Ladle it in spoon by spoon and don't be shy: this is what makes *migas* go down easier. Fold and slash, fold and slash, working the dough

from shaggy clumps to rough spheres to hot
pebbles of toasted grain.

When they're ready, they can be
scooped from the pan and onto a plate and
scattered with the variety of sweet and
savory ingredients people like to eat with
migas: crispy pork fat, salted sardines, fried
peppers, raw onions, fresh oranges, chunks
of chocolate. More likely, though, you will
grab a spoon and a chair and gather around
the pan, eating the warm bits of dough directly from its surface. *Migas* are the fuel of
Spanish shepherds, a way to fill up before
tending to your flock, and in the south of
Spain, where shepherds roam the mountain
ridges and desert planes, they have long
been a food of survival.

Federico Motos Lajara has been surviving off *migas* for the better part of a century. He was born October 3, 1930, six years
before the Spanish Civil War, in Fuente
Nueva, one hundred forty kilometers east
of Granada. He stands nearly six feet tall,
with a wispy wheat stalk for a frame and
smooth brown cheeks that belie a life spent
under the Andalusian sun. He dresses in

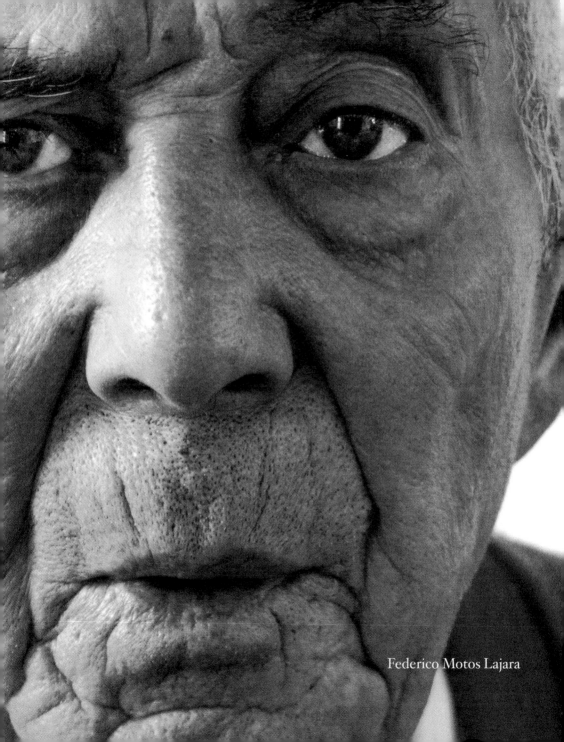

Federico Motos Lajara

wool cardigans and flannel shirts in the winter, cotton button-downs and espadrilles in the summer—an accidental hipster before his time. Besides *migas*, his diet consists mainly of salted pork, homegrown tobacco, and a steady dose of solitude. He is a bachelor by choice and once a shepherd by trade, guiding flocks of goats and sheep through the surrounding sierras. His family calls him Chacho, a term of respect and endearment reserved for older citizens of southern Spain.

Chacho has not seen much of the world. He hasn't seen much of Spain, either. He's never been to the northern coast, never been deeper south in Andalusia, never even been to Madrid. He went to Catalunya once to visit family, but he got lost the first day in town. After hours wandering the streets looking for the way back to his nephew's apartment, he gave up, stepped into a bar, and found that the bar's owner just happened to be from Orce, a few miles from Fuente Nueva, the town that Chacho knows better than any other. He felt right at home.

He left Spain just once, in 1949, across the Mediterranean in the south to serve in Morocco as military police in Franco's army. He worked as a nineteen-year-old patrolman in Fez and Marrakesh, losing himself in the maze of the medina. Chacho has fond memories of those years, but if you press him for details, don't expect much. What sticks with him most from Morocco is the voices he heard. "The Moors sing beautifully," he likes to say.

Beyond this one brief interlude, Chacho has lived his entire life in a cave carved into the side of a hill in one of the smallest and poorest towns in Andalusia. Fuente Nueva, located at the foot of the Sierras de María, is one of a handful of cave communities found around the province of Granada, a remnant from a time when Andalusia was the seat of the Moorish empire in Spain. Beyond religion, architecture, literature, and cuisine, the rulers of Al-Andalus also imported the tradition of making homes inside mountains: spaces that stay warm in the winter and cool in the summer, perfect for the extreme climate of southern Spain.

In the centuries since, scattered pockets of caves have served as a refuge for recluses and a breeding ground for the counterculture—anarchists and gypsies, literally carving out a different way of living. Perhaps the best-known cave community in the region is Sacromonte, a collection of rustic mountain pockets above Granada. Romany people first made a home there in the fifteenth century, but today they share the mountain with a transient community of international hippies and squatters—a place for flamenco music and shared gardens and stunning views of the Alhambra.

But Fuente Nueva is another place entirely. Its name means New Fountain, a reference to the bedrock of the village: a supply of groundwater that brought people here as early as the fourteenth century, when the Moors still ruled southern Spain. The water ensured that the foothills surrounding the caves were covered in crops: wheat and corn, almonds and olives. Life,

though, was never easy, especially in Chacho's youth, as the drumbeat of the Civil War created fissures in the tight-knit community. Though the fighting never got closer than Baza, thirty miles away, the war splintered families as fathers and sons, brothers and uncles often found themselves on opposing sides. Most people in Fuente Nueva wanted nothing to do with the war. Franco drafted from these parts, and men selected for his army often chose desertion, disappearing into the mountains, only to face a firing squad if discovered. In the wake of Franco's victory, the Fascists returned to the village to round up the *rojos*, supporters of the Republicans; many never returned.

If all of Spain went hungry in the wake of the war, Fuente Nueva starved. Already inhabitants of one of the country's poorest regions, the people of the caves sunk deeper into despair as basic resources disappeared. Stories abound about the depths of hunger and desperation felt during the 1940s: families surviving off of weeds and grubs, Franco's men raiding caves to steal food, parents committing suicide because they couldn't feed their families.

Still, the people of the area know how to survive, and as the war's most sinister residue began to dissipate, they transformed a loose confederation of caves and casas into a vibrant community. At its peak in the 1950s, 1,200 people lived in Fuente Nueva, the village so dense that families of ten or twelve would pack into a single cave. The school overflowed with young students of all ages. The town's roster of small businesses grew to include eight bars—places to drink and dance until the early morning. In the warm summer evenings, people would stroll up and down the dirt roads that wrap around Fuente Nueva, dropping into other caves to pay visits to friends and family.

Then, in 1963, something happened that would change Fuente Nueva forever: the water dried up. No one was quite sure how it happened so suddenly; some say an earthquake earlier in the year compromised the fragile geology below. Others entertained spiritual or supernatural suspicions of who

or what was behind the emptying of the wells. Whatever the cause, the calculus was dire: Without water, the crops dried up, the animals went thirsty, and the community lost the ability to sustain itself. An exodus ensued. It didn't happen all at once, but one by one, young and old, the people of Fuente Nueva spread out across the desert in search of life elsewhere in Spain and beyond.

Today there aren't many people left in town—forty-eight in total, according to the last census. There is old Tomás the shepherd, who wears his livelihood in the blisters on his round, red face, and in the hard plastic canteen of water he carries slung over his back when he goes for walks in the afternoon; the French, pockets scattered here and there, including Jean Dumas, who established the first foreign beachhead back in the 1970s; Lina Torres Miron, the last of a large, poor family who survived for years on the generosity of neighbors; Petra, at ninety-three years old the village's oldest resident, who lives with eight cats, two dogs, and a cabinet full of Beefeater to keep her company.

And Chacho Federico, herder of sheep, master of *migas*, the last in a long line of shepherds who once filled the caves of Fuente Nueva.

🍇 🫒 🐖

I first met Chacho in December 2010, when we gathered in a cave to kill a pig. Chacho is the great-uncle to my wife, Laura, and I came with my future father-in-law, Angel, to participate in a *matanza*, the annual pig slaughter observed in small communities around Spain. The trip fell right in the middle of my turbulent courtship with Laura, back when it looked like things between us weren't going to work out. She stayed in Barcelona and I traveled south with her father, whom I had never met—a kamikaze plan forged in a moment of desperation. I hoped my willingness to sacrifice a pig in a cave filled with strangers would convince this girl of our future together. If not, it would be an opportunity to see a special corner of Spain's *campesino* culture before packing up and moving back to the US.

That first morning, Angel gave me a tour of the town he grew up in. We started at the *cortijo*, the home of his birth, where strains of his family have lived for more than one hundred years. *Cortijos* are the large, rustic farmhouses of southern Spain, and they dot the hills of Fuente Nueva and the surrounding area. He showed me where the animals ate, the fireplace around which his family would gather in the mornings and evenings ("our television" he told me), the bed of hay where Chacho slept for so many years. The small school where Angel studied had been abandoned decades ago, but the desks and chalkboards survived. Later we entered the battered village church where Franco imprisoned communists after the war—the roof torn off, a tree rising up from the altar.

Angel left Fuente Nueva when he was fourteen to study in seminary school in one of the province's larger towns. This was the 1960s, a moment of mass migration of Andalusians to the north in search of better opportunities, and after graduating, Angel joined the diaspora. He was on his way to Andorra to look for work when he made a pit stop in Igualada, a midsize industrial town

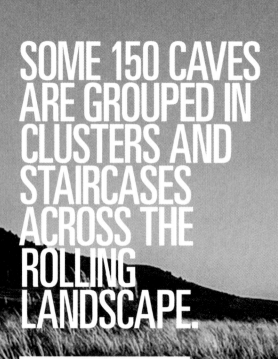

SOME 150 CAVES ARE GROUPED IN CLUSTERS AND STAIRCASES ACROSS THE ROLLING LANDSCAPE.

an hour from Barcelona. He found work as a waiter at a hotel and decided to stay.

At twenty-five, he met Ana Santoyo on the dance floor of Discoteca Scorpia. The daughter of a military policeman from Jaén in Andalusia, Ana worked at the sock factory on the outskirts of the town. They married a year later and had three children: Marta, Laura, and Carlos. Angel embraced life in Catalunya, rising through the ranks of one of Catalunya's largest banks, but he never let himself or his children forget where he came from.

At the far end of the road, we came upon a rustic stone house with an animal pen filled with clucking turkeys and their extravagant plumage. Against the wall of the house, beside an old wooden table, three women in aprons and head scarves stood scrubbing animal viscera—filling intestines like water balloons with ladles of warm water and emptying them out over and over again. Behind them, the splayed body of a dead pig dangled by its hind feet. Angel put a hand on my shoulder: "Welcome to Fuente Nueva."

The *matanza* was held in the cave of Angel and María Ángeles. María Ángeles is my father-in-law's cousin, a spark plug of an *andaluza*, quick-witted and generous, a hurricane of hard work and hospitality. People had warned me about the intensity of the tradition—of the sound and smell of death—and I stepped cautiously into the cave that first morning. A team of men dressed in jumpsuits and rubber boots stood in silence around a table, sipping whiskey from short glasses before the day's work.

It takes a village to kill a pig. Someone to wrangle the hog from the pen, four more to pin it down to a metal table, another to plunge the knife through the base of its neck until it pierces the heart, one to catch and stir the warm blood as it pours from the body, another to break the animal down into a dozen primal cuts, two more to scrub the viscera and flush the intestines, plus a team of three or more to grind, season, stuff, boil, and hang the flesh until every last piece of the pig is in the early stages of preservation.

Despite the depth of the team

assembled—cousins, friends, friends of friends, the town mayor—the roles of the *matanza* are clearly divided along gender lines: the men kill and butcher the pig; the women do everything else. I came dressed in an old tracksuit, sleeves pushed up to my elbows, prepared to earn my keep. When I moved from the butchering into the kitchen with the women to make the various charcuterie, one of the members of the killing team looked up from behind his glass of whiskey: "That's women's work, boy."

Yes, machismo is alive and well in the south of Spain. Men work hard, often physically demanding jobs, but their responsibilities usually stop there. Beyond working full time, women cook the dinner, wash the dishes, pack the lunches, make the beds, feed the pigs, read the books. If you ever walk into a bar here and wonder where the ladies are, they are busy holding the world together.

For two days we salted legs and simmered organs and stuffed intestines with various expressions of protein, fat, and spice. María Ángeles did the work of five men, while her mother-in-law, doña Alberta—her palate trained from seventy years of practice—scattered handfuls of paprika and nutmeg into giant colored buckets of flesh and blood like a farmer scatters chicken feed. We ate *migas* and drank whiskey with Fanta *narajana*. On Saturday night, when all of the work was done, a group of fourteen of us sat down at a long table in the cave and feasted: grilled sausages, tomato salad, jugs of red wine, and plates of the previous season's sacrifice.

When people travel to Andalusia, they come to see the great cities formed during the centuries when the Moors dominated the peninsula: Sevilla, with its towering stone structures, lively bars, and restaurants, its beautiful people; Córdoba, where the splendor of the Umayyad Caliphate survives in the flower-lined courtyards and the austere beauty of the grand mosque; and Granada, the cultural and intellectual center of Al-Andalus, whose sacking in 1492 by Ferdinand and Isabella's army brought the Reconquista to a close. Granada deserves special attention: for the magnificence of the Alhambra, for the soul-stirring strings of flamenco that ring out from bars and private residences; for the remarkable tapas culture, one of Spain's first and finest, where every drink comes with a new free tapa in an ever-escalating ballad of bites and beverages.

But there's only so much you can learn about the culture of southern Spain fighting off selfie sticks under horseshoe arches. You'll need to do what visitors—Spaniards included—rarely do: Take to the open roads of greater Andalusia. Fuente Nueva is ninety minutes by car from Granada, another ninety to the desert beaches of Almería. No, Chacho doesn't list his cave on Airbnb (though my father-in-law continues to toy with the idea of an agriturismo in Fuente Nueva), but you can rent a cave for a week in Orce or Galera, the lovely little cave communities next door, and settle into the rhythms of rural Spanish life.

You'll need to recalibrate your expectations as a visitor. This is one of the poorest corners of the country, and the area doesn't wear its tourism bona fides as conspicu-ously as elsewhere in Spain. You won't find fancy food or nice hotels or establishments brandishing TripAdvisor awards. You won't be entirely alone—Europeans, the French and the British in particular, have bought a few caves in the region over the years and slowly embraced the charms of the *campo*—but you'll never lose the feeling that you're out on the edge of civilization. In many ways, you can see more of Spain from the inside of a cave than from the lookout of the Alhambra.

The beauty for the outsider lies in the little discoveries. You can start your day in Huéscar or María with a basket of *porras*—the crispier, airier analog to the churro—and set sail, bite by bite, in a sea of melted chocolate. You can follow the farmer's market as it moves from town to town throughout the week, buying stone fruit and nightshades and drinking with the locals that fill the bars on market days. You can climb a mountain, sip water from frigid streams, sleep under a bank of stars so bright you can read a book by the light. And when you emerge from the wilderness, you can feast on *cordero segureño*, the famous lamb of the region, lightly blackened over oak and served with lots of crusty bread and local red wine.

This is what I've been doing with Laura since I married into the family. We make at least two trips a year down to Fuente Nueva—usually one in the winter, to partake in the *matanza*, and one in the summer, when a stream of visitors and seasonal residents fill the caves and change the village dynamic considerably. We travel down as a family: Laura's older sister, Marta; her husband, David; and their boy, Lucas; and her younger brother, Carlos. The siblings grew up spending the summers in the south. Carlos loved the mountain trails and the silence of the desert, Laura her grandparents' stable of animals and collection of ghost stories. Marta followed Chacho and his flock into the mountains.

El pueblo, as the family calls it, is located three thousand feet up in the Altiplano de Granada, built around a series of hills, valleys, shelves, and ravines, a muddled topography that creates little pockets of texture and geometry perfectly suited for the construction of caves. In total, some one hundred fifty caves are grouped in clusters and staircases across the rolling landscape— some with crumbling stone entrances, others with smooth white faces like the houses of Mykonos.

Inside, you'll find caves come in many different flavors. On one end, you have the cave that closely resembles its raw definition: rustic and dusty and utterly devoid of the trappings of modernity. On the other end is the fancy cave, often purchased by an out-of-towner and remodeled to contain all of the amenities of a modern house, only built into the side of a mountain. Most caves that are still lived in today, including our family's, fall somewhere in between: electricity, running water, working kitchen, modest furnishings, a ground of cool cement and ceilings of rough plaster. Sometimes you forget you're in a cave altogether; other times—when the smell of damp earth fills the bedroom, when the fire goes out and all you can see are your thoughts—it slaps you across the face.

To call Fuente Nueva a town these days is too generous: There is no commercial business here, hasn't been since Juan Miguel closed his bar El Molino in 2005. The closest civilization is Orce, seven kilometers through a snaking valley, a town of 1,400 organized around a large Catholic church and an even larger Moorish castle, with a shoe store, two butchers, a weekly market, and a handful of bars and restaurants. The Alcazaba of the Seven Towers was built during the eleventh century at the peak of the Caliphate of Córdoba, and later in the fourteenth century, Orce formed a valuable outpost of King Ismael I's southern realm. On the spines of mountains you can still see the crumbling stone towers used by the Moors to send messages across the empire.

The most famous citizen of the area, known as *el Hombre de Orce*, isn't a man at all, but a human skull believed to be more than a million years old. In 1982, the Catalan archaeologist Josep Gibert discovered the fossil in a cave not more than a mile from Fuente Nueva. The area had long been known as an archaeological gold mine, including deposits of ancient mammal fossils and caves filled with Neolithic markings, but these bones, claimed Gibert and his team, belonged to the first citizen of Europe. Controversy erupted in the archaeology community as others rushed to protect their own findings, but science and history appear increasingly to confirm Gibert's central claim: that Fuente Nueva is a cradle of Western European civilization. Everywhere in the area you will see signs for *LOS PRIMEROS POBLADORES DE EUROPA*: the first settlers of Europe.

The line between past and present is razor thin in these parts. Laura and I go for long walks in the mornings with Chacho's dogs, imagining life as it once was. Blink once, and there's María on top of the cave, skinning a rabbit for dinner; Federico below in the garden, tending to his hot peppers; Miguel in the workshop, turning a broken chair into a bedside table. Blink again and it's just me and my wife and the sound of the dogs rustling through the crispy fields of grain.

An abandoned cave under a
bank of Andalusian stars.

Once we found a cave on top of a hill with the kitchen table still set, plates filled with the dust of decomposed food, a half-drunk bottle of wine long since turned to vinegar—as if the owners deserted their home halfway through dinner.

Sometimes the line disappears entirely—like when Chacho sifts through his home-grown tobacco with a handmade sieve, or spends hours weaving clothes and implements from esparto, the straw that has long held this community together. The first paved road came here in 1999; the only streetlight came a few years later, igniting a small but fierce controversy among the few that live within its alien yellow gaze. This isn't like other small outposts of the world, where modern forces shake furiously at the gate; the defining question of Fuente Nueva isn't when will it change, but how will it survive?

The Motos family knows something about surviving in the pueblo. In 1936, forty-year-old Federico Motos—my wife's great-grandfather—was called up by Fran-co's army to fight in the civil war. After serving a few months on the coast of Almería, he escaped and walked a hundred miles through the desert back to Fuente Nueva, foraging and stealing along the way. He arrived hungry and withered and full of fleas; he faced execution for his desertion, but the Fascists never came for him. Federico was a drunk and an idler, but his father had made a small fortune selling fabric and used it to buy land around Fuente Nueva. He married Nieves Lajara and together they had three children: María, Federico, and Faustino.

Chacho Federico's younger brother, Faustino, has the distinction of holding more jobs than anyone from Fuente Nueva. He owned Bar Faustino, one of the village's only watering holes back in the 1950s, but when the well dried up, so did the clientele. Later, Faustino married and moved to Orce. He drove a taxicab, but found the fares in rural Spain too infrequent. He ran a bakery, but couldn't keep up with the other bakers in town. He is sweet and soft spoken, fragile but resilient, a man who has spent most of his life starting over.

María was the oldest of the Motos-Lajara siblings. Born in 1928, she left school at age eleven to care for her younger brothers when her mother fell ill with cancer. At nineteen, she met Miguel Pérez at the winter festival of San Antón, and after Miguel finished his military service, they were married in the church of Fuente Nueva.

To be a mother in Fuente Nueva, you must be made of strong stuff. And that was María: heart of gold, blood of ice. Chicken for dinner; snap its neck. Dog gives birth; drown the puppies. Boy needs medicine; mount the mule. She was determined to make sure her only child had every opportunity she didn't. She raised pigs and turkeys and sold eggs to the neighbors while Miguel worked as a carpenter and mechanic and together they saved enough to pay for their son's education. Angel was the only kid of his generation in Fuente Nueva to go to college, a fact that filled their little cave with pride.

María was eighty-three when we first met at the *matanza*, but she was still stirring pots and stuffing sausages. The cave was her kingdom, and she welcomed me in as if I were her own grandson. Like any good grandma, her principle concern was making sure I ate as much as possible; our bond formed quickly in the kitchen. One sweltering summer day, she taught us how to make cheese. We spent the morning convincing a local farmer to sell us twenty gallons of goat's milk, which we hauled back to the cave in giant plastic buckets. There, María, with a silk scarf wrapped around her head, walked us through the process: inoculating the milk with cultures, stirring and skimming off the whey, then tightly packing the curds into the same plastic baskets she had been using for decades. The next time we came south, a room full of goat cheese awaited: firm and funky and throat-scratching in its cave-aged intensity. María's lips curled upward like a climbing vine as we cut into that first wheel.

When someone dies in this part of Spain, they don't send the deceased to a funeral parlor. The body is prepared by a mortician, then placed in the bedroom of the deceased and left open for observation by friends and family. The *velatorio* is an old tradition loaded with complex social dynamics, where your love for the departed is put on display for the village to see. Some sob wildly and curse the heavens, some sit in sullen silence, others refuse to enter the room at all.

María's passing in the fall of 2014 brought in friends and family from across the region. We lit candles and arranged photos as they packed into the cave and remained there for twenty-four sleepless hours before the final funeral procession to the cemetery in Orce. Those gathered that endless night in the cave mourned María's vigorous spirit, her sneaky sense of humor, her magnificent hand in the kitchen. But they also mourned a way of life, every candle closer to extinction. She was a loyal sister and cherished mother, but also guardian of a special piece of Spanish history, one of the last people who believed in Fuente Nueva. Chacho sat by himself in the corner most of the night, weeping silently for his sister.

Not long after, Angel, Laura, and I went on a walk to the cemetery in Fuente Nueva to look for the tombs of other relatives, but Angel couldn't find who he was looking for.

"Chacho, where did they bury my grandfather?" he asked when we got back to the cave.

"What do I know? I don't ever go there. I don't like it. And the day I die, you don't need to do anything. I'll take a piece of cardboard as long as it doesn't break. Just don't burn me. Someone told me that when you die your soul goes up toward the sky and there you can live on, but not if they burn you."

"But you're in sin, Chacho. We're all in sin."

"I'm not in sin! I never killed anybody."

He sat awhile longer, swirling his drink, staring into the fire.

"What kind of a conversation is this!"

For most of its history, Fuente Nueva was a self-sustaining community: you or your neighbor grew grains, you raised animals, you kept a small garden. Mostly, you baked bread in the communal oven, killed and cured pigs to spread the protein out throughout the year, and made stews with whatever you could cobble together. Cave cuisine is shepherd cuisine, survival cuisine, what people around here sometimes call *cocina de miseria*: misery cuisine. That's not to say that people in the pueblo aren't skilled cooks; try Uncle Angel's goat simmered in olive oil and bay leaf or Rosa's garlic-heavy *salmorejo* or María's *olla*, a stew of chicken, *jamón*, and garbanzos, and you'll taste the very essence of Spanish country cooking. But the primary staples of Fuente Nueva have always been elemental: *migas, ajo de harina, gachas*—combinations of wheat, water, and fat, served with whatever you could spare on top.

Nevertheless, people in these parts are known for living some of the longest lives on earth. You need only walk around Orce at 1:00 p.m. to appreciate just how long: The main plaza and the bars surrounding are occupied almost exclusively by men with gray hair and gravely voices. Or consider the case of Chacho, who survives on a diet of flour,

pork fat, and tobacco, but nevertheless can't remember the last time he's been to the doctor. I don't mean that in the hyperbolic sense; when I press him for the details of his last doctor visit, his eyes roll back as he searches his memory and comes up with nothing but a shoulder shrug.

Part of this fountain of youth can no doubt be explained by the olive oil, the omega-3s in the fatty fish they eat, the moderate amounts of red wine, but much of it comes down to the lifestyle, one historically defined by constant energy expenditure to handle the tasks of the day: caring for the crops, tending to the flock, chopping the wood to keep the fire alive. Those tasks have largely disappeared for many in the area, but the diet remains stubbornly similar; only time will tell if the people of Orce and Fuente Nueva can survive the *migas* without the movement.

Breaking up the monotony of the daily bread is a surprisingly vigorous scene in the bars of the region—made considerably more merry around the first of the month, when pensions and benefits go out and, for a few days at least, the old Andalusians feel rich. From the dead-simple food to the crowds of shepherds and farmers and carpenters sharing stories at the bar, a tapas crawl here is a rare chance for the outsider to see Spain in its most honest state.

In the spring, I sometimes spend time alone with Angel and Chacho in the caves. One morning, while sipping my coffee, Chacho shuffles in wearing his finest button-down shirt and sports jacket. "Put on something decent. We're going to town." We start at the Caja Granada, where Chacho cashes his retirement check for his years as a shepherd (given the sheer number of shepherds in Spain, the government developed a pension system to ease them out of the mountains), then head immediately next door to the butcher to buy a leg of *jamón* ("give me the good stuff, I don't want any of the bullshit you have back there . . ."), a coil of chorizos, and a few small treats for the dogs, which Chacho will never admit are for the dogs.

We head to Huéscar, the biggest town in the county, the place you go when you need to see a doctor or buy a TV. Thursdays are market days and the town teems with people filling up on chlorophyll, the first sign of the coming warmth: thick bunches of asparagus, hills of spring onions and favas and green peas. Chacho hasn't bought a piece of produce in decades, views plant matter with general suspicion, but he loves the energy of market days.

We enter a bar off the main plaza and take stools at the counter. One euro around here will buy you a beer and a free tapa—a perplexing business model, but a necessity for the patrons in these parts. The day's first round comes with slices of toasted bread topped with grilled bacon. For the most part, tapas here share a standard formula: a little protein or vegetable, a lot of salt, garlic, and olive oil, a piece of bread to soak it all up. I tell Chacho that in Barcelona people pay separately for their tapas. "Then they're not tapas."

An old friend of Chacho's spots us at the bar and we have another round as the two catch up. As Chacho pays the bill, the friend invites us over to his house for lunch. "My wife's an amazing cook," he assures me. Chacho tells him we have plans. Back in the car, I mention that a free lunch might have been nice. "Are you kidding me? He can smell the money on me. By the time we finished, he'd be begging us for some. Besides, his wife can't cook worth a damn."

Next we stop at a small bar inside the Shell gas station between Huéscar and Orce, a new spot on Chacho's radar. "You'll like the bartender—I think she's your type." She's in her late forties, stern, and generously proportioned, what people here might call *hermosa*. She pours us sweet wine from nearby Galera and brings us a plate of lamb sweetbreads—robed in olive oil and garlic, each tender gland the size of a gumdrop. *Segureño* lamb, Chacho assures me.

Whatever silences filled the morning slowly disappear as the grapes and glands take effect. Chacho tells me stories of Granada, the place he knows and loves most after Fuente Nueva and Orce. Whenever he goes—it's been a decade since the last trip—he stays in the Hostal Costa Azul. "No matter how full they might be, they always have a place for me." He knows the flamenco bars, the casinos, the strip clubs, the tapas joints. He also knows where to find a good woman, a habit that Chacho has never tried to hide.

"There was always a lot of vice in Granada. Back when I was going, there were two good brothels, one was don José's, the other don Pedro's. Each had fifty-six women in a line. I always counted. Even Fuente Nueva had its vices in its heyday. There were four known prostitutes in town, plus three that were unknown. Even to their husbands." The *hermosa* bartender flashes a nervous smile to the odd couple on the bar stools.

Back in Orce, we settle into one of the town's three main bars, a place they call Los Jubilados, the retired ones, for the seniority of its clientele. More than Huéscar or Galera, Orce is Chacho's turf, and as we take our place at the bar, the men line up to pay their respects to the old shepherd. When he introduces me as family, a warm tingle shoots up my neck.

"This guy would give you the shirt off his back," one tells me. "Federico is a man's

THE SHEPHERDS OF
FUENTE NUEVA ARE
NOT LONG FOR THIS
WORLD.

_____

man," says another. "Still living the dream."

Chacho cares little for money. He's long lived from pension check to pension check, spending everything he has (and then some) on food, booze, women, that unholy trinity of temptation. He's generous when he can be, like today, but nobody is accepting it. A week from now, the old men might happily take him up on the offer, but today, they fight to cover our tab.

The only woman to be found is behind the bar pouring drinks and delivering the tapas flying out of the kitchen: first, a roasted potato slathered in a thick emulsion of garlic and olive oil; next, a plate of fried asparagus and lemon. Juan Ricardo, a farmer and local bon vivant, wins the fight to pay for our drinks, and he spends twenty minutes talking about what everyone in bars these days talk about: *la crisis*, the corrupt politicians, a Spain that will never be the same. Chacho sips and nods.

Then they discuss women in a dialect beyond my grasp. I've learned the hard way over the years the difference between speaking *castellano* and speaking *andaluz*.

The former is the language of Cervantes; the latter, the language of Chacho. Beyond a strain of vocabulary most of the rest of Spain wouldn't recognize, the defining characteristic of *andaluz* is a clipped pronunciation that mashes words together and makes entire syllables disappear. Thus, *más o menos* becomes *ma o meno, tres horas* equals *tre hora*, and *para nada* gets chopped to *pana*.

This happens with varying degrees of severity depending on the speaker. Talk to a young merchant about the weather and you might hold the conversation; speak to an eighty-five-year-old shepherd about unrequited love and you'll beg for a translator.

By 2:30 p.m., the *jubilados* peel themselves from their perches and begin to wobble home to their women, who wait silently in the wings with the midday meal. The siesta hour looms large.

I'm not anxious to drive the curvy road back to Fuente Nueva, but Chacho waves me off. "Are there police around? Probably, but you don't have anything to worry about. I'll tell them you're with me."

🍇 🫒 🐖

One morning, as the sun peeks above the sierras, I spot a roaming cloud of dust on the horizon. I speed over to the source, leave the car on the side of the road, and set out running at full pace until I come to the front of a pack of sheep pouring down the hillside like a ruptured desert dam. The shepherd shows no signs of slowing down, but he doesn't brush me off either. "I'm the son-in-law of Angel Motos!" I yell over the song of sheep. "Yeah? Well, how can I help you?"

I'm not entirely sure. I've seen these clouds move across the plateaus for years now and wondered about the animals and men inside them, but today is the first time I did more than stare. I tell him I just want to chat. "You sure about that?" he says between clouds of cigarette smoke. Maybe chat is the wrong word; for the next two hours, Luis Reche Motos does all of the talking.

"I left school when I was thirteen, learned to be a shepherd from my dad. Everyone owned sheep back then, but small flocks—between fifty and one hundred. Now, you see bigger flocks and fewer shepherds. I have four hundred myself, plus sixty goats. Sheep can't be locked up. They have to get out and eat—mostly grass and barley, which means if it doesn't rain, I'm ruined. In this part of Spain, we have six months of summer and six months of winter. In the summer we climb the mountains in search of cooler weather. The sheep form a ball and stick their heads down into their own shadows and they don't move until the heat breaks. The only time worse than summer is winter. Went down to minus eleven degrees this past season and I lost a few newborns. The births happen all at once—three hundred babies and me. And people in the north say *we're* lazy? They don't know real work. Look at my hands! And I'm not one of the good ones. Up there in the mountains is a guy we call Snails. Now that's a good shepherd—knows the mother of every sheep just by looking in its eyes. What I do have is a good dog. I call her Electrician. She lost one of her front legs in an accident, but that doesn't stop her. The sheep look to her to know what to do, not me. Without her, I'm nothing. You see, sheep have one

great defect: They are the dumbest creatures alive. If you leave them alone, they
will either eat themselves to death or starve
to death. Goats, too, but they're smarter
than sheep. You have to write down everything they do, everything they eat. I have
four or five books going at a time. Later,
people come and check and charge you for
every little service. That's an old tradition
in Spain: one works and five earn. That
will never change. But business keeps getting harder. The price of milk just dropped
from a euro to sixty cents and it will destroy
people. All of these you see here are for
meat. They set the price at the cooperative.
Right now they're paying us seventy-eight
euros per animal, but that could drop ten
euros and my year will be over. They say the
segureño lamb we raise is special, something
about the quality of the fat and the flavor
of the meat. In Madrid they pay a fortune
for it. We don't eat lamb at home much, but
when I do, I just sear it on both sides. The
rest of the people here? They like it burnt
to shit, which never made sense to me. I
was born here in Fuente Nueva back when

everyone had their own garden, but then
the water dried up and now there's just four
families left: Tomás, us, Mercedes, and you
guys. I didn't want to be a shepherd. I sold
tractors, sold butane, tried everything to
avoid it, but my back went out and here I
am. My sons are fourteen and sixteen and
they don't know what to do. They want
to help, but they can't stay. When they're
eighteen, they'll go to Granada or Murcia
and look for work. I don't want this life for
them. I smoke two packets of cigarettes a
day—roll my own with blond duchy. That's
my vice. Well, that and the phone. I spend
all day on it, talking to other shepherds.
But all we talk about is sheep. It's a lonely
life. That's why they say shepherds are a
little bit crazy."

You can tell by the way he talks—the
speed with which he dispatches his facts,
the smoke he blows between sentences—
that the shepherds of Fuente Nueva are
not long for this world. When Chacho
remembers the work, he draws his words
slowly and fills the spaces in between with
shoulder shrugs and hand flicks, as if to say,

What the hell are we really talking about here? Whereas Ramón has a mastery of the fine details, Chacho's memory of the shepherd life is broad strokes of shape and color.

"I started out with my dad's sheep. The other shepherds helped, but nobody teaches you to be a shepherd. If you grow up here, you just become one. I'd leave the house in the afternoon and not come back until the next morning. I didn't eat much when I worked, maybe some wild chard I'd find in the *campo*. I had an incredible dog that stayed with me for many years. When she died I got two big dogs—more wolves than dogs. I didn't give them names, though— you go through too many to name them."

Many dogs, many seasons, many nights with his flock under the stars. You can only imagine the plight of the pastor if you pause sufficiently to let your mind wander over all of its dimensions—not just the romance of the rural landscape, the fidelity to the flock, the growth and decay of the shifting seasons, the ever-evolving journey, but also the dance of the desert: the sear of the sun, the burn of the wind, the fangs of the winter; the silent nights with stone pillows; the soul-stretching solitude, the bone-chattering boredom, the days without distraction from yourself; the impermanence of the mission: knowing that everything will come to a certain end once enough grass and grain disappear, only to be lived again once it regrows. The constant reminder of your place in the circle.

The night sky is a mirror for the idle minds of wandering men. You learn to speak with the world that surrounds you: the sheep, the sun, the stars, the moon. Especially the moon. *If anyone understands, it must be you*, he thinks, *for we share blood ties.*

Chacho didn't fill diaries with the diets of his sheep; he also didn't have a cell phone or a sixteen-year-old boy. His brother, Faustino, had dreams—he wanted to make a family and a business and a life bigger than himself—but Chacho managed to keep his dreams contained within the confines of a cave. He sits by the fire, lights a cigarette, roasts a piece of salted pork over the embers, and doesn't worry about what comes next. *¿Y ahora qué?* What next?

Chacho Federo, the *migas* master of Fuente Nueva.

The two words that drive most of us quietly mad don't prick Chacho's spine the same way they do yours or mine.

Chacho still remembers the number of prostitutes lined up at the most famous brothels of Granada, but can't tell you the last time he's been to the doctor. His brother, Faustino, can tell you the price of a mule in pesetas but not the cost of a ham in euros. Angel can describe his mother's *olla* down to the last garbanzo bean, but doesn't know where his grandfather is buried.

Depending on who you ask, either 400 or 1,500 people lived in Fuente Nueva during its peak in the 1950s; Chacho was either a shepherd for fifteen years or fifty; the well dried up for the third time in 1963 or the second time in 1965; Pepe's dad was either secret police or misunderstood.

It's not a Chacho thing. Not even a Fuente Nueva thing. It's a pueblo thing, the inevitable outcome of a village that runs on oral history—especially a history as pregnant with pain as this one. Inventing and reinventing yourself and the people you love is one way to soften the sting of a troubling past.

One thing that doesn't escape the memory is controversy. In a community this small, people remember. Angélica didn't come to Ana's mother's funeral; now their habit of eating churros with each other on Saturdays has also passed. Jesús borrowed a family heirloom and hung it on his bedroom wall; won't be seeing him for dinner anytime soon. Fifty years ago, José and Juan Carlos had a land dispute; today the opposing family members don't even understand why they're not supposed to talk to each other.

In the 1940s, officials in the area outlawed masks at Carnaval because people were using the cover of costume to settle old scores. The Spanish have a saying: *pueblo pequeño, infierno grande*. The smaller the town, the bigger the hell.

Even in the most tragic details, though, you find a measure of magic realism: Miguel riding his bike for hours to buy ice after his wife's miscarriage; the neighbor burying her pot of honey to keep it from the Fascists' sticky fingers; the great-grandfather of Angel shot in the woods by an angry father who didn't want him seeing his daughter; Chacho saving two separate young women bent on suicide from the town's well. In Fuente Nueva, truth will always be stranger than fiction.

The priest of Orce has the town's vault of written history under lock and key. One day soon I will visit him, but people tell me I will find only scraps of information on Fuente Nueva. I've been to Orce's small museum, seen Europe's earliest fossil—a tooth from 1.4 million years ago—encased in a thick glass cube, but that's not the history I'm after. For better or worse, the stories of this village live on in the heads of its last citizens, and the people who have been listening to them tell these stories for years. Realizing this early on, I started to take notes and record conversations; years later, people still ask why.

Together with Laura and her siblings, we talk a lot about preserving memories. And making our own. One day, these caves will be ours, and to find a life in Fuente Nueva, we will need to bridge the gap between then and now.

Angel's best friend gave us a pig for our wedding in 2013, and that winter we all traveled south and killed and butchered it the way we decided—chorizo and *salchichón* from María Ángeles's recipes, headcheese and bacon from mine. We light the communal oven, but instead of country bread studded with garbanzos, we make pizzas, which Chacho doesn't recognize by name or by sight, but eats nonetheless. Food is a suture between past and present, between them and me.

Every year, Chacho does a little bit less. One afternoon, as the family gathers around the fire and the water begins to boil, he passes me the iron spatula. His brother, Faustino, sits crouched at his side, all 140 pounds rested on the balls of his feet—a habit formed from a lifetime of huddling around the fire. As I work the mass, stirring the water into the grain, waiting for something to take shape that will prompt the brothers to urge me forward, all I can think about is wet cement—the slow, inevitable march toward a foundation. Something about *migas* feels permanent, irrevocable: Once the starch sets, there is no going back. Five minutes into the mixing, I've broken a sweat and I feel the muscles in my right arm grow tight; ten minutes in and a blister on my left hand bubbles to the surface. Faustino spots it, smiles, mumbles something to his brother that I can't understand.

Occasionally Chacho issues a stern mandate—"Turn it faster so you don't see any black marks on the surface!"—but behind the sharp words is something genuine and urgent. When he sees me starting to lose control of the pan, he gently grabs the spatula, and with a few turns of his wrist wrests control back from the hot iron below him.

When the *migas* are done, I bring the pan out to the table set in the patio and everyone begins to build their plates. Angel likes the little crispy pebbles with a good hit of dried chili crumbled on top. Faustino reaches for tomatoes and sardines. Laura takes raw onion and chorizo. When María Ángeles sees the dark edges on the *migas* she looks up at Chacho.

"What happened? They stick?"

Chacho says nothing, but looks up slowly from his bowl and points his spoon across the table at me. The family laughs.

Some day, someone else will make the *migas*.

MATT GOULDING is a cofounder of Roads & Kingdoms and the coauthor of the *New York Times* bestselling series *Eat This, Not That!* He divides his time between the tapas bars of Barcelona and the barbecue joints of North Carolina.

NATHAN THORNBURGH is a cofounder of Roads & Kingdoms, where he puts all his previous careers—as a musician, a foreign correspondent for *Time* magazine, and an accomplished drinker—to good daily use.

DOUGLAS HUGHMANICK is director of design for Roads & Kingdoms. He is also a cofounder of Roads & Kingdoms, as well as ANML, a digital design studio he operates in the San Francisco Bay Area.

ACKNOWLEDGMENTS

It was supposed to be an easy book to write—I've lived in Spain for six years, circled its borders more times than I can count, consumed more food and drink than anyone would deem prudent. But it wasn't easy, not even close, and that's a reflection of the beauty and complexity and nuance that I consistently found myself incapable of capturing. Nevertheless, I keep trying.

Of course, this book would not be possible without the 48 million Spaniards I now call my compatriots—people of boundless humor, hospitality, and vitality. In particular, I owe a special debt of gratitude to the following people:

José Andrés is at the heart of everything I know and love about Spain, and every bite of this book is suffused with his wisdom, generosity, and indomitable spirit.

To Luis and Visi Irizar and the Irizar family, for teaching me the magic of modern Basque cuisine, the beauty of San Sebastián, and the art of hospitality. Albert Adrià and the El Barri crew have for years shown me the pinnacle of modern Spanish cuisine. Thanks for always saving me a seat.

And the dozens of people who welcomed me into their lives: Salvador Serrano, rice guru and cherished amigo, and his friends and family in Valencia; José Manuel Garcerá and José Maza of Team Wikipaella; Joan Picanyol, Santiago Martín, and the whole Fermín family; the Roca brothers, among the most kind and humble and talented chefs in the world; Victor de La Serna, José-Carlos Capel, Diego and Marta Crespo, Pedro and Marcos Morrán, and Quim Márquez, king of the Boqueria. And to the crew at Satan's Coffee, for keeping me caffeinated and focused just long enough to write this.

Back in the US, everything starts and stops with my partner Nathan Thornburgh, the soul of Roads & Kingdoms, who makes all of this happen. *No hay palabras, hermano.*

Douglas Hughmanick, the genius mind behind the look and feel of everything at Roads & Kingdoms. From websites to book series, you continue to break boundaries.

To our photographer Michael Magers, a world-class road warrior and photographer par excellence, who tussled with tuna and shared caves with shepherds to bring this country to life with his lens.

Anthony Bourdain continues to set the bar impossibly high for anyone who wants to tell stories about food and the wide world beyond. His support, guidance, and inspiration are at the center of everything we do at Roads & Kingdoms.

To Kim Witherspoon, who never met a deal she couldn't make. Your collaboration on all fronts makes all the difference.

To Karen Rinaldi and her team at HarperCollins, including Hannah Robinson, Leah Carlson-Stanisic, and John Jusino, for always providing the right balance of freedom and guidance as we bring these books to life.

A special thanks to my friends and family here in Spain, who continue to deepen my love for this country every day. Especially my parents-in-law Angel and Anna, who have given me the gift of another family in the place I wanted it most. (And, of course, to my family back in North Carolina for always keeping the light on.)

And, above all, to my wife, Laura. Home is wherever you are. And I'm glad it's right here.

PHOTO CREDITS

NOW THAT YOU HAVE THE INSPIRATION, GET THE INFORMATION.

Find intel on the best places to eat, drink, and sleep across the nine regions covered in this book, all available in the palm of your hand. For more information, go to roadsandkingdoms.com/spain

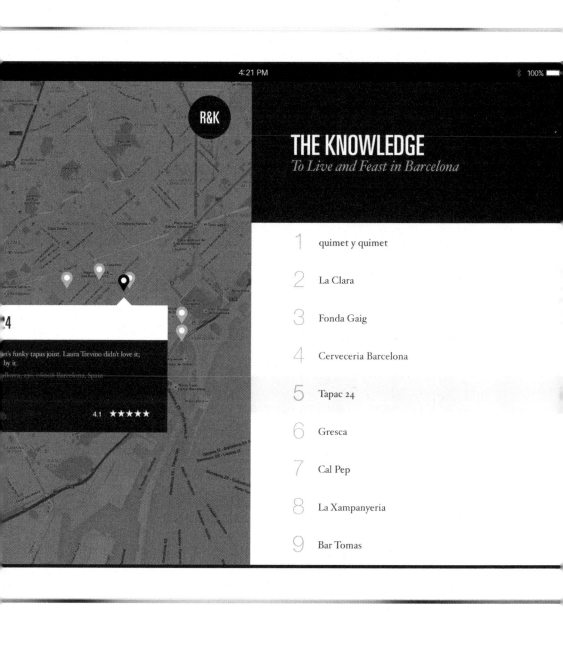

4:21 PM 100%

R&K

THE KNOWLEDGE
To Live and Feast in Barcelona

1 quimet y quimet

2 La Clara

3 Fonda Gaig

4 Cerveceria Barcelona

5 Tapac 24

6 Gresca

7 Cal Pep

8 La Xampanyeria

9 Bar Tomas

‡4

…n's funky tapas joint. Laura Trevino didn't love it;
…by it.

…llorca, 230, 08008 Barcelona, Spain

4.1 ★★★★★

ROADS
& KINGDOMS

Roads & Kingdoms is a digital media company at the intersection of food, travel, politics, and culture. Its partners have included *Time*, *Sports Illustrated*, and Anthony Bourdain. Check out more of our work at roadsandkingdoms.com.